Traditionally amongst the finest in England, farmhouse cooking has mostly been confined to the countryside. From the scrapbooks and private cookery books of our ancestors and from contributions of today's farmers' wives, Mary Norwak and Babs Honey have collected the very best of these country recipes so that everyone, town or country dweller, may enjoy the riches of good English food.

Book One combines a marvellous selection of recipes – for breakfast, soups, pies, meat, poultry and game, butter and cheesemaking, and winemaking – with a description of the basic methods used and the many homely ways in which farmers' wives preserve their products by salting, smoking and freezing.

With the return to fresh, natural foods, these recipes include old favourites as well as unusual dishes that have been handed down over the years and are still made regularly. At last these delicious recipes will enable all lovers of food to rediscover real English country cooking.

D1103436

Farmhouse Cooking

Book One

MARY NORWAK and BABS HONEY

SPHERE BOOKS LIMITED
30/32 Gray's Inn Road, London WC1X 8JL

First published in Great Britain
by Sphere Books Ltd 1973
Copyright © Mary Norwak and Barbara Honey 1973

TRADE
MARK

Set in Monotype Plantin

Printed in Great Britain by
Hazell Watson & Viney Ltd
Aylesbury, Bucks

ISBN 0 7221 6446 7

CONTENTS VOLUME 1

CONTENTS VOLUME 2

* NOTE: All recipes serve 4 to 6 people (according to appetite), unless otherwise stated.

Introduction

Most of us have a child's eye view of farming. We imagine all farms are nice neat buildings, surrounded by orderly fields, grazing cows and scratching chickens. The farmer wears breeches and boots and a soft hat, and strides around with a dog at heel, and sometimes a horse in hand. His wife looks like Mrs Noah, permanently wrapped in a huge white apron, her hair in a bun, living her life in a vast well-scrubbed kitchen surrounded by home-baked bread, honeycombs and cabbages fresh from her well-ordered kitchen garden.

How different is the reality! There are tiny hill farms and vast estates; decrepit cottages and sparkling new bungalows; gloomy Victorian piles and tidy Georgian doll-houses; farmhouses in the centre of village streets and farmhouses miles from anywhere up rough tracks. Farmers and their wives come in different patterns too, but all the men have one thing in common – they like their womenfolk at home, working for and with them. They are traditionalists, bless their hearts, even when they drive sparkling new cars and go abroad for their holidays. Family life is still ruled by the farm. Holidays are taken at odd times of the year, regardless of school terms, because haymaking and harvest are paramount. No farmer's wife will commit herself to village activities between June and September, when her men work all hours of daylight, and food and home comforts are the only things that matter.

All through the year, farmers insist on their hearty breakfasts, potatoes with every meal, pies and puddings, lashings of cut-and-come-again cakes and mouth-watering helpings of their leisure-time game and fish which they dump on the kitchen table.

This collection of recipes reflects this interest in good hearty food during the past two hundred years. We have been sent still-used eighteenth-century recipes; notes of old favourites on the backs of envelopes; Victorian recipes written on black-edged mourning paper; and a number of fascinating scrap-books full of delicious goodies. We received a number of recipes that originated during the 1939–45 war, when many of today's farmers were newly married and struggling to keep up their high standard of food. We have included recipes from an evacuee who grew to love farm life, and from an Italian farmer's wife whose husband was a prisoner-of-war in this country. Some of the recipes reflect the poverty of the country between the two wars of this century; others of the richness of some Victorian farmers, and the 'carefulness' of the Edwardians building up

9

their holdings. Some mirror the interest of today's young wives in foreign dishes, and in labour-saving devices, together with a returning interest in natural foods which discards the synthetic and the standardised convenience product.

Sadly, many of our contributors are unknown to us, for they have left only their names in their friends' cookery notebooks. Three of them, however, left exceptionally interesting collections of recipes. Thomas Train, of Gateshead, left a bound copy of *The Female Instructor; or, Young Woman's Companion*, whose contents ranged through 'Education, Religion, Conversation, Sensibility and the Government of the Passions, Courtship and Marriage, The Management of Children, Family Receipts', but his family had used the book hard, and had written their own recipes on the blank backs of the illustrative plates. They are nice homely recipes which contrast with the rather formal instructions in the book in which they are written.

A little later in time, during the first quarter of the nineteenth century, came Joseph Webb of Kent, who left a neat pocketbook full of recipes 'for horse or man'. There are cures for the mange, nourishing drinks for cows, remedies for milk-fever or scab or inflammation of the lungs (often the same remedy seemed to be applied to Mr Webb's animals and children). There are household hints, and recipes for sauces, wines and soft drinks, methods for pickling fruit and vegetables, ways of improving cider and colouring cheese, and even the costs of preparing some recipes. A basic family cake cost 4/5½d in 1823 (one shilling for 1 lb butter, 10 pence for 1 lb sugar, and eggs 1 penny each).

Mrs Garden, perhaps our most prolific source of Victorian recipes, left a notebook which shows clearly the importance of good country food even in a rich and smart household in the second half of the nineteenth century. Her book started life as an Eton College exercise book, full of Greek and Latin exercises. Later it was used to note down jokes about the clergy, household hints, knitting patterns, instructions for dancing the Lancers, lists of useful shops in London and Paris, and above all, recipes. A few of the recipes are rather grand and expensive, with French names, but the majority are friends' recipes, mainly from East Anglia, for harvest cakes, stewed fowl, surplus game, hashed mutton, gingerbread, apple pudding, and the like. The Gardens, like so many Victorian families, were in the transitional stage from their country origins to life in a town. Their staff would still have been mainly recruited from the country, probably from their own ancestral neighbourhood, and both above and below stairs, country food was normally eaten. This tradition of simple country food maintained by the staff was certainly still evident in well-to-do nurseries until the 1939–45 war, and middle-aged men tend to consider 'nursery food' the only sort worth eating. After a century of country people drifting towards the towns, there is an increasing tendency for middle-class families to seek country homes again, with a consequent revival of interest in wholesome farm-based food. Mrs Garden's notebook is as usable today as the most up-to-date cookery manual.

As far as possible we have avoided the professional technicalities of such subjects as salting and cheesemaking, which can be found in official bulletins, but have included the many homely ways in which farmers' wives preserve their surplus produce. We have let our ancestors and our friends speak for themselves and as far as possible kept their original writing which adds such flavour to each dish. Many of them kept commonplace books in which they recorded their recipes, the names of the houses or friends from which they originated, their reliable household hints and medical remedies and their favourite bits of poetry. We hope that you will enjoy today's version of a commonplace book.

1 Breakfast

A good honest, wholesome, hungry breakfast
Izaak Walton

Farmhouse breakfasts are still pretty solid affairs. They need to be as the farmer often goes out very early after his first breakfast, which is just a snack to 'break his fast'. When the early morning chores have been completed, serious eating begins with the second breakfast. Brawn, faggots and sausages are traditional breakfast foods on the farm, as well as the obvious eggs and bacon; most men like all the fried trimmings as well – potatoes, potato cakes, apples, tomatoes and mushrooms.

FARMHOUSE FAGGOTS

1 lb pig's fry (lights, liver, heart and melt)
1 pig's caul
3 small onions
3 oz breadcrumbs
$\frac{1}{4}$ oz salt
$\frac{1}{4}$ oz white pepper
$\frac{1}{4}$ oz ginger
$\frac{1}{4}$ oz sage

Soak caul in tepid water. Cover the pig's fry and onions with water. Simmer for 1 hour. Drain off liquid. Pour a little of the liquor on the crumbs;

keep remainder for gravy. Mince the pig's fry, onion and breadcrumbs. Add seasoning to taste. Beat to a paste with fork, cut caul into 4-inch squares, form mixture into balls, cover with caul, place on greased tin and cook until brown in hot oven.

Mary Horrell, Exeter, Devon

GRANDMA BOY'S SOMERSET FAGGOTS

½ lb lights
½ lb melt
¼ lb onions
½ lb caul

½ lb liver
6 oz breadcrumbs
Salt and pepper

Put meat and onions through a mincer, mix with breadcrumbs and season with salt and pepper. Shape the mixture into lumps the size of a tea cup. Wrap each in caul, tucking the ends underneath. Place in a tin or pie dish. Half fill with water and bake for 1 hour.

HOG'S PUDDING

2 lb liver, heart, lungs and trimming of meat
1½ lb groats or unpolished barley

2 tablespoons salt
½ teaspoon pepper
½ teaspoon ground nutmeg

Simmer the liver, etc., for approximately 1 hour. Soak groats in the liquor from the pluck for 12 hours. Cook preferably in a double cooker until quite tender. Mince the meat and mix it with the groats and seasoning. There should be sufficient moisture to make the mixture soft. If the groats soak up all the liquor add water to correct consistency. Fill mixture into large intestines, 12 inch lengths, tying ends together to form a ring. Put the hog's pudding into hot water and cook gently for 25 minutes. It is important to cook slowly, otherwise the skins will burst. Hang up the puddings to keep. They will keep up to ten days, and may be eaten cold or fried.

Currants used to be added and they were mixed in, then the boiled hog's pudding hung up an open chimney to smoke. They were eaten all through the winter.

PORK SAUSAGES

Put ½ lb fat and ½ lb lean pork through mincer with ¼ slice of stale bread, 1 teaspoon anchovy essence, pinch powdered thyme or sage, salt and pepper to taste. Mix *very* thoroughly. Shape into sausages – roll in flour and fry. They smell so good you will find the family will eat them straight out of the frying pan, but if they can bear to wait you can add all sorts of exciting things to them, such as fried onions, fried apple rings, tomato sauce, bacon or scrambled eggs. Make them into sausage rolls as they will *not* be too dry – like commercial sausages which are full of that mysterious thing called rusk – or use for Toad in the Hole.

Mrs Chaplin, Finsthwaite, Lancs

PORK SAUSAGES

9 *lb lean pork*	**Seasoning**
3 *lb firm fat from fat bacon*	3 *oz salt*
3 *lb bread (before soaking)*	1 *oz white pepper*
	½ *oz ginger*
	¾ *oz mace (if you like it)*

Soak the bread and wring out. Put lean and fat through coarse plate of the mincer. Mix in seasonings then add the bread and run the whole lot through the fine plate. Attach skins to the filler and fill.

OXFORD SAUSAGES (1)

1 *lb lean veal*	6 *sage leaves*
1 *lb young pork*	1 *teaspoon pepper*
1 *lb beef suet*	2 *teaspoons salt*
½ *lb grated bread*	*Spring of thyme, marjoram*
Peel of ½ lemon	*and savory*
1 *nutmeg grated*	

1. Mince all the meats together.
2. Add flavouring, herbs etc.
3. Mix thoroughly together and press into prepared skin.

1869

OXFORD SAUSAGES (2)

Take equal quantities of veal and pork minced, and add half the weight of beef suet. Season with salt and pepper. Add a small quantity of bread soaked in water and 1 chopped anchovy. For seasoning, add lemon peel, nutmeg, lemon thyme, basil or marjoram.

Eighteenth-Century Notebook

EPPING SAUSAGES

Take equal quantities of pork and of beef suet very finely minced. Add salt, pepper, nutmeg, sage, and some bacon. Mix with egg and fry.

Eighteenth-Century Notebook

SMOKED SAUSAGES FROM SCOTLAND

Salt some beef for two days. Mince with suet and season highly with pepper, onion or shallot. Fill large gut, plait in links. Smoke in chimney. Boil to eat.

Eighteenth-Century Notebook

GLAMORGAN SAUSAGES

1 egg
5 oz breadcrumbs
3 oz grated cheese

Pinch mixed herbs
A little chopped onion
Salt and dry mustard

Combine the dry ingredients, season, bind with egg yolk and form into sausage shapes. Roll in flour, dip in egg white and crumbs, fry in lard and serve alone or with garnishings of chip potatoes, fried apple rings, or tomato.

MRS GILBEY'S SAUSAGES

12 lb sausage meat
4 oz salt
¼ oz mace
¼ oz cloves
½ oz pepper

1 nutmeg
10 oz breadcrumbs
½ pint of hot water, or sufficient to make it of a proper consistency

Boil sausages before frying them.

Mrs Garden, 1847

OXFORD BRAWN

1 pig's head (pickled if possible)
2 feet
2 tongues
2 ears (or 4 if possible)
Some slices of cooked ox-tongue

4 sausages
Dried sage
Salt and pepper
More salt for covering the head

Cut the head in half and soak for one night. Cover it with salt for another night then boil for 6 hours, very gently. Let it get really cold. Take out the bones and put back in the liquor; now boil in this liquor the feet, tongues and ears for 2 hours. Remove all the bones and gristle then chop all the meat into small pieces, including the 4 sausages which have been boiled for ½ hour with the tongues, etc. Season all the meat with sage, pepper and salt and mix up well. Place the ox-tongue, which should be a nice red colour, in a pattern around the mould or bowl, then put in the meat and press down firmly with a weight on top. Let it stand overnight. The tongues may be put in whole, if liked, in the middle of the mould.

Miss Pocock, Headington, Oxon

Miss Pocock was a farmer's daughter with several brothers. Her mother died when they were all quite young and the only girl had to become the housekeeper – and a wonderful job she made of it. Nor did she stagnate or become a martyred drudge – she would ride to town and study in the evenings to further her education and she became very knowledgeable about local history, among other things.

GRANNY HONEY'S BRAWN

This is very simple and quick to make.

Boil a pig's head very slowly for some hours until the meat is dropping off the bones. In the water in which it is boiling put some chopped onion, with salt and pepper to taste, and a good sprig of parsley if available.

When the meat is cooked leave it in the liquor for an hour or so to cool, but before it is at all cold, remove the meat on to a large dish or tin, and start to cut up. Use every scrap of meat and, chopping it as you go, put it into a big bowl. While you are busy doing this have the liquor on the stove and keep it boiling gently, meanwhile throwing in every bone as it comes clean from the meat.

Finally when all the meat is finely chopped add salt and pepper to taste and a good grating from a whole nutmeg, according to taste. If overmuch liquor has come away with the meat, strain it through a colander before putting in a suitable bowl, tin or mould in which the meat reaches right up to the very top. Place a plate with a weight on top and stand on a tray or large dish overnight.

SAGE BRAWN

½ *pig's head*   **10** *sage leaves*
2 *trotters*   *Salt and pepper*

Clean the head and trotters carefully. Cover with water and add chopped sage leaves and seasoning. Boil gently for 4 hours, until the meat leaves the bones. When cool enough to handle, take out all the bones, and chop up the meat. Mix the meat and the cooking liquid and pour into pudding basins to set. Seasoning should be adjusted before the mixture is poured into basins, and a pinch of nutmeg is delicious.

CHICKEN BRAWN

1 *boiling chicken and giblets*
½ *salt pig's head*
12 *peppercorns*
1 *teaspoon salt*
Parsley

Strip of lemon peel
1 *onion*
2 *bayleaves*
Pinch of nutmeg

Put the chicken and giblets into a pan with water, peppercorns, salt, parsley, lemon peel, and *unpeeled* onion (this colours the liquid). Simmer for 2 hours. Put the pig's head into another pan and cover with water. Bring to the boil, and drain. Cover with fresh water and add bayleaves and nutmeg. Simmer for 2 hours. Slice the chicken meat in neat pieces and put round the bowl or moulds. Put in some chopped pork from the head, and then alternate layers of chicken and pork. Season with pepper as you pack in the layers. Mix the two cooking liquids, strain and pour over the meat.

LANCASHIRE BRAWN

½ *salt pig's head*
1 *pig's tongue*
1 *pig's heart*
6 *cloves*

Strip of lemon peel
12 *peppercorns*
Blade of mace
¼ *pint vinegar*

Simmer the pig's head with tongue and heart and all seasonings, except vinegar, for 4 hours in water to cover. Remove meat, and cut half in chunks. Mince the rest of the meat. Strain the stock and return the meat to the saucepan. Pour over the stock and vinegar, bring to the boil, and pour into basins.

RABBIT BRAWN

1 *large rabbit*
2 *pig's trotters*
12 *peppercorns*

Blade of mace
2 *cloves*
2 *hard-boiled eggs*

Cut up the rabbit and leave it to soak in cold salted water. Simmer the trotters in water for 2½ hours. Add the rabbit and spices and continue simmering for about 2 hours until the meat leaves the bones. Cut the meat in pieces. Put slices of hard-boiled eggs in the bottom of a bowl, put in the meat, and pour over the strained stock.

NORFOLK PORK CHEESE

1 salt pork hock with trotter   *Powdered sage*
Pepper

Simmer in water to cover until the meat falls off the bones. Cut the meat
into pieces and toss them in pepper and sage. Put the bones back in the
liquid and boil them until the stock is reduced to half a pint. Strain over
the meat, mix well, and pour into bowls.

SCRAMBLED EGGS WITH KIPPERS

2 kippers   *1 tablespoon butter*
6 eggs   *4 slices buttered toast*
Pepper

Grill the kippers and discard the bones and skin. Flake the flesh and keep
warm. Beat the eggs lightly with a fork and season with a little pepper but
no salt. Melt the butter in a pan and add the beaten eggs. Add the kipper
flesh and cook over a low heat, moving the mixture constantly from the
bottom of the pan but not stirring. While the eggs are still creamy, put on
to the toast and serve at once.

To keep cracked eggs whole
For boiling, simply wrap them in a plastic bag, *tightly*.

BIRDS' NESTS

Stuffing   *Hard-boiled eggs*

Good rich stuffing made with thyme, parsley, egg and lemon rind. Roll
the eggs in the stuffing, wrapping it around neatly. Dip hands in flour to
complete the task. Fry the covered eggs in hot dripping. Serve with fried
tomatoes but cut the eggs in halves to show their colour.

YORKSHIRE DIP

The word 'dip' has several meanings – the one I have in mind is the kind
we have with our breakfast bacon and eggs. Those who can face fried
bacon in the morning may not 'curl up at the edges' at the thought of
gravy as well! I pour a little tea from the teapot into the hot fat and while
sizzling pour it over eggs and bacon. Is this an old Yorkshire custom that
is dying out?

Mrs Alden, Yorks

CADGERY

Boil 3 tablespoonsful of rice till very soft. Strain through a sieve – add a piece of butter and the yolk of an egg, 1 tablespoonful of anchovy sauce, white pepper, cayenne ditto and a little salt. Put it on the fire and mix it well together. Add the fish to it in small pieces, let it heat gradually and serve up quite hot. Fish that has been dressed answers the best.

Mrs Garden, 1847

MORNING SCRAMBLE

2 rashers of back bacon   *2 eggs, beaten*
1 slice bread ¼ inch thick   *Pepper*
1 oz butter

Remove rind from bacon and cut into half-inch strips. Cut bread into half-inch pieces. Heat butter in a frying pan and fry bacon and bread until crisp and golden brown, take care not to burn butter. Turn heat to low, pour in beaten eggs and pepper and stir continuously until eggs are scrambled.

INSTANT BREAKFAST ROLLS

Self-raising flour – one handful for each roll required. Salt. Milk and water, or just water if pushed for milk. Empty the flour into a bowl, add salt generously and then mix to a fairly stiff dough with liquid. Pinch off pieces and fork or roll into rolls and place on a floured baking tray at intervals making a cross on each one before putting into the *hot* oven. Cook for 12–15 minutes or until done to your satisfaction. Eat hot and well-buttered with boiled eggs.

2 Soups

Good broth and good keeping do much, now and than,
Good diet with wisdom, best comforteth man.

Thomas Tusser

Making soup is one of the greatest kitchen pleasures, and there is no doubt everyone really appreciates the time and trouble taken. While a light soup can be a pleasant beginning to a meal, the heavier winter soups are really best for 'meals-in-one'. Serve from an old-fashioned tureen, and ladle into some really large soup plates or bowls so that everyone can have a generous helping of vegetables and all the trimmings.

Trimmings really make a good home-made soup even better. *Croûtons* are just half-inch dice of bread quickly fried golden in butter and well drained; they give a nice crisp texture to contrast with smooth cream soups. *Crusty bread* heated in the oven and pulled apart, with a lot of un-salted butter, makes another good accompaniment – the butter is blended with a crushed clove of garlic before spreading. *Cheese toasts* are good, particularly in onion soups, and are best made with slices of crusty bread, toasted one side, then spread thickly with grated cheese, salt and pepper and grilled until golden and bubbling before putting into the soup bowls with the soup poured over. *Sausage balls* are marble-sized balls of sausage meat flavoured with a little finely-grated onion and herbs, tossed in seasoned flour, then cooked in the soup for the final half-hour before serving. *Egg dumplings* are particularly good in meat soups, made by melting 3 oz butter and stirring in 2 oz plain flour and 4 fluid oz boiling water, cooking over low heat until smooth. Leave this mixture to chill, then stir in 2 egg yolks, $\frac{1}{2}$ teaspoon salt and $\frac{1}{4}$ teaspoon sugar, and fold in 2 stiffly whisked egg whites. Drop by teaspoonfuls into the soup, and simmer until dumplings rise to surface.

To start a stock-pot for the winter

Boil some water, then put in all bones, gristle, etc. at hand, with a little salt and a few vegetables, and cover all with cold water. Let the contents come slowly almost to the boil. Just before boiling point is reached, skim the stock. A little salt and a spoonful of cold water will bring the scum up quickly. A day is not too long to let the stock boil, filling up with water as it boils away. In this manner a good stock is obtained at very little cost and with very little trouble.

Rice, potatoes, bread, cabbage (or similar green vegetables) slightly tainted meat, pork, or veal, should *not* be put in the stock-pot, as they cause the stock to turn sour very quickly.

Mrs Ada Wallace, 1911

Browning for Soup

2 oz of powdered sugar and half a pint of water. Place the sugar in a stewpan over a slow fire until it begins to melt, keeping it stirred with a spoon until it becomes black. Then add the water and let it dissolve. Cork closely, and use a few drops when required. Burnt onions may also be used to give colour to soup, or a piece of bread toasted a dark colour, but not burnt, can be put into the cold stock, heated in it, and taken out when sufficient colour is imparted. It must not be put into boiling stock, as in that case it would crumble.

Mrs Ada Wallace, 1911

ARTICHOKE SOUP

$1\frac{1}{2}$ *lb Jerusalem artichokes*	*1 pint milk*
1 large onion	*1 oz plain flour*
2 oz butter	*1 egg*
1 pint water	*4 tablespoons cream*

Peel the artichokes and slice them. Slice the onion and soften without colouring in half the butter. Add the artichokes and toss over gentle heat for 8 minutes. Put in the water, bring to the boil, and simmer for 15 minutes, then put through a sieve. Return to the pan. Blend the flour with a little water and put into the pan, and stir while cooking gently. Beat the egg and cream together and gradually pour on the hot liquid. Do not boil. Serve with small squares of fried or toasted bread.

CELERY SOUP

1 quart stock
2 heads celery
¼ pint milk

2 oz flour
Salt and pepper

Wash celery and cut into pieces. Simmer gently for 1 hour. Rub through sieve; return to pan. Mix flour with a little milk, throw into soup. Add milk and bring to boil. Season before serving.

TOMATO SOUP

1 lb ripe tomatoes
1 oz butter
1 quart stock or water
4 cloves
2 onions (sliced)

1½ oz flour
1 lump sugar
1 small carrot
½ pint milk

Put onions, tomatoes, carrot, cloves and stock in saucepan; simmer until tender. Rub through the back of wire sieve with wooden spoon. Melt butter in pan, stir in flour; add salt and pepper; gradually pour in liquid. Add milk and sugar. Bring to boil and serve. Taste all soups with extra spoon to see if seasoned enough.

VEGETABLE SOUP (1)

1 carrot
2 onions
4 potatoes
2 pints water or stock
1 tablespoonful tapioca
½ turnip

Bits of celery
1 pint milk
Small bunch of thyme and parsley
Salt and pepper

Wash, prepare and cut vegetables into dice; put on to boil with water and two teaspoonfuls salt; also herbs. When tender add tapioca and milk, and simmer until tapioca is clear. Add quarter teaspoonful pepper, sprinkled through fingers. Taste and serve.

VEGETABLE SOUP (2)

Pare and cut into small pieces 1 small turnip, 1 large carrot, and 1 potato; then chop 1 small savoy cabbage and add with the other vegetables to 3 pints of good stock which has been brought to boiling point. Add 1 tablespoonful of sugar, a cupful of rice, 1 oz of butter, and simmer for 2 hours.

5 minutes before serving add a gill of milk and a pinch each of salt and pepper.

Mrs Ada Wallace, 1911

POTATO SOUP (1)

1 *lb potatoes*	2 *tablespoonfuls sago*
1 *quart stock or water*	1 *oz butter or good dripping*
2 *onions*	*Salt and pepper*
1 *pint milk*	

Melt fat in large pan; peel and slice potatoes and onions; cook in fat about 10 minutes, shaking occasionally. Add water and cook until tender. Rub through sieve or colander and return to saucepan. Half an hour before serving, add milk and sago.

POTATO SOUP (2)

4 pounds of mealy potatoes, boiled or steamed very dry, pepper and salt, 2 quarts of medium stock. Mash boiled potatoes smoothly with a fork, and gradually put them to the boiling stock; pass it through a sieve, season, and simmer for 5 minutes. Skim well, and serve with fried bread.

Mrs Ada Wallace, 1911

EGG SOUP

1 quart of clear stock, 1 egg, $\frac{1}{4}$ oz of flour, 1 small tablespoonful of cream, salt and pepper. Put the flour in a basin, break the egg on to it, and mix them smoothly together; then add the milk and a little salt and pepper. Put the clear stock in a pan on the fire; when it boils, hold a pointed gravy strainer over the pan, pour the batter into it, and stir it through with a spoon, moving the strainer about meanwhile over the soup. Let it boil for about 2 minutes, when the cooked batter should resemble fine threads all through the soup. Serve it up in a hot tureen, with croûtons of toasted bread.

Mrs Ada Wallace, 1911

LENTIL SOUP

1 pint of lentils, 1 quart of liquor in which a piece of pork has been boiled, 2 oz of butter, 2 or 3 cloves of garlic, pepper and salt. Put the lentils in a lined saucepan and boil them in water for quarter of an hour; then pour

off the water, add a little fresh, with the butter and seasoning, and simmer till the lentils are perfectly soft. Stir in the liquor and the garlic (for which a few dried onions may be substituted if preferred), and serve hot, with or without bread fried in boiling fat.

Mrs Ada Wallace, 1911

PEA SOUP

¼ pound of onions, ¼ pound of carrots, 1 head of celery, 1 quart of split peas, a little mint, shredded fine, 1 tablespoon of coarse brown sugar, salt and pepper, 4 quarts of water or stock. Cut the vegetables into small pieces and fry for 10 minutes in a little butter or dripping; pour the water on them, and when boiling add the peas (soaked overnight). Simmer for nearly 3 hours, or until the peas are thoroughly done. Add the sugar, seasoning, and mint; boil for ¼ of an hour. There is not another soup that is more widely liked than this.

Mrs Ada Wallace, 1911

GREEN PEA SOUP

Boil till tender some green peas in water, to which a pinch of sugar has been added. Strain off the moisture, then pass the peas through a fine sieve. Return to the saucepan, add a small lump of butter and a little milk thickened with flour, and allow to simmer gently for a few minutes. When the soup is ready for serving, add a piece of beetroot cut into small squares, and 1 or 2 finely chopped spring onions.

Mrs Ada Wallace, 1911

COUNTRY CARROT SOUP

1½ lb peeled carrots, weighed before peeling
1 large peeled potato
1 skinned onion
2 oz butter
2 pints light-coloured stock or vegetable stock
1 small bayleaf
½ pint milk
Salt and pepper

Chop the vegetables roughly. Melt the butter in a large pan, add the vegetables, and stir them over a gentle heat until the butter is absorbed. Add the stock, bayleaf, salt and pepper, bring the soup to the boil, and simmer it until the vegetables are absolutely tender. Sieve or liquidise the soup, return it to the pan with the milk, reheat and re-season if required.

WATERCRESS SOUP

2 oz butter
1 onion
8 oz potatoes
½ pint chicken stock or water
1½ pints milk
1 bunch watercress

Salt and pepper
Pinch of nutmeg
½ teaspoon cornflour
1 dessertspoon water
2 tablespoons double cream

Melt butter and cooked chopped onion until soft but not browned. Add peeled potatoes and stock or water, bring to boil and cook gently for 15 minutes. Add milk and simmer for 10 minutes. Reserve 4 small sprigs of watercress for garnish, and put remainder into soup. Cook with lid on for 3 minutes, then put soup through a sieve or into a liquidiser. Return soup to pan and season to taste, adding nutmeg and reserved watercress. Blend cornflour with water and stir into soup. Return to boil and cook for a minute. Remove from heat and stir in cream.

TOMATO AND POTATO SOUP

2 leeks
1 oz butter
½ lb tomatoes
¾ lb potatoes
1 teaspoon salt

1 teaspoon sugar
1½ pints water
3 fluid oz single cream
Finely chopped parsley

Remove root and green from the leeks. Split the white part open and wash very thoroughly. Slice finely. Melt the butter and sauté the leeks gently. Chop tomatoes and add these to the leeks, continuing to cook gently for a further 7 minutes. Dice potatoes and add. Season with salt and sugar. Stir well together. Add water, cover and simmer for about 20–25 minutes, or until potatoes are cooked. Sieve and reheat. Adjust seasoning and add the cream and parsley.

BEAN SOUP

2 lb young broad beans
(weighed after podding)
1 small onion (thinly sliced)
6 lettuce leaves (shredded)
Cold water to cover

Salt and pepper
1 pint chicken stock
2 oz melted butter
2–3 tablespoons single cream

Put broad beans, onion and lettuce into a medium-sized saucepan, and add sufficient cold water to cover. Add a little seasoning, cover, bring to the boil, and simmer for about 20 minutes or until beans are tender.

Remove from heat. Strain beans and retain ½ pint of liquid in which they were cooked, add this to the pint of stock. Sieve beans and discard any coarse pieces of skin which will not sieve. (Alternatively, liquidise beans with a little stock.) Add stock to purée, and season to taste. Stir in melted butter. Serve hot or cold; add a little cream just before serving.

CREAM OF ONION SOUP

2 *rashers streaky bacon*	1½ *pints milk*
8 *oz sliced onion*	*Seasoning*
1 *oz butter*	1½ *oz grated cheese*
1 *tablespoon flour*	*Parsley*

Remove rind from bacon, cut up and fry gently to extract the fat. Add onions and butter and cook slowly until onions are soft, keeping lid on to prevent onions from colouring. Sprinkle in flour, mix well and gradually add milk and seasoning. Bring to boil, stirring, cook for about 10 minutes, then sieve and reheat. Put the cheese in a tureen, pour on the soup, and garnish with parsley.

VICTORIAN PEA SOUP

1 *lb dried green peas,*	2 *carrots, scraped and sliced*
soaked overnight	4 *oz swede, peeled and diced*
2 *medium onions, skinned*	1 *ham bone*
and chopped	4 *pints water*
1 *small turnip, peeled and*	*Seasoning*
sliced	

Put soaked peas and prepared vegetables into a large saucepan, add the ham bone, seasoning and water (you can use 2 pints water and 2 pints of liquid in which a bacon joint has been cooked). Bring to boil, cover pan and simmer until the peas are soft.

Sieve the vegetables. Don't worry if you miss a few, as this adds interest to the texture. Return pulp to liquid, stir, re-heat and the soup is ready.

British Farm Produce Council

MIXED VEGETABLE SOUP

2 *oz butter*	2 *medium potatoes*
1 *onion*	2 *leaves cabbage*
¾ *lb carrots*	1½ *pints hot water*
2 *small tomatoes*	*Salt and pepper*
2 *leeks*	1 *oz quick-cooking macaroni*

Melt butter and add chopped onion, cooking until soft but not brown. Add coarsely grated carrots, the choppd flesh of tomatoes, sliced leeks, diced potatoes and water. Bring to boil, season, and simmer with lid on for 15 minutes. Add macaroni and continue simmering for 15 minutes. Just before serving, cut cabbage leaves in thin strips and cook in boiling water for 3 minutes. Drain and add to soup. Serve soup very hot, with grated cheese sprinkled on top.

KING'S SOUP (1753)

4 *large onions*	2 *egg yolks*
4 *pints milk*	*Parsley*
Blade of mace	*Diced toast*
4 *oz butter*	

Cut the onions in very thin slices and simmer in just enough water to cover until soft. Add the milk, mace and butter and simmer for 30 minutes. Put the egg yolks into a bowl and break with a fork. Add a little of the hot milk and stir until smooth. Add to the hot soup but do not reheat. Serve with plenty of chopped parsley, salt to taste and diced toast.

PEAPOD SOUP

Peapods from 1 lb peas	1 *onion*
1½ *pints water*	*Salt and pepper*
1 *tablespoon oatmeal or*	½ *pint milk*
tapioca	

Boil the peapods in water for 45 minutes until tender. Sieve and return the purée to the saucepan. Grate the onion and add to the purée. Bring to the boil and add oatmeal or tapioca and seasoning to taste. Simmer for 5 minutes, then stir in milk. Reheat without boiling. This is nice with a garnish of crumbled crisp bacon or with small squares of fried bread.

CROÛTE AU POT

Cut off the bottom crust of a loaf leaving the same thickness of crumbs as crust. Cut it out in rounds. Soak in consommé or broth. Put them in a tin with some butter into the oven and let them be quite dried up. Then lay in the soup tureen with rounds of carrots, turnips, leeks or cabbage boiled in stock and pour good broth over.

Mrs Garden, 1847

GIBLET SOUP MOST EXCELLENT

One pair of Giblets cut in pieces about an inch long. Put them in a saucepan with as much gravy or broth as will cover them or rather more 3 onions sliced and a bunch of sweet herbs. Let them stew well together till almost done, then strain the liquor from them and mash the Giblets. Add to them a full Gill of white wine and the gravy they were stewed in. Put a piece of butter in a stewpan over the fire and add as much flour as will make it a good thickness. Keep it stirring till it is a fine brown and add it to your soup. Season with pepper, salt and mace. Squeeze in the juice of a Lemon. Let them stew slowly till quite tender, be careful to keep them scumming quite clean. 2 eggs boiled hard the yolks broke and thrown into the Tureen. From Mr Gann, Piazza Coffee House.

Mrs Garden, 1847

OATMEAL SOUP

1 *leek*
1 *oz butter*
2 *oz fine oatmeal*
1 *pint beef stock*

½ *pint milk*
2 *fluid oz cream*
Salt

Slice the leek finely and cook gently in butter until the leek is soft but not coloured. Add oatmeal and stock and stir until it comes to the boil. Simmer for 1 minute. Add milk and cream, and salt to taste and reheat without boiling.

COCK-A-LEEKIE

1 *boiling fowl*
6–8 *leeks*
3 *quarts stock or water*

2 *oz rice*
Pepper and salt
2 *tablespoons parsley*

Clean and truss fowl and wash giblets. Place both in a pan with stock or water and seasoning. Bring slowly to the boil, skim well and simmer gently for a good 2 hours. Wash leeks, discarding outer leaves and chop finely. Add to the pot with rice and cook on for another hour or until the fowl is tender. Cut up meat off bird into neat pieces and place in a hot tureen with the chopped parsley. Remove giblets and skim off any grease from the top of the soup. Pour the soup over the meat and garnish in the tureen. Serve at once. This was traditionally made from an elderly hen which had seen better days.

COTTAGE SOUP

One pound of meat, two onions, two carrots, two ounces of rice, a pint of whole peas, pepper and salt, a gallon of water. Slice the meat and lay one or two slices at the bottom of an earthenware jar or pan, lay on it the onions sliced, then meat again, then the carrots sliced, and the peas, previously soaked all night, and the gallon of water. Tie down the jar and put it into a hot oven for 3 or 4 hours, allowing it to simmer very gently all the time.

Mrs Ada Wallace, 1911

KIDNEY SOUP

Carefully remove the fat from 1 ox kidney, cut into slices, and roll in flour. Place in a saucepan with 1 oz of dripping and fry a deep brown. Peel and slice 2 small onions and add to the kidneys with a generous pinch of salt and pepper. Pour in 6 pints of boiling water and simmer gently for 3 hours, skimming off the fat from time to time. Pare and grate 2 carrots and add to the soup with 2 tablespoons of meat extract. Simmer a few minutes longer and serve.

MARLBOROUGH SHEEP-FAIR DAY 'SOUP'

½ lb lean mutton or lamb	*2 cups of peas (about 1 lb)*
(from neck, shoulder or leg)	*1 cupful shredded lettuce*
1 or 2 onions, or handful of	*1 cupful water*
spring onions using green	*Salt and pepper*
and all	

Cut the meat into very small pieces. Put it into the pan with the peas, sliced onion and shredded lettuce; add the water, and a good sprinkling of salt and pepper. Bring to the boil then cover and cook very gently until the meat is tender (not less than an hour). Add extra, rich stock at this stage but do not make too soupy. Turn into a hot dish or soup tureen and serve with buttered new potatoes, home-made bread, or dry boiled rice. This 'soup' is best eaten in soup plates with spoon and fork.

This was a useful, easily eaten dish for those bygone days when a thriving sheepkeeping community existed on the Marlborough Downs. These days ended in the early thirties, when farming in Britain drifted into the doldrums. The event was held annually in August and the soup made use of the row of late peas.

MUTTON BROTH

5 quarts of water, ½ pound of barley, 1 small turnip, 2 carrots, a little parsley, 1 onion, 4 pounds of scrag of mutton, ½ peck of green peas when in season, 1 teaspoon of salt, 1 teaspoon of pepper. Put the meat into the pot and take off the scum as it rises; then add the vegetables, cut into small pieces, and simmer altogether for 3 hours. Serve very hot.

BEEF BROTH AND PARSLEY DUMPLINGS

8 oz shin beef	Parsley Dumplings
2 pints vegetable stock	4 oz self-raising flour
Salt and pepper	2 oz shredded suet
1 carrot	Salt
1 onion	1 dessertspoon parsley
1 small turnip	
1 stick celery	
1 oz dripping	
Chopped parsley	

Cube the meat and cook with stock, pepper and salt for 1 hour. Dice the vegetables and fry in dripping for a few minutes. Add to the meat and simmer for 1 hour. To make the dumplings, mix the dry ingredients and form into soft dough with water. Add the dumplings to the broth 20 minutes before the soup is done. Sprinkle with chopped parsley before serving.

Joyce Kerr

PIGS' PETTITOES SOUP

8 pig's feet and 4 ears (cleaned)	2 onions
10 pints water	Bunch of herbs

Simmer 4 hours and take out ears. Simmer 1 hour longer and leave to settle overnight. Take off fat. Cut up feet and ears into dice. Season with salt, cayenne, herbs and white pepper. Thicken with flour and butter. Add Madeira and forcemeat balls if liked.

1847 notebook

RABBIT SOUP

1 rabbit, 1 onion, a stick of celery, a turnip, some stock, a bunch of herbs, thickening of flour, a little cream (if at hand), pepper, salt. Skin and wash the rabbit and set aside the head, liver, and kidneys for gravy. Boil the

rabbit in water, then strain it off and add the vegetables and herbs, etc. Cook in the stock till the meat drops off the bones. Take it out, cut the meat into small, neat pieces, putting back the bones and odds and ends into the soup. Boil for another hour, then strain and thicken to a cream-like consistency with the flour. 1 rabbit should make nearly 2 quarts of soup, and milk will answer in it as well as stock; more of whichever is used can be added to make up the required quantity after the soup is strained. When thickened add the pieces of rabbit to the soup to heat through before sending to table.

Mrs Ada Wallace, 1911

MISS BUCHANAN'S IPSWICH PARTRIDGE SOUP

Take a brace or a leash of partridges and nearly roast them, or the remains of partridges dressed the day before. Beat them in a marble mortar bones and all and be careful that all the bones are broken, then take a quart or 3 pints (according to the quantity of soup you wish to make) of good beef broth and put it in a saucepan with the pounded partridges and 6 onions with 2 cloves stuck in each and a carrot. Stew them all together very slowly for 3 or 4 hours, or till the juices are all extracted, and if you have any cold ham in the house add a slice or 2 of the lean. When stewed, strain it through a sieve and press as much of the liquor out as you can do with the back of a spoon. Then take a piece of butter about 2 or 3 ozs and work as much flour into it as you can (at least a tea-cup full) with your hands a little at a time. Then break it in smallish pieces and put it in a basin and take 2 or 3 spoonfuls of the soup when quite hot and put to it. Stir it about till it is mixed and like a thick cream, then put it to the soup and boil it all together, stirring it frequently. Before you send it to table add ¼ pint of cream and a little cayenne pepper, but do not let it boil after the cream is in, as it will curdle. It should be about the thickness of pease soup. Hare soup may be made exactly the same with the remains of a hare that has been dressed.

Mrs Garden, 1847

POACHER'S SOUP

2–4 *lb venison*	1 *blackcock or woodcock*
Shin beef	1 *pheasant*
Mutton with bones	½ *hare or* 1 *rabbit*
1 *head celery*	2 *partridge or grouse*
2 *carrots and turnips*	6 *small onions*
4 *onions*	6 *peeled potatoes*
Bunch of parsley	1 *small white cabbage*
¼ *oz peppercorns*	5 *pints water*

Cut up venison, beef, mutton, celery, carrots, turnips, onions, and put into the water with parsley and peppercorns. Simmer for 3 hours and strain the stock. Cut up the game, dust with flour and brown. Add to the stock with small onions, some more sliced celery, potatoes, and the cabbage cut in quarters. Season with some black pepper, allspice and salt, and simmer 2 hours. Add some red wine, mushroom catsup and forcemeat balls if liked.

1847 notebook

3 Fish

Oh, the gallant fisher's life !
It is the best of any;
'Tis full of pleasure, void of strife,
And 'tis beloved by many.

Izaak Walton

Most of these recipes are for river fish, since angling has always been a popular country pastime. Until a hundred years ago, fresh fish was rarely seen inland, so many popular farmhouse recipes involve smoked or salted fish which kept well. Today our choice is wider, and these basic cooking methods can be employed.

Shallow Frying is useful for cutlets, fillets or flat fish. Dip the fish in seasoned flour, breadcrumbs, batter or beaten egg, and cook in 2 or 3 oz of smoking hot fat, shaking the pan to prevent sticking. Cook on both sides, allowing 12 to 15 minutes according to thickness, and drain on absorbent paper before serving.

Deep Frying can be used for small whole fish, fillets or fishcakes. Rub fish in seasoned flour, shake off surplus and immerse in smoking hot fat in a wire basket (or use batter, having first dipped the fish in flour). Drain well before serving.

Butter Frying is easy and delicious. Use it for fillets of flat fish or small whole fish not more than half an inch thick. Dip in seasoned flour, shake off surplus, and cook on both sides in hot butter. Allow 2 oz of butter for 4 fillets, and 5 to 8 minutes each side.

Oven Frying is marvellous if you cannot bear a smell in the kitchen. Put 2 oz fat in a baking dish and make it very hot in the oven (400°F or Gas Mark 6). Dip fish in seasoned flour, and in batter if liked. Cook in the oven until golden brown. Thin pieces of fish take about 10, cutlets 15-18 minutes.

Grilling is pleasant and simple. Dip fish in seasoned flour and brush with melted fat. Grease and heat the grill tray and put the fish on it. Put a little more fat over fish while cooking. Whole fish take 3-5 minutes each side (cutlets 5-6 minutes, and fillets 5-10 minutes on one side only). Cook the fish about 2 inches from the grill.

Baking is best for large cutlets or whole fish. Dab the fish with knobs of butter, season well and cover with greaseproof paper, baking in a moderate oven on a greased and heated tray. Allow 10-16 minutes per lb for whole fish, 10-30 minutes for cutlets, and 10-20 minutes for fillets, basting well during cooking.

Braising can be used for large cutlets or whole fish and extra items such as tomatoes, mushrooms can be added. Rub in seasoned flour, brush with melted butter, and put in a covered oven dish with a small glass of wine and water (or use vinegar or lemon juice and water), a small chopped onion, a sprig of thyme and a bay leaf. Baste occasionally, and cook as for the baking method.

Poaching of fillets or flat fish makes a light invalid dish. Put the fish in a buttered baking tin with mushrooms or tomatoes, a little fish stock or wine and water and bring gently to the boil on top of the stove. Cover with a lid or greaseproof paper, and cook in a moderate oven, basting occasionally, and allowing 10-12 minutes for fillets and 15 minutes per lb for whole fish.

Foil Cooking is very clean and allows the fish to cook in its own juices giving plenty of flavour. Coat the fish in melted fat, season, wrap in foil, then proceed as for baking.

Boiling for large fish such as cod and halibut is greatly improved if a good fish stock with plenty of herbs and seasoning is used. Allow 1½ pints of liquid to each 1 lb of fish. Bring to the boil, and simmer slowly, allowing 10-12 minutes for a 6 oz fillet of fish. Skin and fillet the fish after cooking, and drain thoroughly.

SALMON

It is the easiest thing in the world to overcook a salmon and that is the surest way to keep your friends up all night looking for the bicarbonate or whatever. Only 5 minutes too much and it will be spoiled. If you have no fish kettle, find the largest possible self-basting roasting tin and half fill it with water. Put in a bay leaf, a handful of salt and 12 peppercorns. Bring it to the boil. Wring out a cloth in hot water, lay the salmon on it and lift it carefully into the water. Leaving the ends of the cloth out, put the lid on and place it either on a simmering mat over the lowest possible heat or into the bottom of the Aga. Leave it simmering 5 minutes per lb for an 8 lb fish up to a 12 lb fish. Over that weight a little longer as the fish will be thicker, but not more than 10 minutes, under that weight 3 minutes. You can take the fish out immediately and lay on its cloth – on the draining board for a moment before putting it on a dish if you want to eat it hot or cold, but if you want to eat it cold it will be more moist if you leave it to cool in its own juice and drain it off next day. If you have had to cut it in half in the cooking, try to mend it on the plate or have it on a baking tin covered in foil if needs be. Cover the join with slices of lemon and cucumber cut very thin and a little hedge of parsley in the cut. Brown bread and butter and salad – not potato.

Mrs Chaplin, Finsthwaite, Lancs

SALMON CHARLOTTE

1 small tin salmon
½ pint white sauce
2 tablespoons parsley
(chopped)

4 tomatoes, chopped and
peeled
Salt and pepper
4 oz white breadcrumbs

Put salmon in basin and mash, add white parsley sauce and salt and pepper to taste. Grease dish and layer with salmon, tomatoes and breadcrumbs. Layer of breadcrumbs on top, cover and put it in a moderately hot oven.

Nel Fielding, Cirencester

SALMON STEAKS FROM WALES

¾ inch thick steak per person
Salt and freshly ground
pepper

Single cream
Bayleaf

This is a very simple recipe which counteracts its dryness. Season fish well with salt and fresh pepper. Choose a dish just the right size, put in fish and just cover with cream. Tuck in bayleaf and cook at 375°F (Gas Mark 5) for 25 minutes.

LITTLE WYLLIE'S SALMON MOULD

1 *lb salmon (cold or tinned)* 2 *teaspoons chopped parsley*
1 *cup breadcrumbs*   *Salt and pepper to taste*
1 *or 2 eggs*   1 *teacup milk*
1 *tablespoon butter*

Break salmon up finely. Add breadcrumbs, seasoning and milk warmed (not boiled). Then add eggs. Pour into a pie dish and beat quite smooth. Put butter cut in pieces on the top. Bake in moderate oven for 1 hour.

COLD SALMON CUTLETS

Cutlets are, I think, the best way to prepare salmon. Cut the portion of salmon into slices 1 inch to 1½ inches thick and wash thoroughly. Drain, dry and salt lightly. Melt equal amounts of butter and cooking oil (not olive oil) in the frying pan, grind in a good seasoning of black pepper and add 2 teaspoons of lemon juice. Remove pan from heat and allow to cool. The cutlets should now be dipped on both sides in the pan then wrapped separately in pieces of greaseproof paper with 1 bayleaf in each. Be careful to keep their shape. Cook in a saucepan, with cold salted water to cover, by bringing them to the boil quickly with the lid on and keeping boiling gently for five minutes. No more. When cool, unwrap the cutlets. Serve with cucumber thinly sliced into diluted white wine vinegar, to which a little sugar has been added.

Lynne Wilson

WEST WALES COCKLE DISH

½ *pint cockles*   1 *pint milk (thickened with*
2 *onions (minced finely)*   *arrowroot or flour)*

Simmer milk and onion and thicken to taste. Stir in cockles, and just before serving put in chives, then season with pepper, salt and a little vinegar.

Mrs L. George

To keep cod-fish
Take out the eyes, fill the holes with salt, and hang the fish up by the head, in a well-aired place.

Mrs Garden, 1847

LEMON BUTTERED PLAICE

8 plaice fillets	*1 teaspoon grated lemon rind*
1 egg	*Salt and pepper*
5 oz fresh breadcrumbs	*3 oz butter*

Wipe fillets and dip in egg. Mix breadcrumbs, lemon rind, salt and pepper. Coat fillets in breadcrumbs and press on well. Melt 2 oz butter and fry fish gently for a few minutes on each side until light golden. Add remaining butter to fry all the fish. Drain and garnish with parsley. Serve with new or French-fried potatoes.

STUFFED PLAICE

4 large fillets skinned plaice	*1 tablespoon chopped parsley*
Salt and pepper	*2 tablespoons melted butter*
4 rounded tablespoons parsley	*Grated rind and juice ½ lemon*
and thyme stuffing	*4 thin rashers streaky bacon*

Season plaice with salt and pepper. Put stuffing, parsley, salt and pepper, butter, lemon rind and juice into a basin and add enough boiling water to give a fairly stiff mixture. Spread stuffing over the skinned side of each fillet and roll up carefully. Remove rind from bacon and roll each fillet in bacon. Put a sheet of foil on a baking tin and grease the centre with a little melted butter. Put the fillets in the middle of the foil, making sure the ends of the bacon are underneath. Fold over foil to make a loose parcel, and bake in the centre of the oven, 400°F (Gas Mark 6), for 40 minutes. Serve very hot with mashed potatoes and a cream sauce.

To bake mackerel

Open them and take out the roes. Wash them and cut off the heads and tails. Wipe them dry and take out the bones, and season them with pepper, salt, mace and nutmeg mixed. Lay them as close as you can in a long pan and cover them with red wine and good vinegar of each an equal quantity. Cover the pan with paste and bake in a *slow* oven.

Mrs Garden, 1847

WHITING

'The price of whiting fresh from the sea, to be used as dinner fish, fluctuates extremely. Sometimes they fetch 4d and 6d apiece even by the seaside, whilst at other times they are as cheap as 3d a score, but the low price holds good only during the great "glut" caught in the herring season.'

A peculiar way of preparing Whiting for breakfast called 'plumping'

A number of moderate-sized whitings are cleaned and washed, laid in salt for a few hours (more or less according to taste) and afterwards hung up in the sun for about 2 days, *not longer*. When wanted for use, boil them lightly on a very clear fire, and serve very hot. The middle-sized are the best for table; the smaller ones bony and the very large of too great a size to fry.

Mrs Garden, 1874

WELSH SOUSED HERRINGS

4 *herrings, deheaded and*	*Juice of ½ orange*
tailed, boned and rolled	1 *bayleaf*
1 *onion*	*Peppercorns*
1 *teaspoon browning*	¼ *pint water*
1 *teaspoon mixed spice*	¼ *pint vinegar*
Orange rind	

Roll herrings up very gently. Cover with other ingredients and cook slowly for 3 hours at 300°F (Gas Mark 2).

CIDERED BLOATERS

4 *whole bloaters*	2 *red-skinned apples, cored*
½ *pint cider*	4 *tablespoons oil*
1 *teaspoon salt*	1 *tablespoon lemon juice*
1 *teaspoon dill seeds*	*Salt and pepper*
(optional but good)	½ *bunch watercress*
½ *lb new potatoes, cooked*	

Cut heads off bloaters, place bloaters in ovenproof dish. Pour over cider, 1 teaspoon salt and dill seeds. Cover with lid or foil. Bake in moderate oven, 375°F (Gas Mark 5), for 15–20 minutes.

Remove bloaters and cool slightly. Cut each one down the back, exposing 2 fillets. Remove bones and skin. Arrange fish down the centre of large oval serving dish.

Cut apples and potatoes into ½ inch dice and mix together. Beat oil with 4 tablespoons of strained cider and lemon juice. Season. Toss potato salad in half of sauce and pour remainder over fish.

Arrange potato salad around outside of dish. Garnish with line of watercress between potato salad and bloaters.

SWEET-SHARP SOUSED HERRINGS

4 *fresh whole herrings*	3 *bayleaves*
¼ *pint malt vinegar*	6 *peppercorns*
¼ *pint water*	2 *oz demerara sugar*
1 *tablespoon tomato ketchup*	1 *teaspoon turmeric or*
1 *teaspoon chervil (or*	*mustard*
parsley)	

Remove heads and wash herrings. Bone. Place in an ovenproof casserole dish about 9 inches square. Mix vinegar, water, tomato ketchup, chervil, bayleaves and peppercorns in a jug. Pour over herrings and cover with lid or foil. Bake in moderate oven, 350°F (Gas Mark 4), for 1 hour. Remove herrings from oven and uncover. Mix together sugar and turmeric and sprinkle on top of each herring. Return to oven and continue baking for 15 minutes. Remove and leave herrings to cool in the liquor. When cold, drain fish carefully and serve on a prepared salad.

SOUSED MACKEREL

4 large mackerel　　　　　　*Bayleaf*
Wine vinegar　　　　　　　*Salt and pepper*
Pickling spice

Split, bone and roll up mackerel. Pack into an ovenproof dish and cover with equal parts vinegar and water. Add a dessertspoon of pickling spice, bayleaf, salt and pepper. Cover and bake in a slow oven, 300°F (Gas Mark 2), for about 30 minutes, or until tender. Drain off liquid, add fresh vinegar, and leave in a cool place for 24 hours. Serve with salad, brown bread and butter.

BAKED STUFFED HADDOCK

1 medium haddock　　　　　*2 teaspoons chopped onion*
(about 2 lb)　　　　　　　*2 tablespoons melted dripping*
2 tablespoons oatmeal　　　*Salt and pepper*
2 teaspoons chopped parsley　*1 oz melted butter*
2 teaspoons chopped thyme

Clean fish and mix the remaining ingredients except the butter. Stuff fish with this mixture and sew up with needle and cotton. Truss by placing tail through eyeholes. Melt 1 oz butter in a baking dish, put fish in dish and baste. Cook at 375°F (Gas Mark 5) for 40 minutes, basting frequently. When half-cooked, sprinkle with breadcrumbs and parsley and dot with butter. Cover with greaseproof paper and bake at 400°F (Gas Mark 6) for 20 minutes.

HERRINGS WITH MUSTARD BUTTER

4 herrings　　　　　　　*Salt and pepper*
3 oz butter　　　　　　　*4 tomatoes*
1 teaspoon dry mustard

Split and bone the herrings and open out flat. Cream butter, mustard, salt and pepper and spread on each fish. Fold fish in half and wrap in foil. Put on a baking sheet with tomatoes cut in half and dotted with butter, and bake in a moderately hot oven, 375°F (Gas Mark 5), for 25 minutes. Serve with brown bread and butter.

KIPPER CREAMS

1 *large egg*   *Breadcrumbs*
1 *kipper*   *A little butter*
1 *tablespoon cream*

Scrape the kipper and rub through a wire sieve. Stir in breadcrumbs, butter and cream, make into a soft mixture with the egg, three parts fill small buttered moulds. Steam until firm.

Mrs Page, 1899

BLOATERS À LA SEFTON

2 *bloaters*   1 *egg*
1 *oz grated cheese*   *Lard*
3 *oz breadcrumbs*

Put the lard in a saucepan, fillet the fish and cut in nice pieces, dip in flour, then in egg, and then roll in the breadcrumbs and cheese mixed together; when the lard smokes put them in and fry a nice brown, then take up, drain on paper, serve in a circle with parsley in the centre.

Mrs Page, 1899

MRS DOWSON'S STEWED EELS

1 *teaspoon black pepper*   ½ *an onion*
2 *teaspoons salt*   *Chopped parsley*

Simmer eels in 1 pint of milk for ¼ of an hour. Braid a piece of butter in some flour and add to it about 5 minutes before it is served up. A little lemon juice to be added. The eels are not to be put into water and not skinned – to be wiped with a cloth.

Mrs Garden, 1847

EEL PIE

Clean, skin and cut 1¾ lb eels into pieces 2 inches long. Dry each piece separately, placing a piece of butter inside, with a little pepper, salt and chopped parsley. Lie them in a pie dish with a cupful of vinegar and water mixed. Thicken with a teaspoon plain flour (or cornflour). Cover with a good puff pastry, and bake in a hot oven. Serve cold for Sunday tea.

PIKE

Boil the pike and let it get cold. In the same water boil macaroni. Take the pike carefully from the bones. Mix the macaroni and fish together with a sauce made of flour, butter and milk, pepper, salt and a little Cayenne. Arrange it in a flat dish *au gratin* and set in a quick oven to be creamy underneath, brown on the top.

Mrs Garden, 1847

CURRIED PIKE

Pike are coarse, ugly fish and not particularly good to eat; try one this way. Cook 1 lb of pike, break into flakes and place in a casserole. Fry 1 finely chopped onion in butter and when brown add a teaspoon of flour and a level tablespoon of curry powder. When mixed cook a further 2 minutes, then add ½ pint milk. Boil slowly for 5 minutes, season the sauce and add lemon juice. Pour over cooked fish in casserole, heat through in the oven or under the grill and serve.

Lynne Wilson

TROUT IN JELLY

After the fish have been cleaned and emptied, form them into circles by skewering their tails into their mouths. Put them into warm water, with salt, vinegar to taste, 2 shallots, a clove of garlic, cook them gently until tender – the time depends on the age of the fish, but a fine knitting needle or a clean matchstick may be stuck into the flesh, but make as small an incision as possible on account of wanting to keep the juices in the fish. Remove from the liquor and place carefully on a suitable dish to get cool. Meanwhile reduce the liquor by half, and following makers' instructions, take some well-known gelatine and make a thick jelly. Baste the fish with this, coat after coat, until they are nicely covered. When set garnish with rings of cucumber and radish, or according to taste.

TROUT CASSEROLE

When the fish are biting and he returns with at least six, this dish is the answer. Medium fry 2 chopped onions, add salt. Line a baking dish with olive oil then brush with a garlic clove. Place the 6 filleted trout in the dish and season. Make a layer with the onions then another of buttered crumbs.

Bake at 350°F (Gas Mark 4) for 15 minutes. Test with a fork and when done sprinkle with chopped parsley and chopped bacon and serve.

Lynne Wilson

TROUT IN BEER

If his luck has only run to a solitary, but good-sized trout, try cooking it in beer. Put ½ pint beer, 1 cup of white wine and 3 tablespoons of vinegar into a saucepan.Bring slowly to the boil. Add the cleaned and gutted fish with a teaspoon of horseradish, a flavour of leaf thyme, ground ginger, and a slice of lemon peel. Simmer until tender and serve fish separately. Strain the sauce and add to taste.

Lynne Wilson

TROUT IN TOMATO

Put 3 filleted trout in an ovenproof dish. Melt 2 oz butter and pour over fish, then add seasoning and some parsley with finely chopped onion. Cook in oven for 20 minutes then drain off butter and cover all with ½ pint of heated tomato sauce. Grill for a few minutes and serve.

Lynne Wilson

CRABTREE FARM FISH PUDDING

1 lb haddock or bream
1 chopped onion
2 eggs
½ pint milk
3 oz butter

3 oz breadcrumbs
Juice of ½ lemon
Salt and pepper
Grated cheese

Poach the fish and cool. Flake the flesh and mix with the finely chopped onion, beaten eggs, milk, softened butter, breadcrumbs and lemon juice. Season well and put into a greased pie dish. Sprinkle with grated cheese. Bake at 375°F (Gas Mark 5) for 40 minutes. Nice with mushroom or tomato sauce. This recipe was invented by a member of the Young Farmers' Club (for the 'TV snack' class) at the Cheshire County Rally. It could be baked in individual dishes.

Margaret Bennion, Malpas, Cheshire

STABLE HOUSE FISH PIE

1 lb halibut
8 oz lobster
4 oz button mushrooms
2 peeled and seeded tomatoes
4 oz peeled shrimps

8 oysters
4 eggs
½ pint good white sauce
Salt and pepper
1 lb potatoes

43

Steam the halibut and flake the flesh in large pieces. Mix with lobster meat, mushrooms and tomatoes tossed in a little butter, shrimps and oysters. Whisk the eggs into the white sauce and season well. Bind the fish mixture with the sauce and put into a pie dish. Boil the potatoes and mash them with butter and a little milk, salt and pepper. Pipe them on to the pie, or mark them with a fork. Bake at 350°F (Gas Mark 4) for 30 minutes. This is delicious and rich; some of the shellfish may be omitted if necessary, and it can be fresh, canned or frozen. If time is short, the fish can be heated on top of the stove in the sauce and put into the pie dish, and the potato topping can be browned quickly under the grill.

INVALID'S FISH PUDDING

1 *small whiting*   1½ *oz breadcrumbs*
1 *egg*   1 *tablespoon cream*
¼ *pint milk*

Scrape fish and mix with the crumbs boiled in milk. Add the egg yolk and cream, and light seasoning. Whip the white to a stiff froth and fold into mixture. Put mixture into a buttered basin, cover with a buttered paper, steam until firm.

Mrs Page, 1899

COLD FISH SALAD

The ingredients vary according to taste. You can make it from left-over fish, but Signora Beglia prefers shrimps and, as they are easy to get in her part of the world, she uses mussels as well.

For 4 people you need shelled shrimps, cooked mussels (optional), any amount of cooked fish, olive oil (or other vegetable oil), a clove of garlic, parsley and lemon.

Mix the fish well together in a large bowl. Chop the parsley very finely, then crush the garlic and mix with the parsley. Signora Beglia used a mortar to do this, but an electric mixer is also first class. Next mix in the oil, the chopped parsley and crushed garlic into the fish, add the juice of 2 lemons and season to taste.

This makes an excellent main dish or a first course if it is spread on toast. This recipe comes from Signora Beglia, wife of an Italian farmer who was a prisoner-of-war in England.

STUFFED SPRATS OR HERRING

Large sprats or small herrings, bread soaked in milk (the quantity depends on the number of herrings and as this is eaten cold any amount can be made), mashed potatoes, garlic, grated cheese and breadcrumbs.

Open the fish and clean it. Mix together soaked and squeezed bread and the mashed potatoes in equal quantity. Now mix in finely cut parsley, 2 cloves of crushed garlic (not essential but very good) and the grated cheese. Place this mixture on the fish which are left open. Sprinkle with breadcrumbs and moisten with oil or butter. Bake in a medium oven until the breadcrumbs are brown. Allow to cool and serve with tomato salad.

FISH BAKED IN MILK

$1\frac{1}{2}$ lb of halibut or any kind of fresh fish, 1 pint of milk, $\frac{1}{4}$ of a teaspoon of dried herbs, 1 oz of butter, and salt and pepper to suit taste. Place the fish in a well-greased tin or dish, and cover it with the milk. Add the herbs tied in a small piece of muslin, and the seasoning of salt and pepper. Place a dish over the top, and then bake the fish slowly in a fairly hot oven for $\frac{3}{4}$ hour or until it is tender. The milk, thickened with a little flour, should be used for the sauce, the herbs being taken from the muslin and added too.

Miss Butcher, Newport, 1913

GRILLED GRAYLING

This popular river fish possibly ranks second to trout. Thoroughly clean, split fully and open out. Brush with salad oil, season well with salt and pepper and cook under a hot grill until golden brown. Serve with sliced lemon.

Lynne Wilson

4 Meat

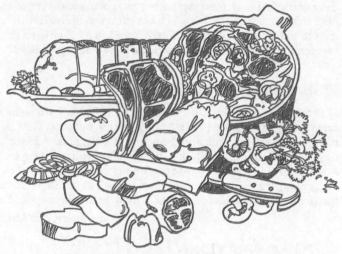

There's no want of meat, sir,
Portly and curious viands are prepared,
to please all kinds of appetites.

Massinger

A friendly swarry consisting of a boiled leg of mutton and the usual trimmings.
'Pickwick Papers'
Charles Dickens

The Vicarage Mutton
Hot on Sunday,
Cold on Monday,
Hashed on Tuesday,
Minced on Wednesday,
Curried Thursday,
Broth on Friday,
Cottage pie Saturday

Old Jingle

GETTING THE MOST FROM A ROAST

Before a joint can be successfully roasted, there are a number of factors to consider. First, the type of meat – such as beef, lamb, mutton, pork or veal. Second the cut, and every family has its favourite. Third, the amount of fat. Finally, the age and probable ancestry of the meat, and the length of time it has been hung.

Personal preference plays a large part in preparing a roast joint. Beef takes the least time, according to the 'doneness' liked. Lamb should not be overcooked, and should have a faint pinkness. Veal and pork must be thoroughly cooked. If you do not use a meat thermometer, a 'touch test' will help to assess the doneness of the meat. If the meat feels firm, it is well done. If it responds like a cake, soft but resilient, the meat is medium rare. Pricking meat loses valuable juices, but if this is done, the meat is rare when the juice is red, medium rare when pink, and well done when colourless. Pork and fowl with light meat must be cooked until the juice is colourless, but most other meats are overdone at this point.

In roasting, everything is done to preserve the dry quality of the heat, and meat should be cooked on a rack which allows air to circulate. Potatoes are best cooked separately in a few spoonfuls of pan drippings. In top quality meat which has a good fat content, there is sufficient moisture in the meat, and no basting is necessary. To start the joint, just rub a little fat over the pan. Very lean meat may be larded with lengths of fat, or brushed with melted fat or oil and then basted, but stock or water used in a pan creates excess steam and spoils the flavour. The best and safest method of basting is with a bulb type baster rather than a spoon.

There are many theories about times and temperatures in roasting, but the latest is that the flavour is best retained by quick browning, followed by cooking at medium heat. The juices are sealed in by the initial hot searing of the meat at 500°F. After 3 minutes, reduce the heat to 350°F and cook for the required time. By this method, no basting is really needed, and there is little pan juice. It is particularly suitable for really choice meat.

With a solid fuel cooker, it is sometimes difficult to reduce oven-heat quickly. Get the oven heat up to the required temperature, put in the meat, then open up the oven door for a minute or two, close up the damper and spin wheel and make up the fire and the temperature quickly reduces, and heat can also be reduced by using the top-plates for cooking.

A really labour-saving and trouble-free method of roasting is to use a meat thermometer. This is marked with the various temperatures and degrees of doneness for various joints. The thermometer is inserted right into the meat on the rack, put into the preheated oven, and checked from time to time until the correct temperature is recorded.

Timing in meat cookery must be a matter of choice depending on the doneness required. At the moderate temperature, beef needs 25 minutes per lb, but for a rare joint take off 5 minutes per lb. Lamb needs 30 minutes per lb as this meat is usually preferred a little more cooked than beef; while pork and veal must always be very well-cooked, so they need 35 minutes per lb. Nowadays, many of us take meat from the freezer, and human nature being what it is we usually forget to allow plenty of time for thawing. If you want to cook meat straight from the freezer, allow double cooking time, and wrap the meat in foil, or cover it with another baking tin. A well-thawed joint has a much better flavour, and it's a good idea to leave the meat to thaw in a well-greased oven tin so that the juices are not lost.

If the joint has been carefully prepared to eat hot, it will also be very good cold. A joint brushed with salad oil, then liberally rubbed with dry mustard and sprinkled with pepper, salt and flour, will have a delicious brown and tender crust. While meat roasted on the bone has the reputation of being sweetest, a boned joint can be stuffed to extend the meat and make more servings.

A roast joint can be made more attractive by basting with a mixture which will give a rich glaze. A $\frac{1}{4}$ pint of fruit juice blended with a tablespoon each of brown sugar and made mustard, and a spoonful or two of the pan drippings, should be spooned over the roast twice during the last 30 minutes of cooking.

Well-chosen accompaniments add to the pleasure of a good joint. Yorkshire pudding, horseradish sauce and mustard, of course, with beef; mint sauce with lamb; redcurrant jelly with mutton; orange or apple with pork and veal. A quick piquant sauce for any hot roast can be made by whipping 1 tablespoon made mustard with 3 tablespoons reducrrant jelly. A creamy gravy is very good with veal or lamb, made by adding milk instead of water to the flour stirred into the pan drippings. Hot fruits are a very good extra, such as hot peach slices with baked ham, hot pineapple slices with lamb, and hot orange slices with veal. Everyone knows how good small baked apples are with pork, but they are equally good with beef.

After taking the roast from the oven, stand it for 15 to 20 minutes before carving; it will cut better and hold the juices.

When a joint has been carefully prepared and served on the first day, the succulent remains will be welcomed on reappearance.

How to make tough meat tender

Soak it in vinegar and water; if a very large piece, for about 12 hours. For 10 lb of beef use $\frac{3}{4}$ pint of vinegar, and soak it for 6 to 7 hours.

Edwardian notebook

VICTORIAN SIRLOIN OF BEEF

Allow $\frac{1}{4}$ hour to each pound of beef.

Make up a good fire; spit or hang the joint evenly, at about 18 inches from it. Put a little clarified dripping in the dripping pan and baste the joint well as soon as it is put down to dress; baste again every $\frac{1}{4}$ hour till about 20 minutes before it is done; then stir the fire and make it clear; sprinkle a little salt, and dredge a little flour over the meat, turn it again until it is brown and frothed. Take it from the spit, put it on a hot dish, and pour over it some good gravy (made) or mix the gravy left at the bottom of the dripping pan with a little hot water and pour it over.

Garnish with fine scraping of horse-radish in little heaps. Serve Yorkshire pudding with it on a separate dish. Sauce: horse radish.

VICTORIAN RIBS OF BEEF, ROLLED AND ROAST

Allow 20 minutes to the pound, or 15 minutes and 30 minutes over.

Order the butcher to take out the bones of the joint; roll it into a round, and fasten it with skewers and a broad piece of tape in the shape of the round. Place it at the distance of 18 inches before a large fire until it is partly dressed; then move it gradually forward towards the fire. Put some clarified dripping in the pan; baste it the moment the dripping melts and do the same every $\frac{1}{4}$ hour. Just before it is done, i.e. about 20 minutes before you remove it from the spit, dredge it with flour, and baste it with a little butter. Remove the tape and skewer, and fasten it with a silver skewer instead. Serve it with good gravy over. Horse radish sauce.

To boil beef

Reckon the time from the water coming to a boil.

Keep the pot boiling, but let it boil very slowly. If you let the pot cease boiling you will be deceived in your time; therefore watch that it does not stop, and keep up a sufficiently good fire. Just before the pot boils the scum rises. Be sure to skim it off carefully, or it will fall back and adhere to the meat, and disfigure it sadly. When you have well skimmed the pot, put in a little cold water, which will cause the scum to rise again. The more carefully you skim, the cleaner and nicer the meat boiled will look.

Put your meat into cold water. Liebig, the great German chemist, advises us to plunge the joint into boiling water, but the great cook Francatelli, and others of the same high standing, recommend cold; and our own experience and practice are in accordance with the cook rather than the chemist. Put a quart of cold water to every pound of meat. Allow 20 minutes to the pound from the time the pot boils and the scum rises.

It is more profitable to boil than roast meat.

Twentieth-century beef

British beef is the best in the world, but, because of its size, the variation in the texture of the muscles and the cooking requirements of the different cuts, it is more difficult for the housewife to understand than other types of meat.

The demand today is for much leaner beef, but it must also be tender and have a good flavour. With modern methods of breeding, feeding and livestock management, it is possible to achieve this, and more and more beef of this standard is being produced annually.

Beef when first cut is dark red, but on exposure to the air the colour brightens. When choosing it, look for a bloom, small flecks of fat in the lean (this is called 'marbling'). It indicates that the animal has been fully prepared for marketing and acts as an internal baster bringing flavour and tenderness to the meat. The fat should be creamy in colour and cuts should be clean and pink in the bone.

A side of beef is divided into two quarters between the tenth and eleventh rib. Most of the roasting joints and steaks come from the hind-quarter.

Hind-quarter cuts

Sirloin: Roast on the bone or, to get the most out of the joint, remove the fillet and use separately cut in steaks for grilling. The loin can also be boned and rolled for roasting. Steaks can be cut from the upper part of the sirloin, e.g. entrecote steaks.

T-bone steak: A trimmed slice of sirloin with the fillet and bone left in, weighing about $\frac{3}{4}$–$1\frac{1}{2}$ lb.

Fillet: Weighs 3–5 lb and is the undercut of the loin. It is very tender and delicately flavoured. Usually cut into steaks and grilled. The whole or half the fillet can be trimmed, neatly surrounded and tied, with beef or pork fat for roasting. This is a luxury dish as it is very expensive.

Porterhouse steak: Defined in the USA as the first cut from the hip end of the loin. Sometimes cut from eye or fore-rib; sometimes from eye of loin. Grill.

Rump steak: Grill or fry.

Silverside: The best joint for salting and boiling and for making pressed beef. Needs long, slow cooking.

Topside: Being lean and containing no bone this is an economical joint. Excellent for slow roasting, pot roasting, braising or boiling. Ask the butcher to tie some fat all round the roasting joint to keep moist.

Thick flank (or top rump): Very lean, and comes from the lower and inner portion of the hind leg. Best for braising, stewing or pot-roasting.

Fore-quarter cuts

Fore rib (chine), middle rib and thick rib: Fore and middle rib are adjoining cuts and both are best roasted on the bone or boned and rolled. The fore rib bone is the longer but the end of it can be cut off to make a separate joint (thick rib). An alternative use for middle rib, when boned, is as a first-class stewing or braising steak.

Porterhouse steak: See description in hind-quarter cuts.

Chuck steak and neck: These cuts are also very good for pies and puddings.

Rolled brisket: Pot roast or braise; otherwise it can be salted and boiled like silverside. It requires long, slow cooking. The fat from the braised joint is excellent for making pastry. The fore leg is called 'shin' and the hind leg is referred to as 'leg of beef'; both are gristly and full of tissue but the meat on both is lean, has a good flavour and is excellent for stewing or for making brawn. Both give a thick jellied stock. It is worth noting that, when roasting meat, the bone helps to conduct heat to the middle of the joint and adds greatly to the flavour and makes the gravy more nutritious. If joints are boned and rolled for easier carving, sit the bones on top of the joint during cooking.

BRISKET CASSEROLE

2½–3 lb boned rolled brisket	1 bayleaf
1 oz plain flour	Sprig of thyme
1 oz butter	1 lb new carrots
1 glass red wine	1 lb small onions
¾ pint stock	Salt and pepper

Brown the brisket on all sides in melted butter in a saucepan. Remove meat and stir in the flour. Add the wine and gradually pour in the beef extract stock. Bring to the boil and stir until thickened. Return the brisket to the saucepan, add salt and pepper, bay leaf and thyme and cover tightly. Simmer over a low heat for 1¾ hours. In the meantime scrape the carrots and peel the onions, leaving both vegetables whole. Add these to the meat and gravy and continue cooking gently for a further 45 minutes, or until tender. Serve the joint on a hot plate surrounded by the vegetables and hand the gravy separately.

BERKSHIRE BAKED BEEF

Take a lean piece of beef – chuck steak or whatever can be afforded. Mix well together 1 teaspoon flour, 1 teaspoon sugar, pepper and salt to taste, and rub it on the meat. Lay it in a pie-dish and pour 1 teaspoon vinegar, 1 dessertspoon sauce (Worcester sauce or mushroom ketchup) and ½ cupful water over it. Cover closely with another pie-dish and bake for 2 hours, basting frequently. Serve with jacket potatoes.

DORSET 'DAB-OF-BEEF' STEW

1½ lb stewing beef
Marinade of teacup of cider
vinegar seasoned with a good
pinch of pepper
1 oz lard (melted in frying
pan)

1 good onion
2 cloves
1 bayleaf
Parsley

Cut the beef in good dabs i.e. thickish slices and soak in marinade for
about ½ hour. Melt the lard and make it hot. Cook the drained beef on both
sides for a minute or two, then put a plate over the top of pan and keep just
ticking over for 10 minutes on a low heat. Pour the marinade into a
casserole (or thick saucepan) and add the onion, a bayleaf, 1 or 2 sprigs of
parsley, the cloves and lastly the meat. Cover to top of meat with water.
Cook slowly in oven, or on top of stove, for 3 hours.

CHUCK STEAK – ROLLED AND STUFFED

Take a good slice of chuck steak, about 1 inch thick, lay it flat on the
board and put in the centre a mound of sage and onion stuffing such as
would be used for duck or goose; roll the steak lightly around, skewer it
securely and bind with fine string or yarn, so that the forcemeat cannot
escape, fasten a paper greased with dripping over it, lay in a baking tin
placed in a moderate oven, and let it cook gently for about a couple of
hours. Baste it well from time to time. A ¼ hour before it is to be dished,
remove the paper and allow the meat to brown. Serve well seasoned brown
gravy with it.

OVEN BEEF AND DUMPLINGS

3 lb salt brisket
½ lb carrots
½ lb onions
4 celery sticks
2 bayleaves
6 peppercorns

Dumplings
6 oz plain flour
1½ teaspoons baking powder
1 level teaspoon salt
1 level teaspoon mixed herbs
3 oz shredded suet

Soak the meat in cold water overnight, and drain. Line the inside of a
roasting tin with foil and put the joint in the centre. Cut onions, carrots
and celery in large pieces, put round the joint, add bayleaves and peppercorns, and put ¼ pint water over the meat. Cover the tin with a second
piece of foil, tucking the edges well under the tin. Cook in the centre of the
oven 400°F (Gas Mark 6) for 1 hour 50 minutes. Make the dumplings by
sifting flour, baking powder and salt into a bowl with herbs and suet,

mixing to a fairly stiff dough with cold water and dividing into 8 pieces. Form each piece into a ball. At the end of cooking time, take foil off meat, put dumplings on vegetables round joint and re-cover with foil. Continue baking for 40 minutes until dumplings are well risen and cooked. This is an old favourite, but it is particularly useful to cook such a meal in the oven when a solid fuel cooker is in use, and there need be no anxiety about the saucepan boiling dry when the cook is coping with something else.

JUGGED BEEF

$1\frac{1}{2}$ *lb shin beef*
2 oz plain flour
Salt and pepper
4 oz chopped streaky bacon
2 onions stuck with 4 cloves

Grated rind $\frac{1}{2}$ lemon
Bayleaf, thyme and parsley
6 small mushrooms
3 beef cubes in $\frac{3}{4}$ pint hot water

Cut meat into 2-inch pieces and roll them in flour seasoned with salt and pepper. Fry bacon lightly, and add the meat, browning lightly. Add onions, lemon rind, herbs, mushrooms and stock. Cover and cook slowly on top of the stove or in a slow oven at 300°F (Gas Mark 2) for 3 hours. Remove onion and herbs before serving. Serves 4 people.

PRESSED BEEF

2 lb boned and rolled salt
brisket of beef
1 pint stock

1 onion
Pepper

Soak the brisket in cold water for 2 hours. Drain and put in a saucepan. Pour in the stock and add the finely chopped onion and pepper. Cover closely and bring to the boil. Simmer gently for $1\frac{1}{2}$ hours.

When cool enough to handle press the meat into a 1 lb loaf tin and fill up with a little of the cooking liquid. Put a plate with a weight on top over the tin and when cold keep in the refrigerator or a cool larder.

Turn out on to a serving dish the following day and surround with crisp lettuce leaves.

POTTED BEEF

1 lb stewing steak
5 oz bacon

Salt, pepper and nutmeg
1 bunch mixed herbs

Slice stewing steak very thinly, and also the bacon. Arrange alternate layers in an oven dish, seasoning with salt, pepper and nutmeg. Add herbs

53

and just enough water to cover. Put the bacon rinds on top. Cover tightly and cook in a very slow oven for 3 hours. Remove herbs and bacon rinds. This dish will set into a clear pink jelly with very soft meat. If the weather turns cold, it is also delicious served hot.

BEEF IN BEER

4 *lb brisket of beef*　　　　　$\frac{1}{2}$ *pint beef stock*
6 *rashers lean bacon*　　　　 $\frac{1}{4}$ *pint wine vinegar*
1 *lb onions*　　　　　　　　*Salt and pepper*
$\frac{1}{2}$ *pint brown ale*　　　　　　*Bayleaf*

Have the beef rolled and tied. Cut bacon into thin strips and put into casserole. Put in the meat. Slice the onions thinly and put round the beef. Add salt and pepper, depending on possible saltiness of bacon, and bayleaf. Heat together ale, stock and vinegar and pour over the meat. Cover tightly and cook at 300°F (Gas Mark 2) for $3\frac{1}{2}$ hours. The gravy is rich and delicious, and the meat has a good flavour when eaten cold or in sandwiches.

HUNTER'S BEEF

3 *lb rolled ribs of beef*　　　 $\frac{1}{4}$ *pint dry red wine*
3 *rashers streaky bacon*　　 1 *beef cube dissolved in* $\frac{1}{2}$ *pint*
2 *carrots*　　　　　　　　*water*
2 *onions*　　　　　　　　*Thyme, bayleaf and parsley*
1 *stalk celery*

Cut bacon in dice, put in a heavy saucepan or casserole, and cover with chopped vegetables. Season with salt and pepper, put on lid and put on gentle heat to soften vegetables in bacon fat. When they are just soft, add wine and stock made with beef cube. Put meat on top of vegetables, add herbs, cover and cook for $2\frac{1}{2}$ hours at 325°F (Gas Mark 3). Slice the meat and serve on vegetables, and reduce gravy by fast boiling before handling separately. This makes a good Sunday meal if there isn't much time to attend to a joint with all the trimmings.

STEAK AND MUSHROOM CASSEROLE

$1\frac{1}{2}$ *lb chuck steak*　　　　　*Bay leaf*
2 *oz dripping*　　　　　　*Parsley and thyme*
4 *small onions*　　　　　 $\frac{1}{2}$ *pint stock*
4 *oz button mushrooms*　　1 *dessertspoon cornflour*

Cut the steak in cubes and lightly brown in melted dripping. Put into the casserole with onions cut in quarters, mushrooms, herbs and stock. Cover tightly and cook at 350°F (Gas Mark 4) for 2 hours. Before serving, remove herbs and thicken with cornflour. Garnish with a little freshly chopped parsley.

BOILED SPICED BEEF

Choose a piece of beef with as little bone as possible, sprinkle it well with salt, and let it drain for 24 hours. Then prepare the following mixture: 1 lb of common salt, 1 ounce of saltpetre, ½ lb of sugar, and a mixture of pounded mace, cloves and nutmeg. Rub this well into the beef, and let it lie in a crock for a week, turning and basting it daily. Leave it in the pickle for 3 days longer, turning it each day, but not rubbing it. Then drain it well and cook. When cold, this makes very excellent sandwiches.

SPICED BEEF

10–12 lb pickled beef *1 saltspoon grated nutmeg*
1 dessertspoon black pepper *½ saltspoon ground mace*
½ teaspoon ground ginger *1 glass claret or port*
1 saltspoon powdered cloves

Drain the beef from the pickle. Mix together the other ingredients (except the wine) and sprinkle them over the entire surface of the meat, which must then be rolled, bound and skewered into a good shape. Put the meat into an earthenware stew-pot with a lid, pour the wine over it, cover the top of the vessel with 2 or 3 thicknesses of greased paper and put on the lid.

As no other liquid than the wine is added, it is absolutely necessary that the steam generated should be kept within the vessel, and for this purpose the lid is frequently covered with a paste of flour and water. The meat should be cooked slowly in the oven for about 4 hours, and then pressed between 2 boards until cold.

A SAVOURY POCKET STEAK

1 small onion and 3 *1 lb or more of rump steak,*
mushrooms chopped finely *1 inch thick*
  1 oz butter and breadcrumbs

Cook vegetables in the butter a few minutes, add the crumbs and seasoning. With a sharp knife give the steak a slit through, leaving the bottom of each side ½ inch thick, fill the pocket as a pincushion with the mixture, and skewer up, pour over a little oil, and grill or bake 10 to 12 minutes. Serve with potato chips, and glaze poured over.

Mrs Page, 1899

CORNISH UNDERROAST

2 lb shin beef
8 oz ox kidney
1 lb onions
1 oz plain flour

Salt and pepper
1 pint stock
Potatoes

Cut up beef and kidney into very small pieces. Slice onions. Toss meat in flour and season well. Fry meat and onions in a meat tin with dripping until meat has changed colour. Pour on stock and leave to simmer while the potatoes are prepared. Peel the potatoes and cut them into pieces about the size of an egg. Put them all over the meat, half below and half above the gravy line like icebergs. Cook at 325°F (Gas Mark 3) for 2 hours until the potato tops are brown and the bottoms soaked in gravy. Serve with plenty of vegetables.

SCOTCH COLLOPS

1 lb fresh minced beef
1 large onion
1 oz butter or dripping

Salt and pepper
1 tablespoon oatmeal
1 breakfastcup water

Brown the beef and finely chopped onion in the fat. Season with salt and pepper, add the oatmeal and water. Cover with a lid and simmer for 30 minutes. Put into a serving dish and surround with mashed potato. Poached eggs may be served on top.

SUFFOLK NESTS

1 small onion
1 lb minced beef (raw)
Pinch of mixed herbs
3 tomatoes
1 oz butter

Salt and pepper
4 eggs
4 tablespoons cream or top milk

Chop the onion and cook in butter, then add meat, herbs, tomatoes and seasoning. Cook gently for 15 minutes and put into greased oven dish. Make 4 hollows, drop an egg into each, and top with a tablespoon of cream. Bake at 375°F (Gas Mark 5) until eggs are set (about 10 minutes).

VEAL FRICASSEE

2 lb breast of veal
2-3 oz cooked peas
1-2 egg yolks
1 stick celery
2 large carrots

2 potatoes
Parsley
$\frac{1}{2}$ gill cream
Cornflour
Salt and pepper

Trim the meat and cut into small squares; place them in a large saucepan. Sprinkle with salt and cover with cold water, bring gently to the boil, removing scum as it rises to the surface. When the water boils clearly, add the celery, carrots and potatoes cut into small squares. Allow to simmer until the vegetables are cooked, then remove them from the pan. Continue simmering the meat until it is quite tender, then transfer it to the dish on which you will serve it, and keep it hot while preparing the sauce. Strain the liquid into a small pan; blend in 1 dessertspoon of cornflour previously dissolved with cold water. Reheat the sauce, stirring all the time, then remove from the heat. Blend into the sauce the egg yolks and ½ gill cream. Add the cooked vegetables and the cooked green peas to the sauce and reheat all together gently, without allowing it to boil. Pour this all over the cooked meat and dredge generously with chopped parsley before serving.

VEAL FILLETS WITH SEMOLINA STUFFING

1 lb veal, cut in the thinnest
possible slices
Semolina

Bacon, chopped
Nutmeg
Fresh parsley, chopped

Cook the semolina in the usual way, leave to cool a little, then add the chopped bacon, a little nutmeg, and chopped parsley. Leave to set. When cold, cut the stuffing into fingers. Place a finger of stuffing on a slice of veal, roll round tightly and secure with a cocktail stick or tie with string. Heat some butter in a pan and fry the rolls until brown all over. Place meat in a casserole, dot with butter and cook for 35–40 minutes or until tender, 350°F (Gas Mark 4).

VEAL WITH SHERRY

4 veal cutlets or chops
6 tablespoons olive oil
1 stalk celery
1 carrot
1 onion

1 tablespoon tomato paste
¼ pint dry sherry
Salt and pepper
Chopped parsley

Heat the oil and fry the meat until brown; add the vegetables and mix well. Cover and simmer for about 10 minutes or until the vegetables are tender; mix with tomato paste and sherry together and add to the meat, together with the seasoning. Cover and cook until the meat is tender – about 20 minutes, add water during cooking time if necessary to prevent burning. Sprinkle with chopped parsley.

VEAL FILLETS IN YOGHURT

For each person allow one small round or 'steak' of veal (escallop or 'collop'). Fry the veal 'collops' in butter until tender and cooked and browned lightly on both sides. Sprinkle with salt. Remove the meat and keep hot; meanwhile cook some mushrooms, as required, in the butter. Put the meat back into pan with the mushrooms and pour over sufficient natural yoghurt to cover each escallop. Sprinkle liberally, or to taste, with paprika. Heat most carefully for a few minutes and serve right away.

Mrs Hutchins suggests serving this dish with new potatoes, if in season, or mashed or Duchesse potatoes, peas or French beans and carrots. Garnish with parsley.

Mrs Hutchins, Norfolk

COLD STUFFED BREAST OF VEAL

For 4 people you need 2 lb breast of veal cut in 1 piece, and for the stuffing about 1 lb cut into very small cubes the size of a finger nail or smaller, 4 oz chopped ham, 3 eggs, 4 oz cooked green peas, the same amount of cooked carrot, a cup of grated cheese and oil (or a good knob of butter) and hard-boiled eggs.

Mix all the ingredients well together, excepting the large piece of veal, the oil and the hard-boiled eggs but including the raw eggs; season and then place in a pan and lightly fry in the oil, turning over all the time so that the veal cubes are cooked through and the whole well mixed. Cut open the breast of veal and then alternately fill with a layer of the stuffing and a layer of hard-boiled eggs cut into slices (any number of hard-boiled eggs can be used). When full, sew up the breast, wrap in a white cloth and boil for 3 hours.

Allow to get cold and then serve with salad or with the green sauce.

Signora Beglia, Italy

VEAL BIRDS

You need veal escallops, flour, oil, garlic, small black olives and a little white wine. Dip the escallops in flour. Crush the clove of garlic into the oil so that it becomes quite liquid, mix in wine and some small black olives and pour into an oiled pan over a very hot fire. Drop in the lightly floured escallops. Cook for 5 or 6 minutes. Allow 1 escallop per person.

Signora Beglia, Italy

LANCASHIRE HOT POT (1)

Lamb chops, onions, potatoes. The lamb would be from the neck end. To every $\frac{3}{4}$ lb meat allow $\frac{1}{2}$ lb sliced onions and 1 lb sliced potatoes. Into your casserole put potatoes, then onions, then meat, then start again, adding salt and pepper on top of second lot of potatoes (salt sprinkled on meat makes it tough). Finish with a layer of potatoes. Cover with water. Place lid on top of all and cook in hottish oven for a bit, then in cooler oven for 2–3 hours. Take off lid for about $\frac{1}{2}$ hour before serving to brown top layer of potatoes. (Modern ovens – first $\frac{1}{2}$ hour at 400°F, Gas Mark 6, then 2–3 hours at 250°F, Gas Mark 1.) Add more water if and when it is needed.

LANCASHIRE HOT POT (2)

2 lb potatoes, $1\frac{1}{2}$ lb scrag of mutton, 2 sheeps' kidneys (optional), 1 large onion, about $\frac{1}{2}$ pint water, dripping or butter, pepper and salt. You grease an earthenware casserole or hot pot jar and put in a thick layer of sliced potatoes and then the meat cut into suitably sized pieces. Cover with the sliced onion and season with pepper and salt. Pour on about $\frac{1}{2}$ pint water. Finally place on top of the rest of the potatoes cut in halves to cover the meat etc., completely. Dot the dripping or butter over the top. Cook slowly for $2\frac{1}{4}$ hours adding more water between times and keeping lid or butter paper on top to keep from getting too dried-up. Uncover for last 30 minutes to get brown and crispy.

LAMB AND POTATO HOT POT

1 lb boned shoulder lamb	*1 beef cube in 1 pint hot water*
1 lb breast of lamb (also	*2 bayleaves*
boned)	*Parsley*
$\frac{3}{4}$ lb floury potatoes	*1 teaspoon rosemary*
2 large onions	*12 shallots*
Salt and pepper	*12 small potatoes*
1 stick celery	*4 oz grilled streaky bacon*

Cut the meat into 2 inch chunks. Peel and slice floury potatoes and onions and put in alternate layers with the meat in a casserole. Season well with salt and pepper, and add the celery, stock, bayleaves, parsley and rosemary. Cover and simmer for 1 hour. When cool, remove meat to a clean casserole, discard celery, bayleaves and parsley, and mash onions and potatoes into gravy. Pour this gravy over meat, and add peeled shallots and small potatoes. Snip grilled bacon into small pieces over the top and continue cooking uncovered for 30 minutes.

LAMB AND MUSHROOM HOT POT

1½ lb best-end lamb cutlets   ¾ pint stock
1 oz plain flour   Salt and pepper
2 oz butter   Pinch of rosemary
1 onion   1 lb potatoes
6 oz button mushrooms

Trim fat from cutlets and coat them with flour. Melt the butter and fry cutlets and sliced onion until golden. Put into a casserole with mushrooms stock, salt and pepper and rosemary. Peel the potatoes and cut in ¼ inch slices. Arrange potatoes on top of meat, cover and bake at 300°F (Gas Mark 2) for 1½ hours. Take off the lid and continue baking for 30 minutes. Good with peas and young turnips.

LAMB CASSEROLE

1½ lb middle neck lamb chops   Pinch of marjoram
2 large onions   Stock
2 lb potatoes   Salt and pepper

Take off excess fat and arrange the chops in alternate layers in a casserole with sliced onion and potato, seasoning each layer with a sprinkle of marjoram, salt and pepper, and ending with a layer of potatoes. Half fill the casserole with stock and cook at 375°F (Gas Mark 5) for 2 hours. Take off lid and brown potatoes for 30 minutes.

BOILED MUTTON

Half a leg of mutton, a large onion, carrot, turnip, bunch of herbs, parsley, 12 peppercorns, a little mace, salt.

Weigh the meat, wipe it over with a clean cloth and put into a saucepan containing sufficient boiling water to entirely cover, and let it boil for 5 minutes. Then pour in a little cold water to lower the temperature, and add vegetables, herbs, and spice. Lower the burner and let the meat simmer only till done. 20 minutes to each pound should be allowed and 20 minutes over from the start of the simmering. Remove scum from time to time and close saucepan quickly as possible. About ½ hour before serving, add some salt.

It may be served with a nice thick melted butter sauce poured all over, and with the vegetables cut small, arranged in neat piles round. Celery is good with it.

Mary Bull, 1914

BOILED MUTTON AND BROTH

Leg or shoulder of mutton
2 teaspoons salt
Boiling water
2 oz pearl barley

1 large onion
½ lb sliced carrot and turnip
1 oz shredded cabbage
1 tablespoon parsley

Weigh meat, place in pan of salted boiling water. Boil fast for 10 minutes. Skim and allow to simmer; pour boiling water on the barley, rinse and add to the pan. Simmer for 1 hour; then add the sliced onion and vegetables. The cooking time is calculated as 25 minutes per pound of meat plus 25 minutes for the bone. Remove the meat and ½ pint of the liquid. Add the cabbage to the soup pan, boil for 3 minutes. Skim and check the seasoning. Add the chopped parsley. The meat is good with caper or parsley sauce.

MUTTON IN WINE

This is a good way of turning a leg of mutton into a special dish. Put the joint into a saucepan with a wineglass of water, over strong heat, till the water has evaporated and the meat coloured. Add 1 wineglass of red wine and 2 cups of meat stock, with ½ grated onion, a bunch of parsley and thyme, a bayleaf, salt and pepper. Cover tightly, and simmer on a low fire for 3 hours. Just before serving, remove the joint to a serving plate. Strain the gravy, mix in ¼ pint of cream and 2 egg yolks, and warm without boiling. Pour over the meat on the serving dish.

STEWED SHOULDER OF MUTTON

Mutton is not sold much today but lamb is usually one of the cheaper meats and could be used for this.

Remove bone from a shoulder of small mutton or lamb. Make seasoning of breadcrumbs, herbs, onions, butter and a little milk (seasoning in this context is simply the old way of saying 'stuffing'). Mix well together and fill up the space from which the bone has been taken. Sew up tightly, put in a boiler pan (or big saucepan with some sort of tray effect on which to stand meat). Cover meat with hot water and add a little salt to the water. Boil for 1½ hours slowly with lid on. Take the meat from water and skim all fat from liquor; put in some peeled onions, also the mutton and simmer slowly for a further ¾ hour. Just before dishing blend some flour with a little cold water sufficient to thicken the gravy in which the meat has been stewed. Serve with boiled, minted, new potatoes, if possible, and green peas.

HASHED MUTTON

Make a white sauce not too thick. Cut up rather fine 2 heads of lettuce and 3 green onions – the white part only of the onions. Put these in the sauce to cook about ½ an hour. Add with pepper and salt the juice of half a lemon. Then put in the sliced-up mutton; leave it to simmer a short time. Then put in the yolks of 2 eggs well beaten with a little cold water. Serve as the eggs begin to thicken.

Mrs Garden, 1847

PORK AND APPLES

4 pork chops　　　　　　　　　*Pinch of mixed herbs*
1 large onion　　　　　　　　　*Salt and pepper*
2 apples

Wipe pork chops and cook gently in thick frying pan until the fat runs. Turn over chops and surround with sliced onions and apples, sprinkle with herbs and seasoning and continue cooking gently until pork is cooked through, onions are soft and apples reduced to a pulp. Serve with mashed potatoes or with well-drained buttered noodles.

STUFFED APPLES AND PORK

Small joint of pork　　　　　　*1 breakfastcup dry sage and*
Lard for 'dotting' and 1 oz for　*onion stuffing*
stuffing　　　　　　　　　　　*1 large onion, peeled and*
4 Bramley's Seedling apples　　*grated*
(all about the same size)　　　*Salt and pepper*

Put joint in a roasting tin, with about 2 tablespoons of water. Dot with lard. Allow 30 minutes to the pound and 30 minutes over at 375°F (Gas Mark 5) cooking time, with the joint towards the top of the oven. Baste frequently. Core apples, and gently cut through the skin round the middle of the apple. Mix the onion with the stuffing mixture. Put the apples in a lightly greased pie dish. Fill core cavities with stuffing and spread the rest over the top of the apples. Melt the lard, pour over the stuffing and season. Put the apples in the lower part of the oven 1½ hours before the meat has finished cooking, basting frequently with juices from the meat tin.

TENDERLOIN IN BRANDY AND CREAM

Cut your slices of tenderloin slightly on the bias so that they hold together. If you can't cut them ⅛ inch thin – bash them with your husband's mallet or the flat of a heavy knife. Melt a piece of butter in a frying pan – fry the pieces gently on both sides. When you have cooked about 2 or 3 lots the butter will begin to darken – quickly pour in a tablespoon of brandy and set it alight. When the flames have died down pour over half a carton of double cream and let it bubble till it turns dark gold, scraping up the juices meanwhile. Now if you can serve at once do so – if you can't, flatten a sheet of buttery greaseproof paper over the fried pieces and put them to cool quickly and pour the sauce into a separate bowl. Wash the pan and do it again as many times as necessary. When I did it one summer for a silver wedding party we gave for some friends, we had 18 people and most of them came from Scotland. The last people arrived 2 hours late having had an accident and we sat down to dinner at 10.30 instead of 8.30. While we ate the first course the dish of meat was in the slow oven of the Aga and the sauce in a pan on the slow ring. When we were ready the sauce was quickly boiled up and poured over and all was well.

Mrs Chaplin, Finsthwaite, Lancs

PORK CHOPS WITH LEMON

Leave chops to marinate in lemon juice with a pinch of thyme and melted butter in a fireproof dish turning them once or twice during the process. Cook them in the same dish as they are, fairly gently so that they absorb the juice as much as possible. I serve them straight from the dish with mashed or boiled potatoes or just home made bread. A green salad goes well.

Mrs Chaplin, Finsthwaite, Lancs

PORK CHOPS IN ORANGE SAUCE

4 pork loin chops 1 inch thick
2 dessertspoons flour
½ teaspoon salt
2 tablespoons lard
1 dessertspoon soft brown sugar

Pinch of ginger
1 tablespoon grated orange peel
⅓ pint orange juice

Wipe chops with damp kitchen paper and coat with a mixture of flour and salt. Heat lard and brown chops on each side, about 10 minutes in all. Mix together sugar, ginger, peel and juice and pour over chops. Cover and simmer for 45 minutes until chops are tender. Serve with peeled orange rings, mashed potatoes and a green salad.

STUFFED BELLY OF PORK

2 lb belly pork   *1 pig's kidney*
Sage and onion stuffing   *Salt*

Stuff the pork with sage and onion, adding the chopped kidney to the
mixture. Rub the scored skin with a little melted lard, sprinkle well with
salt and roast for 1½ hours at 375°F (Gas Mark 5).

PORK AND APPLE CASSEROLE

4 spare rib pork chops   *¼ pint stock*
1 medium onion   *Pinch of sage or basil*
1 cooking apple   *Salt and pepper*
4 oz tomatoes

Lightly brown the chops on both sides. Surround with sliced onion,
cover with stock and season to taste, adding chosen herb. Cover tightly
and cook at 325°F (Gas Mark 3) for 1 hour. Put sliced apple and tomatoes
on top, and continue cooking for 20 minutes. Remove lid and allow meat
to brown for 15 minutes.

KIDNEYS

The most delicious way of cooking kidneys is to cook them in their own
fat. Put the kidneys surrounded by their fat into a casserole or baking tin,
and bake in a moderate oven (350°F, Gas Mark 4) for 30 minutes. Cut off
the fat, season the kidneys with salt and pepper, and plenty of chopped
parsley and return them to the oven for 5 minutes surrounded by their
own gravy.

HEARTS

Simmer gently in a little seasoned stock in a casserole until tender, then
cut into pieces, removing tubes, and return to the stock with plenty of
onions and a little sage. Simmer until onions are cooked, then thicken the
gravy.

Those who like the traditional ox heart stuffed with sage and onion,
sometimes known as 'mock goose', can vary the stuffing by using a mixture of chopped walnuts and breadcrumbs, or by using bacon and plenty
of mixed herbs.

BRAINS

Put brains in a basin under a cold tap for an hour, then remove all skin, ligaments and blood vessels. They should then be cooked by simmering in a little water to cover with a spoonful of white vinegar and a pinch of salt for 30 minutes, before draining and drying.

They are delicious cut in large squares, dipped in batter and deep fried until golden, then served very hot with salt and parsley. They can also be served with a squeeze of lemon, or with home-made tomato sauce.

The most elegant accompaniment is *Black Butter* served over brains which have been simmered, then cut up in pieces and kept warm. This is made by browning 2 oz butter, adding 1 dessertspoon chopped parsley and pouring over the brains, then swilling out the pan with 1 dessertspoon vinegar or lemon juice and pouring this over the brains too. A little chopped garlic or a few capers may be added.

SWEETBREADS

Put sweetbreads in a basin under cold running water for an hour, then remove any skin, hard pieces or blood and dry them well. Blanch them in a saucepan of boiling salted water for 10 minutes, then drain and dry them, and leave to cool.

To serve simply, they can be cut into thick slices, seasoned and floured and fried until golden in butter or olive oil, then garnished with parsley or lemon.

The pre-cooked sweetbreads may also be cut in pieces and threaded on skewers with pieces of thick bacon and small mushrooms, then seasoned and rolled in melted butter and breadcrumbs before grilling under low heat for 10 minutes.

LIVER

Liver can be cut in thin slices, lightly floured, then cooked quickly in butter or bacon fat, to serve with crisp bacon. If onions are also served, clear the pan with a little red wine to make a good gravy, and finish the dish with chopped parsley and squares of fried bread.

The liver can be cut in cubes and threaded with squares of bacon on skewers, finished off with small tomatoes, brushed with oil, salt and pepper and chopped thyme and grilled. Alternatively, cut the liver, bacon and onion in very small pieces, cook them separately and quickly in a little butter or oil, then toss them with plenty of hot buttered boiled rice, a few button mushrooms cooked in butter, plenty of salt and pepper, and herbs, preferably thyme and rosemary.

Liver is particularly juicy cut in cubes and cooked quickly in deep hot fat. Some people like to dip the cubed liver in batter first. If you have a large family, try cooking roast liver, cutting a gash in the solid piece and filling it with a stuffing of bacon, onion, breadcrumbs and egg, then roasting the liver in a moderate oven with a covering of streaky bacon rashers.

This is delicious with a good gravy made from the pan juices, and with redcurrant jelly.

OXTAIL STEW

2 oxtails	Salt and pepper
1 oz dripping	1 teaspoon tomato purée
1 lb carrots	1 tablespoon lemon juice
8 oz onions	Bunch of mixed herbs
1 oz flour	

Chop the oxtails into joints, wipe and dry them and fry lightly until golden in dripping. Add thick slices of carrot and sliced onions, and when lightly coloured, sprinkle in flour, and mix well. Add water to cover, or a mixture of water and wine, or cheap red or white wine. Add herbs, salt and pepper, bring to the boil. Simmer or cook in oven set at 300°F (Gas Mark 2) for 2 hours.

Strain off liquid and leave until cold, then take off fat – this can be done the evening before the meal is needed. Put meat and vegetables into casserole, pour on liquid and bring to the boil. Adjust seasoning if necessary, and stir in tomato purée and lemon juice. Cover and cook at 300°F (Gas Mark 2) for 3 hours, and serve sprinkled thickly with chopped parsley.

STEWED OXTAIL

1 oxtail	1 tablespoon lemon juice
6 cloves	2 carrots, cut finely
¼ teaspoon whole white pepper	1 large onion, sliced
2 oz butter	Bunch of herbs
1 oz flour	Salt to taste

Fry the onion slices in the butter, remove from pan when brown; fry the joints of tail in same butter. Take out the joints, stir in the flour, and allow it to get light brown. Return the joints and onions, cover with stock or water, add the seasonings and vegetables, simmer slowly for 3 hours, and add the lemon juice just before serving. The meat should leave the bone easily when sufficiently stewed. Skim off as much fat as possible before serving and arrange the joints neatly in the dish before pouring over the gravy.

WELSH STEWED OXTAIL

1 good sized oxtail   ***Sufficient Old Ale to cover***

Leave soaking overnight, before cooking the following morning with suitable vegetables to accompany it according to the time of year. Plenty of onions or shallots, sufficient for one whole one per person. It is best to cook the oxtail alone until nearly tender, then add the vegetables at a suitable time – finishing with sliced potatoes which will also help to thicken the rich gravy. If wished, a dumpling-type covering can be added about 20–25 minutes before dishing.

Dumpling Mixture	*As much good dripping as you*
8 oz self raising flour	*can scoop on to your fingers,*
½ eggspoon salt	*twice*
1 level teaspoon baking	*Water*
powder	

Rub dripping (2–3 oz lard may be used if preferred but is not as tasty) into the dry ingredients and mix with sufficient water to make a nice soft dough. This dough can either be used to cover the whole stew in one whole piece, or it can be divided into individual dumplings by flouring the hands and dividing into suitable number of portions. Serve as soon as dumplings are fluffy and cooked.

    While on holiday may years ago, this delicious recipe was given to the Honey family by 'Billy the Butch' or Thomas-the-Meat in Haverfordwest, Pembrokeshire. He said that as farmers they would fully appreciate this dish, 'Only,' he warned, 'don't let father get at the ale before you can cook the oxtail.'

FFAGOD SIR BENFRO

1½ lb pig's liver	2 teaspoons salt
2 large onions	½ teaspoon pepper
3 oz suet	1–2 teaspoons sage
4 oz breadcrumbs	½ oz flour

Mince the raw liver and onions. Mix thoroughly with the suet, breadcrumbs, seasoning and sage. Form into small balls. Bake in a moderate oven for about 30 minutes. Remove from the tin and keep warm. To make gravy, stir the ½ oz flour into the pan juices and add boiling water or vegetable stock, and seasoning.

    This is a Pembrokeshire recipe. It was very popular fifty or sixty years ago after pig killing. The English equivalent would be 'Savoury Ducks' but Ffagods are very much nicer.

Many Welshmen were hill-farming people. Because of this their recipes contained a good deal of carbohydrate, which besides being cheap, provided the energy needed for the hard manual labour of farm work.

HAGGIS

The thrifty Scots would not, indeed could not afford to, waste anything so when a sheep was killed every little bit was used.

The paunch and pluck of a sheep
2 large handsful of oatmeal
1 lb onions
½ lb grated suet

1 tablespoon chopped parsley
1 teaspoon grated nutmeg
½ pint 'pluck' stock
Salt and pepper to taste

Wash the paunch thoroughly in several cold waters, turn inside out and wash and scrape in very hot water. Leave overnight steeping in cold, salted water. Wash the 'pluck' thoroughly and blanch, then boil gently for 2 hours. Remove windpipe and gristle and mince the heart, liver etc. finely. Toast the oatmeal a little in a warm oven or in front of a fire, chop the onions and mix all ingredients together very thoroughly. Fill the paunch almost full (to allow for expansion), tie or sew up, prick well and place in a pan with sufficient boiling water to cover. Boil steadily for 3 hours.

LANCASHIRE KIDNEY CASSEROLE

I usually use pigs' kidneys, 1 for 2 people, plus onion, carrots and potatoes. Slice and roll in seasoned flour. Brown in saucepan, also 1 onion. Put in casserole, plus carrots and top with sliced potatoes. Add some stock and cook for about 2 hours in a medium oven.

BLACK DISH

To every ½ lb liver, allow 1 large onion, 1 cup water, salt and pepper and a teaspoon of chopped sage. Put all this together in a 'reet gud' dish (a casserole) and cook well with the lid on. And don't be mean with the salt and pepper and add more water if necessary. Serve with mashed potatoes and carrots. In Victorian days, offal was seldom served to the gentry, and the poorer people benefited from this silly fad. These 2 recipes were told to her great-granddaughter by a very old Lancashire lady. She says they were traditional in her childhood and she made them all her life, and she insists they are still good enough for anyone.

OX TONGUE

Put tongue into tepid water with salt; boil for 3 hours, or until the skin is easily removed. When skin is peeled off, curve tongue round in a suitable glass or chrome dish and cover with a flat plate. On plate stand a very heavy weight and leave to cool till the following morning. Ease tongue around with a curvey knife and slide out on to an oval meat dish. Garnish with fresh parsley.

The flavour of the tongue is improved if onions or other suitable vegetables are cooked in the water with the tongue. The resulting liquid is excellent for soup.

TONGUE WITH CUMBERLAND SAUCE

1 salted ox tongue (4-6 lbs)
½ lb root vegetables
Bayleaf, thyme and parsley
Peppercorns

Cumberland Sauce
2 large tablespoons
redcurrant jelly
1 glass port
Juice of 1 orange and ½ lemon
1 teaspoon shredded,
blanched orange rind

Wash the tongue and put in a large pan. Cover with cold water, and bring slowly to the boil. Skim well, add chopped vegetables, herbs and peppercorns, and simmer until the bones at the root of the tongue will pull out easily (about 3 hours). Cool in the liquid, then take off skin and trim away root and bones. Curl the tongue round in a cake tin, and cover with a plate and a weight. Leave 24 hours before turning out. To make the sauce, heat the redcurrant jelly until dissolved, then stir in the rest of the ingredients. Serve cold with tongue, or with ham.

DEVILLED KIDNEYS

4 lambs' kidneys
2 onions
2 tomatoes
1 level tablespoon cornflour
1 level teaspoon curry powder

½ pint beef stock
1 tablespoon chutney
Salt and pepper
Squeeze of lemon juice

Slice kidneys, onions and tomatoes and toss in a little hot oil until onions are just golden. Add cornflour and curry powder, cook for 1 minute, stir in stock and bring to the boil. Add chutney, salt and pepper and lemon juice and simmer for 15 minutes. Serve on toast or with rice or mashed potatoes.

BRAISED LIVER

1-1¼ lb ox liver	Bacon trimmings
2 oz dripping	1 teaspoon flour
2 oz onions	Cup of water
8 oz carrots	Salt and pepper
4 oz turnips	1 heaped teaspoon arrowroot
Stick of celery	

Cut thick slices of liver and fry in very hot dripping; remove and next fry the onions and rough-cut vegetables and bacon trimmings. Place in a casserole, lay the liver on top and sprinkle on the flour. Add the water and seasoning and cook, covered, for 1¼ hours, in a moderate oven. Mix the arrowroot with a little water and pour into the casserole; colour with browning if necessary. Cook for another 15 minutes.

A SUBSTITUTE FOR LAMB'S FRY

Lamb's fry is a very expensive dish, but here is a substitute which few can tell from lamb's fry. Cut neat small strips of calf's liver and a lamb's sweetbread into slices; well butter a dish, and screen it with breadcrumbs. Then arrange the calf's liver upon the crumbs, then the slices of sweetbread, and scatter bits of butter here and there. Dust over a little pepper, cover it with a piece of buttered paper, put the dish in a moderately heated oven, and serve with a dish of nicely mashed potatoes.

Mrs Herbert Newton, Norfolk 1913

TRIPE AND ONIONS

1 lb dressed tripe	1 oz flour
4-8 oz onions	Salt and pepper
1 pint milk	

Put tripe in cold water and bring to the boil. Remove from the water and cut into small strips. Cut up the onions, place them in cold water and bring to the boil; strain off water and put the onions with the tripe and milk, add seasoning. Simmer for 2 hours. Mix the flour with a little water or milk; add to tripe etc. and boil for a few minutes.

TRIPE ROLLS

1 lb cooked tripe	Bunch of mixed herbs
8 oz bacon pieces	Nutmeg
3 onions	1 pint cider
3 carrots	

Cut the tripe in neat slices and cover with slices of bacon. Season with salt and pepper, nutmeg and a sprinkling of herbs, and roll up, tying with cotton. Slice the onions and carrots into a casserole, add a bunch of herbs, put on the tripe rolls and pour on the cider, adding a little water to cover if necessary. Cover and cook at 325°F (Gas Mark 3) for 3 hours. Serve very hot with a purée of potatoes.

THE DOCTOR'S TRIPE HOT POT

1 *lb pre-cooked tripe*	3 *tomatoes*
1 *oz flour*	*Beef stock*
1 *lb onions*	*Salt and pepper*
2 *lb potatoes*	1 *tablespoon beef dripping*

Wipe the tripe and cut it into squares. Dip in flour lightly seasoned with salt and pepper. Peel the onions and potatoes, and remove skins from tomatoes. Cut them all in slices. Grease a deep casserole and fill with alternate layers of tripe and vegetables, seasoning each layer, and ending with a layer of potatoes. Pour in the stock so that it comes half way up the dish. Dot with dripping and put on a lid. Cook at 375°F (Gas Mark 5) for 1¼ hours. Remove lid and continue cooking for 15 minutes to brown the potatoes.

TRIPE AND BACON

1 *lb pre-cooked tripe*	¼ *pint water*
8 *oz bacon rashers*	1 *dessertspoon tomato sauce*
½ *oz plain flour*	*Salt and pepper*

Fry the bacon slowly so that the fat runs. Put the bacon on a warm dish. Slice the tripe and fry it until golden in the bacon fat. Put the tripe with the bacon on the dish. Sprinkle the flour into the fat and cook for 1 minute, stirring well. Add the water, sauce and salt and pepper, stirring all the time. When hot and thick, pour over the tripe and bacon. Serve with mashed potatoes and peas. A few sliced onions cooked with this are very good.

IVERSON GRILLED TRIPE

1 *lb pre-cooked tripe*	1 *tablespoon chopped onion*
1 *tablespoon finely chopped parsley*	2 *tablespoons melted butter*
1 *tablespoon vinegar or lemon juice*	*Salt and pepper*
	Browned breadcrumbs

Wipe the tripe and cut it into bite-sized pieces. Mix together the parsley, onion, vinegar or lemon juice, butter and seasonings. Dip the tripe pieces into this and coat them with breadcrumbs. Brown under a hot grill for 5 minutes each side. This is good with crusty bread and butter, and a winter salad of watercress, chicory and celery.

COTTAGE PIE

A $\frac{1}{4}$ lb of cold meat, 1 lb of cold potatoes, a little gravy, $\frac{1}{2}$ oz of dripping, $1\frac{1}{2}$ teaspoons of flour, $\frac{1}{2}$ an onion, $\frac{1}{4}$ pint of water, and a little salt and pepper. Put the meat through a mincing machine, and mash the potatoes. Then grease a pie-dish, and put in alternate layers of potatoes and meat, seasoned with pepper and salt, also a little gravy and onion, until dish is full. The top layer should be of potatoes. Put the pie in the oven, and bake it until it is brown.

Miss P. Smith, 1913

DORMERS

An old, well-tried way of using up cold meat for hungry, growing teenagers. Chop up 1 lb scraps of cold lamb, 4 oz or less of suet, $\frac{1}{2}$ lb boiled rice, pepper and salt to taste, and mix. Roll up as sausages, cover with egg and breadcrumbs, fry in hot dripping until golden brown. Serve on a dish of mashed potatoes with carrot 'strips' and peas, with some hot gravy.

MEAT CAKES WITH TOMATOES

Take $\frac{1}{2}$ lb cold meat and chop up finely, or mince. In a saucepan melt a tablespoon of good, tasty dripping and in it gently fry a well chopped, or minced, onion. Then stir in, first, about $\frac{1}{2}$ lb of mashed potato, then the minced meat and finally salt and pepper to taste. Using a little flour on your hands, mould the mixture into rounds and place on a baking dish with a tiny nob of dripping on top. Cook in good oven until light brown, then place on top a slice of tomato or half a small tomato and continue baking until this is cooked. Serve on dish with parsley to garnish. If the meat is a bit scarce, serve the dish without tomatoes and send to table with poached eggs on top of the meat cakes.

PORK RISSOLES

Cut the meat off the bone of cold roast pork. Mince the meat or cut into very small neat pieces; mix it with a well-chopped onion, pepper and salt, breadcrumbs and 1 egg, well beaten, to bind the whole together. Form into shapes the size of an egg, and fry in hot dripping until golden brown. Meanwhile stew the pork-bone in a little water with an onion, salt and pepper and add flour and water thickening. Arrange the rissoles on a dish and pour the gravy round them. Serve with peas and mashed potatoes.

1911

MEAT LOAF

1½ lb raw lean meat (beef, veal, rabbit, mutton or a mixture of any of these)	Salt and pepper
	Nutmeg
	½ teaspoon mixed spice
3 oz fat bacon	2 eggs
1 tablespoon chopped onion	Stock
6 oz breadcrumbs	Brown crumbs

Cut the meat into small pieces and pass it, with the bacon, twice through the mincing machine. Chop the onion and add to the meat with the breadcrumbs and seasonings. Add the beaten eggs and sufficient stock to moisten. Press tightly into a greased bread tin, cover with greased paper, and steam for about 2 hours. Take off the paper, press the meat mixture down with weights, and leave until cold. Turn out, toss in brown crumbs, and serve cut in thin slices.

PORK SAUSAGE GALANTINE

1 lb pork sausage meat	1 tablespoon chutney
2 oz lean bacon	1 teaspoon Worcester sauce
1 egg	1 level teaspoon dried mustard
4 level tablespoons dried breadcrumbs	1 beef extract cube crumbled and dissolved in ¼ pint hot water
2 teaspoons chopped parsley	
Pinch mixed herbs	

Remove rind and chop the bacon finely. Beat the egg. Wash and chop the parsley. Make the stock. Mix all the ingredients together in a basin adding enough stock to make a fairly soft mixture. Grease a 1-pint pudding basin or a 1 lb loaf tin. Pack the mixture into it and cover with aluminium foil.

Steam for 1½ hours or pressure cook 15–20 minutes allowing the pressure to drop before removing the galantine. Leave the galantine to cool. Turn out, slice and serve.

73

CURRY

1 *lb meat (uncooked)*	2 *oz coconut*
2 *oz fat*	2 *teasponns chutney*
1 *oz plain flour*	*Pinch of sugar*
1 *onion*	1 *teaspoon redcurrant jelly*
1 *apple*	*Squeeze of lemon juice*
1 *dessertspoon curry powder*	*Stock*
Raisins or sultanas	

Cut up the meat and slice the onion and apple. Put the coconut to infuse in a little boiling water. Fry the meat, onion and apple in the fat, and remove to another pan. Fry the curry powder, then the flour. Add the stock and the strained coconut infusion. Boil well, and add chutney, sugar, redcurrant jelly and lemon juice. Pour over the meat and simmer for 2 hours.

Jean Clark, Cherington, Glos.

CAWL

Use any meat from the joint. Bring to the boil and simmer 30 minutes. Add carrots, swedes, cabbage etc. and simmer 30 minutes. Add potatoes and simmer until they are nearly cooked, and then add leeks. Simmer until leeks are tender. This is called Cawl Twmo (Welsh); Cawl 'Warmed Up' (English) and is eaten for a midday meal and warmed up for supper. Mr Raggett says the family were given this every Friday night when they reached home from school in Haverfordwest. When his sister Penny made it she thickened the gravy, whereas his mother did not. He preferred Penny's version. *Everyone* has cawl once a week, he reckons, in those parts.

Mark Raggett, Solva, Pembs

BUBBLE AND SQUEAK

Cut from boiled beef, slices the thickness of a penny piece. Trim and cut them as you please, partly underdone are the best. Plain boil 1 large cabbage, 1 onion, 1 carrot. When cooked, drain and mince very fine, removing any hard parts of cabbage. Put into a sauté pan a piece of butter as large as an egg when melted. Put in beef to warm, taking care it does not dry. This done, remove the meat and put in the vegetables. Stir on the fire till very hot, moisten with stock, add salt, pepper. Place them and the meat on the dish the same as cutlets. Pour a little stock over and serve.

Mrs Garden, 1847

DEVILLED MEAT

1 teaspoon mustard powder
1 teaspoon Worcester sauce
1 teaspoon chutney
½ teaspoon curry powder
1 teaspoon tomato sauce

2 teaspoons vinegar
Pinch of Cayenne pepper
Pinch of sugar
1 oz butter
Cooked meat or poultry

In a small, strong pan, mix together mustard, Worcester sauce, chutney, curry powder, tomato sauce, vinegar, Cayenne pepper, sugar and butter. Melt together and bring to the boil. Pour over slices of meat or poultry and put into a moderate oven, 350°F (Gas Mark 4), for 10 minutes, turning once. Remove the meat and grill on each side for 3 minutes. Serve very hot.

BEEF HASH

3 onions
1 tablespoon fat
1 lb cooked beef

½ lb cooked potatoes
¼ pint beef stock
Salt and pepper

Cut onions in cubes and fry in fat until brown. Add diced cooked beef and diced cooked potatoes, together with stock, and season well with salt and pepper. Continue simmering for 15 minutes.

5 Ham and Bacon

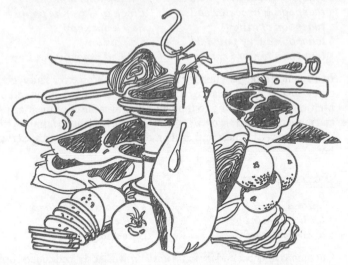

They sowes great with fare that come best for to rere
Loke dayly thou seest them and count them full dere.
And yet by the yere have I proved ere now
As good to the purse is a sow as a kow.
And he that will rere up a pig in his house
Shall eate sweter bakon and cheaper fed sowse.

Thomas Tusser

If you're lucky enough to have a whole ham you can store it in a cool dry place by the shank; uncooked hams should not be stored in a refrigerator or a damp atmosphere. Once a ham is cooked, it can be stored in a refrigerator, but the temperature shouldn't be below 40°F. When it's time for cooking, an old-fashioned fish kettle will substitute for a ham pan. Soak a ham for at least 24 hours, though 2 days may be necessary if the ham is very dry and well bloomed. Scrub off the bloom, weigh the ham, put in cold water and bring to boiling point. Simmer very gently (the actual temperature should be 185°F) allowing 15 minutes a lb, and leave the ham to cool in the water for an hour after cooking. To give extra flavour, I like to put a couple of bayleaves in the water and a tablespoon of brown sugar.

After cooling the ham for 24 hours to allow it to set, skin it, and trim off any discoloured meat, and dress the ham with rusk or breadcrumbs. One of the most important things about a whole ham is to see it is carved properly so that everyone has a share of lean and fat meat, and there is no waste. Use a thin-bladed sharp ham slicer for really tempting thin slices, and take the first slice from the knuckle end. Turn the ham round and carve the flank until the knife reaches the small covering bone over the leg joint. Take out this small bone, then turn the ham over and start carving the undercut. Go on cutting alternate slices from these 3 faces, until only the prime face is left, and go on carving this until the bone is clean.

Boiling bacon is a fairly everyday affair, but careful choice and cooking of the original joint can make all the difference between a stringy, salty piece of meat, and a succulent tender and sweet joint.

Forehock is one of the cheap boiling cuts, which can be boned and rolled to save time and trouble; one end is fatter than the other, so carving should be from alternate ends.

End of collar is another cheap piece which can be boiled and pressed lightly; two pieces may be pressed together. Another cut which is good for boiling and pressing is *flank*, rather fatter, which is very good served with rabbit or chicken. These three joints are particularly useful if you like to use up the end pieces in pies or puddings. *Prime Collar* is a middle price cut which is very good if long slits are cut in the meat and a stuffing of chopped herbs inserted. *Slipper* is a small lean joint which is good as a hot joint with spinach or broad beans. *The three gammon joints, middle, corner and hock,* are all choice cuts which respond particularly well to the treatment of boiling, then finishing in the oven with a glaze.

The usual complaint about bacon is that it is too salty. Always allow time for the joint to be soaked for at least 12 hours. If you still have doubts, cook a potato in the water, which will take up the salt. Simmer the joint very gently, allowing 20 minutes a lb. If you want to glaze and decorate the bacon, strip off the rind while the meat is still warm, then put the joint on a rack in a roasting tin before the glaze is used.

CIDER GLAZE

Stud the diamonds with 3 cloves each and sprinkle with 2 tablespoons demerara sugar. Pour over ½ pint medium sweet cider and continue to cook, basting regularly. When joint is cooked and fat golden brown, thicken juice with cornflour and serve with the joint.

APPLE AND MARMALADE GLAZE

Spread the scored fat with ¼ lb fairly thick marmalade. Peel, core and slice 1 large apple. Immerse in lemon juice for 10 minutes. Drain. Attach slices of apple on cocktail sticks to the fat. Brush with more marmalade and continue to cook, basting several times and covering with foil if the apples gets too brown.

RAISIN GLAZE

4 oz raisins
Grated rind and juice of 1
lemon

¼ pint water
4 tablespoons honey
Black pepper

Place the raisins, lemon rind, juice and water in a pan and simmer covered very gently for 10 minutes. Strain and add the honey to the liquid with a little pepper. Pour over the joint and continue to cook basting regularly until 10 minutes before the end. Return raisins to the liquor round the joint and serve spooned over the joint when completely cooked.

TREACLE GLAZE

Mix 2 tablespoons plain flour and 2 tablespoons demerara sugar with 2 tablespoons golden syrup and 3 tablespoons warm liquid from bacon. Spread over bacon, put in a hot oven, 400°F (Gas Mark 6), for 20 minutes.

HONEY GLAZE

Spread 2 tablespoons clear honey over the bacon and sprinkle with 1 tablespoon fine breadcrumbs. Mix ¼ pint pineapple juice and ¼ pint vinegar and pour over joint. Bake for 20 minutes at 400°F (Gas Mark 6) basting occasionally.

MUSTARD GLAZE

Mix 2 teaspoons French mustard, 2 tablespoons wine vinegar and 2 tablespoons cooking liquor, and pour over bacon. Mix together 2 tablespoons fine breadcrumbs and 1 tablespoon demerara sugar, and sprinkle over the joint. Bake at 400°F (Gas Mark 6) for 20 minutes.

CLOVE AND SUGAR GLAZE

Score the fat surface of the joint criss-cross and stud with cloves. Mix 1 teaspoon powdered cloves with 2 tablespoons soft brown sugar, and make a smooth paste with ginger ale. Spread on the bacon and bake at 400°F (Gas Mark 6) for 20 minutes.

A whole ham or a bacon joint always looks attractive with a special garnish. Canned or fresh pineapple rings, sprinkled with demerara sugar and quickly grilled until the surface caramelises, can be arranged on or round the bacon, with maraschino cherries in each circle. Sliced canned peaches and cherries make another garnish, or orange slices dipped in French dressing and sprinkled with chopped parsley. Half maraschino cherries can be fixed into the diamonds scored on a glazed bacon joint with whole cloves.

One of the best things about a joint of bacon or a ham is that there is never a scrap of waste. Use the remains to stuff large firm tomatoes, mixed with a few breadcrumbs and herbs, and a little chopped onion. Or bind the same mixture with an egg, fry and put between buttered baps as 'baconburgers'. Scotch eggs can be covered with minced cooked bacon instead of sausage meat, or apples can be stuffed with minced bacon well seasoned with herbs, and baked in the oven. Most of us know how delicious is bacon and egg pie, but bacon also goes well with onions in a creamy sauce for a supper-time flan (sprinkle the top with grated cheese and give it a golden finish in the oven or under the grill). An old-fashioned bacon roly-poly pudding is usually made with chopped uncooked bacon pieces, but minced cooked bacon is equally good with a little sweet pickle, chopped onion and mixed herbs, rolled up in a suet pastry and steamed for 2 hours, then served with hot tomato sauce. If you have a lot of sandwiches to prepare, make your own sandwich spread with minced cold bacon mixed with a little sweet pickle and onion, mayonnaise to bind and a spoonful of fine white breadcrumbs to stiffen the mixture. This is specially good for brown bread sandwiches with a few slices of tomato or cucumber.

BACON RASHERS

Bacon should have an adequate layer of white, firm fat over the rasher so that it will cook in its own delicious flavour. Remove rind from rashers and fry or grill 'shingled' so that the fat overlaps the lean; fat on top for grilling, underneath for frying. If your pan gets overheated, use a little best pork lard to prevent sticking, but don't allow the fat to smoke while cooking or the bacon will taste burnt. Don't add cooking oil or fat to bacon. Flavour will be at its best and shrinkage at a minimum if you allow 6–8 minutes for frying and 4–5 minutes for grilling. The rashers are cooked when crisp – but not brittle.

Drain off excess fat and use to add flavour when cooking other foods. Use up smoked bacon rinds, crisply fried and crushed, for seasoning soups or stews.

Middle Gammon: Perfect for boiling, or baking, and can also be baked in a crust. Cut into thick rashers ($\frac{1}{2}$ inch) it can be served as delicious gammon steaks.

Top back: Should be grilled in thin rashers, boiled or braised in the piece. A perfect lean cut.

Long Back: Good and lean. Slice thinly to fry gently, or grill quickly, for generous servings.

Streaky Back Rashers: Lean and deliciously streaky at end of rasher, best sliced thin. Perfect for grilling crisp.

Prime Collar: Besides making excellent rashers, this can be served as a whole joint – boiled, well seasoned – it makes a good joint, hot or cold.

BACON AND APPLE ROLL

8 oz flaky pastry
12 oz minced cooked bacon
1 large cooking apple

1 small onion
2 tablespoons of water

Roll the pastry into a rectangle. Mix together bacon, peeled and chopped apple, chopped onion and water. Spread bacon mixture on dough and form into a roll, putting on baking sheet so that the join is underneath. Brush roll with beaten egg, cut slits in surface to allow steam to escape, and bake in a hot oven for 20 minutes until the pastry is beginning to colour. Reduce heat and continue cooking until pastry is golden and crisp (about 1 hour in all). Serve hot or cold.

BACON AND LIVER LOAF

1$\frac{1}{2}$ lb minced lean bacon
$\frac{1}{2}$ lb minced liver
1 teacup fine breadcrumbs
1 egg
Salt and pepper

1 dessertspoon brown sugar
1 dessertspoon ground cloves
$\frac{1}{2}$ teacup milk
4 thin streaky rashers bacon

Mix together bacon, liver, breadcrumbs, egg, salt and pepper, sugar and cloves, and stir in milk. Grease 2 lb loaf tin and line with streaky rashers from which rind has been removed. Bake at 325°F (Gas Mark 3) for 1$\frac{1}{2}$ hours. Cool and unmould. For a picnic, wrap loaf in foil, and serve in slices or on buttered baps.

BACON GALANTINE (1)

8 oz cooked bacon	Pinch of mixed spice
4 oz stewing steak	1 teaspoon Worcester sauce
4 oz fresh white breadcrumbs	Pepper
1 large egg	Stock or water
½ teaspoon nutmeg	

Mince bacon and stewing steak together and mix with breadcrumbs, spices, sauce and egg, using just enough water or stock to bind. Shape in a rectangle, wrap in greased greaseproof paper, then in a cloth, leaving a little room for expansion. Steam for 1½ hours in a steamer, keeping water beneath boiling steadily. Lift out galantine, take off cloth and paper, and leave to cool. When cold, glaze the galantine with ½ gill stock flavoured with a little meat extract and thickened with 1 level teaspoon gelatine, using the glaze when it is just on the point of setting. For a party dish, decorate the galantine with a piped pattern of softened butter.

BACON GALANTINE (2)

½ lb collar bacon	Salt and pepper
½ lb beef sausage meat	2 eggs
4 oz white breadcrumbs	¼ pint strong beef stock
1 teaspoon chopped parsley	¾ oz gelatine
½ teaspoon mixed herbs	

Mince together bacon and sausage meat, and mix with breadcrumbs, chopped herbs, salt and pepper. Mix with eggs, then with the stock. Form into a roll, wrap in a floured cloth and tie with string. Cover with boiling water and cook gently for 2 hours. Remove and cool in cloth, preferably overnight. For the glaze: mix ½ pint strong beef stock with ¾ oz gelatine softened in 2 tablespoons cold water, and use the jelly just as it is setting.

BACON CASSEROLE

1 lb bacon	1 lb tomatoes
2 lb potatoes	1 gill milk
1 large onion	Seasoning

Arrange a layer of thinly sliced potatoes on the bottom of a well-buttered casserole. Cover with a layer of chopped bacon, sliced onion and sliced tomatoes, season well with salt and pepper and add a little sage if liked. Repeat these layers until the casserole is full, ending with a layer of potatoes, pour the milk over the top, add some pieces of butter, cook in a moderate oven for about 2 hours.

BACON AND TOMATO CASSEROLE

2 lb gammon slipper
2 large onions or leeks
14 oz tin tomatoes

1 teaspoon basil
Pepper

Soak the piece of bacon for 6 hours (2 hours if unsmoked). Put into casserole and cover with sliced onions or leeks, and tomatoes. Season with basil and freshly ground black pepper, cover tightly and cook, 350°F (Gas Mark 4), for 1 hour.

WELSH BACON

1-2 lb potatoes
4 rashers bacon
2 large onions

Pepper and salt
1 oz dripping
1 lb broad beans

Peel and wash the potatoes, and cut into equal-size pieces. Cover the bottom of a saucepan with half the bacon, cut into pieces. Add layers of potatoes and onions, finishing with potatoes. Season. Add the dripping and enough water to cover the bottom of the saucepan well. Cook very slowly until the potatoes are cooked. Add the beans, and cook faster for 15–20 minutes, to brown the potatoes.

BACON AND BEER CASSEROLE

2½ lb bacon collar
1 carrot
1 onion
Pepper
1 tablespoon black treacle

1 bayleaf
1 pint ale
1 oz butter
1 oz flour

Soak bacon for 6 hours (2 hours if unsmoked). Put in casserole, and add sliced carrot and onion, a shake of freshly ground black pepper, treacle, bayleaf and beer. Bring to the boil, skim, and simmer for 1 hour (or cook at 350°F, Gas Mark 4). Remove bacon, take off skin, and keep joint hot. Blend butter with flour and thicken the strained liquid. This is very good with baked parsnips.

SOMERSET GAMMON STEAKS

4 slices gammon about ½ inch thick
A little made mustard

2 medium-sized cooking apples
Fat for browning
¼ pint cider

Remove the rind from the gammon and spread each slice with mustard. Brown on both sides in a little hot fat in a frying pan. Lay each slice of gammon on a piece of foil, large enough to wrap it completely, on a baking tin or meat tray. Peel, core and quarter the apples then cut in thin slices. Lay the apples on top of the gammon pieces. Add the cider to the fat in the pan and simmer for a minute then pour over the meat. Wrap in the foil and bake about 30 minutes at 425°F (Gas Mark 7).

BACON ROLL

1 lb minced ham (left over from a gammon joint)
1 lb minced beef
1 small onion, finely chopped
1 stick celery, finely chopped

Salt and pepper to taste
Pinch of mixed herbs
1 egg
½ lb streaky bacon rashers

Mix together in a large bowl the minced ham, minced beef, onion, celery, seasoning, herbs and beaten egg. Work together well with the hands and shape into a roll 3–4 inches in diameter. Remove the rinds and bone from the bacon rashers, flatten the rashers well with the back of a knife then wrap firmly around the roll of meat. Overlap the ends of the rashers and try to keep the joins on the underside of the roll.

Lay the roll on a piece of foil, large enough to wrap it completely, on a meat tin or baking tray. Wrap and cook at 425°F (Gas Mark 7) for about 45 minutes then open the foil for about 15 minutes to complete the browning.

WEST COUNTRY OATCAKES WITH BACON

½ tablespoon bacon fat
3 tablespoons water
4 level tablespoons medium oatmeal

Pinch of salt
4 bacon gammon steaks, rinded and slashed
4 tomatoes, halved

Melt the bacon fat with the water in a pan and sprinkle in oatmeal and salt. Work well together until smooth. Roll out the oatmeal on a board dusted with oatmeal to several cakes the size of a small saucer and very thin. Cook slowly on a pre-heated griddle or heavy frying pan for about 10 minutes. Remove to a tea towel in a warm place and leave to harden. Serve quickly with grilled gammon steaks and tomatoes.

YORKSHIRE PEASE PUDDING WITH BOILED BACON

8 oz split peas
Salt and pepper
1 oz butter
1 egg, beaten

Pinch of sugar
3 lb joint of bacon forehock
or collar

Wash the peas and soak overnight in cold water. Tie loosely in a cloth and place in a saucepan with a pinch of salt and cover with boiling water. Boil for 2½–3 hours till soft. Sieve the peas or liquidise in a blender and add the butter, egg, pepper, salt and sugar. Beat together till lightly mixed, then tie up tightly in a floured cloth and boil for another 30 minutes. Serve the pease pudding with the hot bacon joint boiled for 25 minutes per lb, and 25 minutes over with bayleaves, cloves and sliced onion added to the cooking liquor.

COLLAR BACON HOT-POT

3-4 lb collar joint bacon,
boned and rolled
1½ oz dripping
12 button onions, peeled
12 small carrots, peeled

4 leeks, chopped
Stock or beer
Bouquet garni
Bayleaves

Soak bacon in cold water overnight. Place in saucepan, cover with cold water. Bring to boil and simmer for half cooking time, allowing 25 minutes per lb and 25 minutes over. Remove joint, skin and score the fat into squares. Melt dripping in a large fireproof casserole and fry vegetables until lightly browned. Add sufficient stock or beer to cover. Place the joint in the casserole. Add bouquet garni and several bayleaves. Cover and bake at 350°F (Gas Mark 4) for remaining cooking time. 10 minutes before ready remove lid to brown, increasing oven temperature to 425°F (Gas Mark 7). Serve, if liked, with parsley sauce made with the stock from the vegetables.

BACON PANCAKES

Pancakes:
¼ pint pancake batter
Lard for frying

Filling:
2 oz lard
8 oz chopped bacon

2 oz chopped onion
Sprinkle of mixed herbs
Lemon juice
Seasoning
2 oz chopped prunes or
cooking apple

Make the pancake batter. Melt lard in a frying pan and make 6 thin pancakes, leaving the pancakes flat. Put lard, chopped onion, bacon and prunes into a frying pan and cook for 4 to 5 minutes. Add seasoning and mixed herbs to the bacon mixture and divide into 6 equal portions. Reheat the pancakes and place a portion of the bacon mixture in each. Roll the pancakes and serve piping hot.

CIDER-BAKED FOREHOCK WITH CIDER SAUCE

3-3½ lb forehock (boned and rolled)
⅓ pint cider
1 tablespoon brown sugar
Cloves

Cider Sauce
Cider
1 teaspoon cornflour

Soak the bacon in warm water for 1 hour. Rinse and put in saucepan with cold water. Boil gently for 30 minutes. Take out, remove rind and put bacon in baking tin. Mix cider with half the sugar and pour over bacon. Leave to stand for about 30 minutes, basting from time to time. Sprinkle remainder of sugar on top and put cloves in lines across top. Bake at 400°F (Gas Mark 6) for 30–40 minutes, basting occasionally, but not for the last 15 minutes. To make the sauce, put the cider in which the bacon was cooked into a saucepan, and make up to ½ pint with more cider. Bring to the boil. Mix cornflour with a little water and add to the cider. Simmer until thick and serve with the bacon. Apple rings can be served with this dish.

Joyce Kerr

6 Poultry

It was a turkey. He never could have stood upon his legs that bird. He would have snapped 'em short off in a minute, like sticks of sealing-wax.

'A Christmas Carol'
Charles Dickens

CHICKEN

Flavour comes from age (hence the distinction between lamb and mutton, veal and beef), so it can hardly be expected that a 10-week bird can have a full flavour. Hanging time before dressing also gives flavour, and to-day's birds do not remain with their innards so long as the old-fashioned roaster. Set against this loss of flavour are the advantages of reasonable size, tenderness and keen price.

The only way to keep a good flavour in today's birds is to cook them very carefully. Overcooking, particularly in roasting, is the worst crime against good flavour, and better results are often obtained by frying, grilling or casseroling chicken.

The best way of roasting the traditional chicken was with a bunch of herbs and plenty of butter, but today's broiler needs a less subtle approach. In winter, stuffings containing sausages and bacon, or the chicken liver, will give a better flavour. In summer, lighter mixtures which include pineapple, walnuts or sweetcorn, are more acceptable.

Before roasting, the bird's weight should be carefully checked, and cooking time calculated to suit the oven-ready weight. Cook at 375°F and allow 20 minutes a pound plus 20 minutes for all birds up to $3\frac{1}{2}$ lb in weight. The bird should be completely thawed, or cooking will take longer. A giblet gravy will also help to give flavour, or a garnish of streaky bacon rolls filled with pieces of chicken liver.

A jointed bird is often more useful in the kitchen but it's often just as simple to do it yourself – you need a strong sharp knife, a chopping board and a weight. For halving, choose a $1\frac{1}{2}$ to 2 lb bird; for quartering choose a 2 to $2\frac{1}{2}$ lb bird. Remove the giblets, then put the bird on a chopping board. With a sharp knife cut through and along the length of breastbone.

Open the bird out, then cut through along length of backbone, removing it entirely if you like by cutting close along to either side. Tap back of knife sharply with a heavy weight to cut through the bony sections. The bird is now in half.

Put the chicken halves skin side up on a board, and divide each half again by cutting diagonally across between wing and thigh, so that the bird is in quarters (2 wing and breast joints, 2 thigh and drumstick joints). The joints are neater if leg shanks and wingtips are removed.

Chicken joints grill or fry in less than $\frac{1}{2}$ hour, and bake or casserole in less than an hour. For grilling, frying and baking, they need to be moistened frequently with butter or a sauce, and are cooked at a moderate temperature.

ROAST ROSEMARY CHICKEN

1 *roast chicken, 3-$3\frac{1}{2}$ lb*	$\frac{1}{4}$ *pint stock*
trussed weight	*Salt and pepper*
A small sprig of rosemary	*A little butter*

Put the giblets back into the carcass of the chicken with the rosemary – they help to flavour the gravy. Put the chicken into a roasting tin, sprinkle it with salt and pepper, and dot a knob of butter over it, then pour the stock round the chicken. Roast the chicken in a fairly hot oven, 400°F (Gas Mark 6) for 1 to $1\frac{1}{4}$ hours. Remove the giblets and serve the chicken on a hot dish, surrounded with Duchesse potatoes or potato croquettes. Serve the gravy, which should be thin, separately.

LANCASHIRE CHEESY CHICKEN

1 *hot roasted chicken*	3 *oz butter*
1 *pint milk*	3 *oz plain flour*
A sliced carrot	$\frac{1}{2}$ *pint stock*
A sliced onion	6 *oz Lancashire cheese*
A sprig of parsley and thyme,	*Pinch of grated nutmeg*
and one bayleaf	*Salt and pepper*

Cut the chicken into joints, removing the legs at the thigh joints and dividing the thighs from the drumsticks. Cut off both wings with a slice of breast. Cut off the wishbone with some meat, then cut the breast off either side of the bone. Arrange the joints on a hot dish and keep them warm.

Put the milk into a saucepan with the carrot, onion, sprig of parsley, thyme and bay leaf and heat this very slowly to extract the flavours of the vegetables into the milk. When it is almost boiling, take it off the heat.

Melt the butter in a large saucepan, take it off the heat and stir in the flour. Add the stock and whisk or stir the sauce briskly over a very gentle heat until it is warm enough to melt the butter and make the sauce smooth. Strain the hot milk into the sauce and stir it briskly over a moderate heat until it comes to the boil. Take the sauce off the heat and crumble the cheese into it, beating it well to make it smooth, then coat the chicken. Put the chicken under a hot grill for a few moments to brown the top. If the chicken is to be served later or next day the dish can be finished completely, but it will have to be heated thoroughly in a fairly hot oven about 400°F (Gas Mark 6) for about 20 minutes before browning it under the grill.

FRICASSEE OF CHICKEN

Cut the remains of a cold chicken and 2 or 3 oz of ham into neat pieces, season them with pepper, salt and a little lemon juice. In a saucepan put a little white sauce, about $\frac{1}{2}$ pint, stir until hot, and then put in the chicken and ham. Stir over a mild heat until the meat is well warmed in the sauce. Serve it on a hot dish with snippets of toast placed round.

DEVILLED CHICKEN

Remove the skin from the wings and legs of a chicken. Cut a deep incision in several places of the flesh, make a fiery mixture of Cayenne pepper, salt, mustard, anchovy (paste) and butter, and rub it all into the cut parts of the flesh. Broil over a clear fire, and serve on a hot serviette.

If required for breakfast, this could be prepared overnight. The modern version of this is to cook on an electric spit. Otherwise it could be carefully grilled or wrapped in foil and cooked in a hot oven.

The Good Wife's Cook Book, 1870

HONEY GLAZED CHICKEN

1 *roasting chicken (3-3$\frac{1}{2}$ lb)*
1 *cooking apple*
1 *large onion*
4-5 *tablespoons oil*

3-4 *tablespoons clear honey*
Salt and pepper
Watercress to garnish

Remove giblets from chicken and sprinkle inside lightly with salt and pepper. Peel the apple, cut into quarters and remove the core. Place inside the chicken together with peeled and halved onion. Brush with a little oil and place in a roasting tin. Season. Pour the honey over the chicken and put the remainder of the oil in the base of the roasting tin. Cook at 375°F (Gas Mark 5) allowing 20 minutes to the pound and 20 minutes over. Baste the chicken from time to time. When cooked arrange on a serving dish and garnish with watercress.

Miss Margaret McFarlane, Bath

CHICKEN WITH BAKED RICE

1 roasting chicken, 3 lb in weight	*1 teaspoon salt*
2 oz lard, cooking fat or oil	*4 oz streaky bacon*
2 large onions	*2 teaspoon black pepper*
Pinch of herbs	*4 oz chipolata sausages*
	8 oz rice

Boil rice in salted water for 15–20 minutes, drain. Melt fat in baking dish add onion, cut in slices, add chicken and place breast downwards in oven 375–400°F (Gas Mark 5 or 6) and cook for 30 minutes. Remove chicken, mix rice with onion, mixed herbs, salt and pepper, replace chicken on rice resting on its backbone, and continue to cook till bird is tender, $1\frac{1}{4}$ to $1\frac{1}{2}$ hours, turning rice over from time to time and brushing breast of bird with oil.

Meanwhile, roll up bacon and secure on a skewer, bake with sausages in shelf below chicken for 20–30 minutes. Serve chicken on bed of rice garnished with sausages and bacon rolls.

CHICKEN IN TARRAGON

This tarragon chicken recipe is very good with bought chicken joints. It is original and easy, and our sons often make it without cream for a quick easy supper. But it's honestly good enough for dinner.

Fry your chicken joints in half butter and half oil with a sprinkling of dried tarragon. The amount of tarragon is a matter for personal taste. The pan used should have a lid for preference. When done, remove the chicken to serving dish and keep warm. Now add enough cream to absorb or fully blend with the fat (you have to stir like hell). Season, add lemon juice to taste and having got it right, pour it over the chicken and return relaxed, if not smug, to your sherry.

Joan Dampney, Christchurch, Hants

VIENNA CHICKEN

Cut up a chicken into pieces; lay them in a pie dish in a mixture of ½ pint olive oil, the juice of 4 lemons, 1 bayleaf, 2 or 3 sprigs of parsley, and pepper and salt. Let them remain soaking for 4 or 5 hours.

Take each piece of chicken, drain it, dip it in egg and breadcrumbs, and fry to a nice golden colour. When all the pieces are fried, put them in a stew-pan with sufficient white stock to barely cover them, then add the yolk of 1 egg, and ½ a breakfastcup of milk, 24 button mushrooms, salt, pepper etc. to taste. Let them gently stew for ½ hour, thicken the sauce, add the juice of 1 lemon and serve.

CHICKEN MARSEILLAIS

Chop finely ½ lb cold chicken; put it in a basin and mix with it a teaspoon of flour and butter, 2 tablespoons of cream, the yolk of an egg, a teaspoon of chopped parsley, salt and pepper to taste. Thoroughly mix this to a paste. Roll out some flaky type pastry as thinly as possible cut into 6 inch squares, fill with the mixture and fold over and pinch the edges. Bake to a light golden brown in not too hot an oven. Serve hot.

CHICKEN POMPADOUR

Boil ½ lb spaghetti in salted boiling water, but do *not* break up. Drain it in a colander, well butter a basin or mould, line it with spaghetti, twisting it around and fill the centre with 1½ cups of cold chopped chicken, salted and peppered to taste. Pour on top of this ½ cup of cream, 1 oz fresh butter, the yolk of one egg, and a teaspoonful of finely chopped parsley, then cover over with some more spaghetti. Steam it for 1 hour, then turn it into a hot dish, and serve with tomato sauce

SURREY CHICKEN CASSEROLE

1 nice plump chicken, onions, potatoes, thyme and parsley (or dried mixed herbs), leftovers of bacon, not too fat; 1 or 2 hardboiled eggs, if liked, ½ lb sausage meat.

Cut chicken in suitably-sized pieces and fry lightly in dripping or if bacon is fairly fat, fry this first then fry chicken joints, dipped in wholemeal flour, in the resulting fat. Drain well, then taking a good thick casserole dish, put first a layer of sliced potatoes, then a layer of onions; sprinkle this with a little salt and pepper, then put a layer of chicken, potato, onion, sausage meat, potato, onion, chicken, sliced hardboiled egg, bacon, onion and lastly sliced potato, in that order. Pour on ¾ pint water or thin stock, sprinkle with salt and pepper, dot with dripping or butter, cover with buttered paper and casserole lid. Cook gently for 1½–2 hours, before removing lid and paper; return to oven to brown the top layer of potatoes.

GLOUCESTERSHIRE CASSEROLED CHICKEN

1 cooked chicken
1 pint white sauce
2 cups cooked rice
½ cup chopped nuts, almonds
for preference but

home-grown cobs or walnuts
would do
Cooked green peas and/or
carrots
1 cup chopped mushrooms

Remove chicken from bone and dice. Add to the white sauce and season with pepper and salt. Put layer of cooked rice in casserole dish, scatter chopped nuts, peas and mushrooms over, add layer of chicken and sauce. Continue in layers, finishing with last drop of sauce. Bake in a moderate oven until done through – about ¾ hour; serve with small snippets of dry toast and garnish with parsley.

CHICKEN MARYLAND

Fry portions of boned chicken (you need not bone the wings) in egg and breadcrumbs and lay in a flat dish. Fry mushrooms, also drained pine-apple pieces and banana, if you like, in halves. Sometimes a few extra frozen chicken livers make it extra good. This is all done in one fry pan – then begin the sauce by either flour or cornflour mixed in a bowl with cold water, make this rather thick as you will be adding more liquid, pour some into the hot fry pan, and make a roux, and as it will be much too thick add white wine or cider (I nearly always add cider), and some of the tinned pineapple juice. This sauce takes more time to make than the rest of the meal – as soon as it is like a *thin* sauce pour it over the chicken etc. and cover the dish with foil and put in oven for ½ hour or longer if guests are late. Peas and mashed potatoes go well with this as it is rather rich. Salt and pepper must be added to the sauce.

DOYNTON CHICKEN

4 chicken joints
3 tablespoons olive oil
4 rashers unsmoked streaky
bacon, chopped
6 oz long grain rice
2 tablespoons tomato purée
3 oz onion, chopped

2 cloves garlic, crushed
1 pint chicken stock
10 oz frozen peas
Salt and pepper and sugar to
taste
Rings of carrots and parsley
to garnish

Heat the oil in a heavy pan and fry the chicken joints until golden all over. Remove chicken and keep it hot. Add onion and garlic to pan and cook gently for several minutes, then add bacon and rice. Stir and fry until rice begins to brown. Add the stock, tomato purée and seasoning and bring to the boil. Turn the mixture into a casserole, place the chicken joints on top and cover tightly. Bake in a moderate oven, 350°F (Gas Mark 4), for about 40 minutes until rice and meat are tender. Meanwhile, cook the peas, drain and stir into rice. Serve very hot garnished with olives or strips of pimento.

GRILLED FOWL

The remains of cold fowl, juice of $\frac{1}{2}$ lemon, breadcrumbs, pepper and salt, grated lemon peel.

Cut the remains of some cold fowl into pieces, season them with pepper and salt, squeeze over them the juice of $\frac{1}{2}$ lemon, and let them stand for $\frac{3}{4}$ hour. Wipe them dry, dip them into clarified butter, and then into breadcrumbs with a little grated lemon peel. Put them on a gridiron and broil them over a clear fire. When fried instead of broiled, use the yolk of egg, well beaten, instead of the butter.

TO STEW A FOWL WITH RICE

1 fowl; about 1 quart of mutton broth; pepper and salt; mace; a large cupful of rice.

Truss the fowl for boiling, and stew it in about 1 quart of mutton broth, seasoned with pepper, salt, half a blade of mace, for as long as it takes to cook it tender, letting it simmer as *slowly as possible*, which will improve the fowl's appearance more than fast boiling as it renders them plump and white. Skim the liquor as often as need be; then about $\frac{1}{2}$ hour before the fowl will be quite ready, add a large cupful of rice, and when this too is tender, remove the fowl and keep hot. Meanwhile strain the rice from the liquor and place it on a sieve in front of the fire, to dry and swell; then place it in the centre of a hot dish and hollow out a place for the fowl, arranging the rice rather high in a border around the bird. Serve parsley and butter sauce in a tureen.

STOVED CHICKEN

3 *lb chicken joints*
2 *large onions*
2½ *lb potatoes*
2 *oz butter*

1 *pint giblet stock*
Salt and pepper
Chopped parsley

Wipe the chicken joints. Cut the onions in slices, and the potatoes in medium-thick slices. Brown the chicken pieces in half the butter. In a casserole, put a thick layer of potatoes, then onions and chicken pieces. Season well with salt and pepper and add knobs of butter. Put on another layer of potatoes, then onions, chicken and finally potatoes. Season again and pour on stock. Put on a piece of buttered paper and a lid. Cook at 300°F (Gas Mark 2) for 2½ hours, adding a little more stock or water if needed. If an iron casserole is used, this dish may be simmered gently on a low heat on top of the stove. Sprinkle with parsley before serving.

COUNTRY-STYLE GRILLED CHICKEN

4 chicken joints   *Salt*
½ large lemon   *2 rashers streaky bacon*
1½ oz butter   *2 oz mushroom caps*

Rub chicken pieces with cut lemon. Melt butter and brush generously over chicken, then sprinkle with salt. Put chicken, skin side down, in a grill pan with the rack removed, and cook under low to medium heat, with pan 6 inches below heat, for 10 minutes. Turn pieces, brush with butter, and continue grilling for 15 minutes, with 1 or 2 more applications of butter. When cooked, the skin should be crisp and golden, and the juices, when the thigh is pierced with a fine skewer, should be colourless. Cut the bacon in fine strips and fry with sliced mushrooms in remaining butter. When cooked, add the squeezed lemon juice. Serve chicken with this dressing, garnished with watercress, and crisps.

CHICKEN IN THE POT

3–3½ lb chicken   *1 lb potatoes, cut in small*
Salt and pepper   *cubes*
2 oz butter   *4 oz sausage meat*
1 tablespoon cooking oil *1 tablespoon fresh*
¼ lb diced bacon   *breadcrumbs*
12 button onions   *1 chicken liver*
                          1 tablespoon chopped parsley

Season chicken inside and out with salt and pepper. Mix together sausage meat, breadcrumbs, chopped chicken liver and parsley, and insert into the neck of the bird. Heat butter and oil in a flameproof casserole and lightly brown the chicken all over. Add bacon and onions, cover closely and cook over a gentle heat for 15 minutes. Baste the chicken, add the potatoes, turning them in the fat and replace the lid. Continue cooking in a moderate oven, 350°F (Gas Mark 4), for 1½ hours. Serve in the casserole, sprinkling the potatoes with chopped parsley and chives.

QUICK CHICKEN CASSEROLE

4 *chicken quarters*
3 *tablespoons cooking oil*
1 *can condensed mushroom*
soup

¼ *pint creamy milk*
Chopped parsley

Heat oven to 350°F (Gas Mark 4). Heat the oil in a frying pan and cook the chicken pieces over gentle heat until golden, about 15 minutes. Put into a casserole. Drain surplus oil from the frying pan, then pour in soup and milk. Heat gently, stirring until boiling. Pour over chicken, cover and cook in centre of oven for 30–40 minutes. Sprinkle with parsley before serving.

CRISP BAKED CHICKEN

4 *chicken joints*
2 *rounded tablespoons flour*
1 *rounded teaspoon salt*
½ *level teaspoon curry powder*

A little evaporated milk
2 *oz potato crisps (or coarse*
breadcrumbs)

Pre-heat oven to 350°F (Gas Mark 4). Wipe chicken joints, and coat with a mixture of flour, salt and curry powder. Dip the joints in evaporated milk, then coat thickly and evenly with crushed potato crisps or breadcrumbs. Arrange skin side up on a baking sheet and bake for 45 minutes. Serve hot or cold, with green salad. These chicken joints can be wrapped in foil and carried on a picnic without damage.

BARBECUED CHICKEN

2 *chicken halves (about 1 lb*
each)
2 *oz butter*
4 *tablespoons malt vinegar*
1 *tablespoon Worcester sauce*
1 *tablespoon tomato purée*

1 *level tablespoon brown*
sugar
1 *teaspoon finely grated onion*
1 *teaspoon paprika*
½ *teaspoon salt*

Skewer each chicken half as flat as possible. Melt the butter and brush liberally all over chicken. Arrange skin side down in a grill pan with rack removed, place pan 6 inches below the heat, and grill gently for 15 minutes. Meanwhile add the remaining ingredients to the butter in the saucepan and simmer together for 2 minutes. Turn the chicken, brush with this sauce, and continue grilling gently, with frequent applications of sauce, for 15 minutes, or until the joints move freely. Serve the chicken with the remaining sauce, garnished with watercress, and with crusty rolls and butter.

DEVONSHIRE CHICKEN

4 *chicken joints*
2 *oz butter*
2 *oz finely-chopped onion*
1 *stick sliced celery*
2 *rashers streaky bacon*

1 *oz plain flour*
Salt and pepper
¾ *pint chicken stock*
3 *tomatoes*

Melt butter in a frying pan and fry chicken joints slowly until golden (about 10 minutes). Put chicken into casserole. Add onion, celery and bacon cut into small pieces, and cook until onion is soft but not coloured. Sprinkle in flour and seasoning. Stir for a minute, then add stock and continue cooking until boiling. Add tomatoes skinned, cut in quarters and de-pipped. Pour over chicken, cover and cook at 350°F (Gas Mark 4) for 45 minutes. Garnish with chopped parsley.

HOUSEWIFE'S CHICKEN

4 *chicken joints*
2 *oz butter*
2 *oz bacon*
2 *oz mushrooms*
12 *very small onions*
½ *oz plain flour*

½ *pint stock*
½ *pint dry cider*
Salt and pepper
Parsley, thyme and bayleaf
12 *new potatoes (or 1 can of new potatoes)*

Melt butter and brown chicken pieces all over. Remove chicken and put into casserole. Into fat put bacon cut in strips, mushrooms cut in quarters and the whole onions, and cook until bacon and mushrooms are just soft. Dust with flour, and continue cooking, season with salt and pepper, then add stock and cider. Bring just to the boil, then pour all ingredients into casserole. Add herbs, cover and cook for 45 minutes at 350°F (Gas Mark 4). 15 minutes before serving time, add the potatoes (or the drained can of potatoes) and continue cooking. If new potatoes are not available, use large potatoes cut into small olive shapes. This is a very useful meal-in-one which needs no accompaniments at all except some crusty bread to 'mop up'. The recipe can be used for a whole chicken instead of pieces, if preferred.

GINGER CHICKEN

4 *chicken joints*
2 *oz butter*
2 *medium onions*
Salt and pepper

2 *tablespoons made mustard*
1 *teaspoon ground ginger*
2 *tablespoons orange juice*
1 *bottle ginger ale*

Melt butter and brown chicken all over, then fry sliced onions in same fat until just soft. Smear chicken joints with mustard, then sprinkle with salt and pepper, then return to the pan with all other ingredients. Bring to the boil, cover and simmer for 45 minutes. Thicken the sauce with a little flour if liked. An unusual dish, which is excellent with plain boiled rice or mashed potatoes and a green salad.

DUCK

Roast duck is the traditional Easter treat, and these days birds are bred with broader breasts so that a duckling becomes a reasonable proposition for 6 people. If you want a really delicious bird which is not greasy, but has a crisp skin and full-flavoured meat, try roasting it with $\frac{1}{2}$ inch of water, and with salt on the breast, but no extra fat. The bird should be turned halfway through cooking to brown the breast.

For people who might miss the traditional stuffing, try putting 6 cored apples round the bird, stuffing them with sausage meat and cooking for about 30 minutes. Another good garnish is 12 small whole onions tossed in butter with a rasher of diced bacon, then simmered in a little giblet stock with salt, pepper and a pinch of summer savory.

A delicious sauce to go with duck can be made by adding $\frac{1}{2}$ pint each of good stock and white wine to the pan drippings, stirring in $\frac{1}{2}$ teaspoon each of shredded orange and lemon rind, the juice of 1 orange and 1 teaspoon of lemon juice, simmering for 10 minutes.

When the first new potatoes come in, they are very good with a duck casserole. Joint the bird, dip in flour, and fry in butter until golden, then put into a casserole with $\frac{1}{2}$ lb chopped mushrooms, 1 teaspoon each of minced onion and mint, salt and pepper and $\frac{3}{4}$ pint stock. Cook in a slow oven, 300°F (Gas Mark 2), for $1\frac{1}{2}$ hours, then add $\frac{1}{2}$ pint green peas and continue cooking for 45 minutes.

The First Portion: Place the point of the knife into right leg between tail end of breast, bringing knife forward round thigh part of the leg to middle of back. Turn bird on its side and bring the knife down the centre of the back to the parson's nose, and back between the leg and the tail end of the breast. This is the right leg portion.

The Second Portion: Repeat on the opposite side to give the left leg portion.

The Third Portion: Place the knife on the centre of the tapered part of the breast back, bringing the knife right along the breast in a straight line. Turn bird over, continuing the cut along the back to the end of the meat and tear. This is the right wing portion.

The Fourth Portion: Repeat on the opposite side to give the left wing portion.

The Fifth and Sixth Portions: Bring the knife to the centre back breast as near the breast bone as possible, cutting right along the breast bone and into carcass. Repeat on the opposite side.

GOOSE

September 29, Quarter Day and the beginning of a busy farming year. The day when rents are paid, farms change hands, and servants by tradition are hired. Above all, the feast of St Michael, when the goose was celebration food.

Geese are sadly neglected today, when so many country traditions are dying out, but what can be better than a really tasty bird, with its crisp skin, rich fat and dark flesh? This very richness makes a lot of people wary, but cunning cooking turns a goose into a feast, and there are endless ways of using the remains and offal.

On average, a goose loses half its weight in waste and cooking, so a 12 lb bird would come down to about 6 lb at the table. It needs more cooking for its size than turkey or chicken, but care must be taken to crisp the outside fat without drying the meat.

Start the bird at a high temperature, 450°F (Gas Mark 8), for 30 minutes, then reduce the oven to 400°F (Gas Mark 6) for the rest of the cooking time, allowing 20 minutes for each lb plus 20 minutes. One of the nicest things about a goose is the crisp skin, and this is improved if the bird is rubbed all over with flour before cooking begins, and the oven is turned a little higher for 15 minutes before serving time.

There's a lot of fat in a goose, so cook it on a rack in a large tin, and 20 minutes after you begin cooking, prick the skin with a fork to allow the fat to run out. Drain some of the fat off during cooking to avoid accidents, and baste the bird 2 or 3 times during cooking.

Sage and onion stuffing is usual with goose. Try it with a chopped apple included and a spoonful of made mustard. Those who don't like onions will enjoy Scandinavian fruit-stuffed goose, made by simmering 24 stoned prunes in a little water or red wine, and mixing them with 8 peeled and quartered apples to stuff the bird. Another good stuffing is Scottish, consisting of a mixture of 2 tablespoons chopped onion fried in butter, 2 oz chopped suet, 1 dessertspoon chopped sage, a beaten egg and 5 oz fine oatmeal cooked in a little water. To help 'cut' the fatness of the bird, red cabbage makes a good vegetable accompaniment, or a few baked rosy apples.

Goose 'extras' are particularly useful in the kitchen. The liver can be turned into a rich pâté, or can be soaked in milk, then sprinkled with seasoned flour and cooked in butter until lightly brown, before being simmered with sliced apples and onions until tender. A wineglass of Madeira added at the last minute makes this a very special dish.

The giblets can be turned into an old dish called *Gallimaufry*. Simmer all the giblets except the liver with a little water, seasoning, bayleaf, parsley and thyme until tender. Cut the giblets into walnut-sized pieces and mix with 1 lb steak and the liver cut into cubes. Brown all the meat in a little dripping and sprinkle lightly with flour. Simmer in the giblet stock for another hour, adding a wineglass of port half-way through cooking, and serve very hot with forcemeat balls and small triangles of toast.

Poultry left-overs in our house never present any problem, and indeed have usually been nibbled away by the time a second-day dish is called for.

ROAST GOOSE

1 goose   *2 slices bread soaked in milk*
4 oz pork   *1 egg yolk*
4 oz veal   *Parsley, thyme, sage*
1 large onion   *½ wineglass Burgundy*
½ oz butter

Chop the pork, veal, onion, and the goose liver very finely and brown them in butter. Squeeze the milk out of the bread and mix together all the ingredients, chopping herbs finely, and using only a little of the wine to moisten. Season with salt and pepper to taste. Stuff the goose and put into a very hot oven for 15 minutes. Reduce heat to 350°F (Gas Mark 4) and cook for 15 minutes per lb basting with the remaining wine.

GLAZED GOOSE

Take a goose, stuff it, roast it, and then glaze with a packet of aspic enlivened with a little sherry. Glazing is a bit fiddly as you have to catch it just as it is sliding off and it does not easily adhere to the fatty skin of a goose. To show off, try to imprison some decorative foliage or flowers in the glaze. For the stuffing, Theo just takes an arbitrary quantity of chopped onion, sage, white breadcrumbs, seasoned and shovels it into the back-end of the bird. Nothing fanciful.

Joan Dampney, Christchurch, Hants

TURKEY

Take the measurements of your oven first. Your turkey may have to go on the bottom of the oven instead of a runner. A 10–13 lb turkey will serve 10–12 people for one hot meal. Larger birds have a higher proportion of flesh to the bone. Hen birds are preferable to cock birds; and a good bird should have a broad breast. Avoid fresh birds which look dark and scrawny; on a frozen bird watch for browning areas of 'freezer burn' which can indicate long and improper storage, or dehydration.

Many people like to cook the turkey in foil, which speeds up cooking time and gives a moist tender bird. This is not true roasting, however, and sometimes results in a stewed taste, particularly with a frozen bird which may contain a lot of excess moisture. The advantages of slow over quick roasting are debatable. Quick cooking seals the birds and gives better flavour, while the slower and more carefree method reduces shrinkage. The best compromise is to put the bird into a hot oven, 425°F (Gas Mark 7), for 20 minutes, then reduce heat to 375°F (Gas Mark 5) for remaining cooking time. The breast should be covered with bacon, and the turkey basted at intervals. For a bird under 14 lb allow 15 minutes a lb and 15 minutes over. For a larger bird allow 10 minutes a lb and 10 minutes over.

Allow frozen turkeys to defrost naturally before cooking (about 36 hours for a 9 lb bird). Cook the turkey on a rack in a shallow tin and brush the bird with melted butter. Cut the string around the drumsticks after 1 hour when they should be set, so that the heat circulates. Test with a skewer in the thickest part of the drumstick to see if cooking is finished; this can be judged when the skewer goes in easily but no liquid runs out. To prevent the breast drying out before the legs are cooked, cover the breast after the first hour of cooking with a cloth dipped in melted butter.

Allow 20–30 minutes for dishing up and making gravy.

Be sure the dish is large and the knife sharp. Put fork firmly into 'knee' joint, and slice thigh flesh away from body until ball-and-socket hip joint is exposed. Cut joint between thigh and drumstick. Repeat with other leg. Take off wings and divide at major joint if bird is large. Slice the breast beginning at the neck area, and slice thinly across the grain the entire length of the breast. If the bird is large, use only one side, so the rest remains moist for cold serving.

Stuffing is important for turkey. Melted fat or cold water used to bind the bread will give a light loose texture. For a crumbly stuffing with a delicious flavour, fry the breadcrumbs in a little butter. For sausage meat stuffing, add a little chopped parsley or onion. For chestnut stuffing, mix cooked chestnuts with a little fried bacon and minced onion, and put through a sieve or vegetable mill for fine texture. For easy cranberry sauce, cook cranberries in a little boiling water until they pop, and add plenty of sugar.

PRESSED TURKEY

This is a useful way of preparing a bird so that it can be easily sliced, and so that everyone gets a fair helping of light and dark meat. Cook the turkey in foil so that the meat is just cooked but not dry. Carve and pack meat into 2 lb loaf tins. Fill tins to the top and press under heavy weights. Break up carcass and cook in very little water to which has been added generous seasoning and herbs. Cook liquid until it is well flavoured and reduced by half, then pour stock on to meat and press again. Turn out when cold and serve in slices.

SPECIAL SAVOURY STUFFING

Partly cook some onion. Add celery leaves, a liberal helping of parsley, egg and seasoning. Put into the liquidiser and blend. Add breadcrumbs and put into a buttered dish. Pour on a little melted butter or dripping. Cook in oven with poultry or joint.

Pat Brown, Keynsham, Somerset

CELERY AND GIBLET STUFFING

1 *medium-sized head celery (chopped)*
1 *small onion (chopped)*
2 *oz butter*
Turkey giblets (cooked and chopped)
Rind of 1 *orange*
3 *oz breadcrumbs*
¼ *teaspoon mixed herbs*
Salt and pepper

Lightly fry celery and onion in the butter. Remove from heat, and stir in giblets, orange rind, breadcrumbs and mixed herbs. Season well, and use to stuff the neck end of the turkey. (Sufficient for 10–12 lb turkey.)

SAGE AND ONION STUFFING

4 oz bread, brown or white, without crusts if these are too tough, 1 large onion, freshly chopped sage if possible – if not, dried, rubbed sage, salt, pepper, drippings. Soak the bread, crusts and all in hot water. While this is soaking peel and chop the onion; fry it in enough dripping to keep it from catching. When onion is golden brown take it off the heat. Mash the bread with your hands until no lumps are left, pouring off surplus water as necessary. Add the mashed, smooth, bread to the onions in the frying pan. Chop the sage and add to the rest with pepper and salt, not stinted. Mix well and use as required. If cooking separately in a dish, add more dripping, but for fat birds like duck and goose don't overdo the dripping.

Great-Aunt Anne's version from Cork

Great-Aunt Anne was the youngest of five children, living in the farmlands behind Cork. They were the only Protestants in a Roman Catholic area, and left Ireland in the Troubles. The eldest sister had gone to Cornwall to farm, and Aunt Anne followed her. She is now eighty-two and still going strong.

CHESTNUT STUFFING

1 *lb chestnuts*	*Little melted butter*
½ *pint milk*	*Grated lemon rind*
2 *oz bacon*	*Sugar*
3 *oz breadcrumbs*	1 *egg*
1 *teaspoon chopped parsley*	

Make 2 slits in each chestnut, boil them in water for 10 minutes, then skin them. Put the nuts into a pan with enough milk to cover, simmer till tender then rub through a sieve. Pound with finely chopped bacon, add the breadcrumbs, parsley, butter and lemon rind. Season, then blend with the beaten egg.

SAUSAGE STUFFING

1 *oz dripping*	1 *large onion*
4 *oz breadcrumbs*	1 *lb pork sausage meat*
1 *teaspoon parsley*	½ *teaspoon mixed herbs*

Melt the dripping, chop the onion and mix with the sausage meat, lightly fry this mixture in the dripping for a few minutes, add the other ingredients and use as required.

PARSLEY, THYME AND LEMON STUFFING

4 *oz breadcrumbs*	¼ *teaspoon thyme*
2 *tablespoons chopped parsley*	*Grated rind of half a lemon*
1 *egg*	*Seasoning*
2 *oz suet*	

Chop the suet and mix with the breadcrumbs, add the herbs and lemon rind, season well, bind with the beaten egg and use as required.

SAGE AND ONION STUFFING

4 *onions*	6 *sage leaves*
4 *oz breadcrumbs*	*Salt, pepper and boiling water*
1 *oz margarine*	

Peel the onions, put them into a pan of cold water and bring to the boil. Boil for 5 minutes. Strain off this water, cover with fresh boiling water and cook till tender. Drain, chop finely, mix with rest of the ingredients and use as required.

7 Game

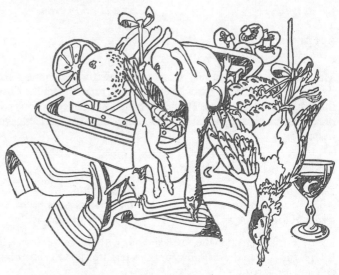

Now soften'd suns a mellow lustre shed,
The laden orchards glow with tempting red;
On hazel boughs the clusters hang embrown'd
And with the sportsman's war the new shorn fields resound.

Bacon

Once the first excitement of the shooting season is over, the country wife is faced with a mounting pile of carcasses, and a waning appetite for plain roast game with all the trimmings. While some men will firmly eat nothing else, and object to casseroled birds, some birds are badly shot or too old to be fit for simple cooking, so that ingenuity must be brought to the task of turning them into tempting puddings, casseroles and pâtés.

A lot of families might find it very odd that others can actually get tired of game. But those with menfolk whose lives revolve round magic dates like 'The Twelfth' or October 1 will know the increasing strain as the winter months continue. Men, and small boys, have a passionate interest in the ultimate eating of any fish, flesh, fowl or good red herring which they have actually done to death themselves – a heritage from the cavemen, perhaps. Their womenfolk, sickened by mounting piles of feathers, gory pelts, or undisposable fish-scales, would sometimes more cheerfully settle for an hygienically wrapped and utterly tasteless chicken trapped in the supermarket.

Nothing can truly beat plainly roasted game with all its delicious accompaniments of crumbs and chips, currant jelly, rich gravy, chestnuts, cabbage or celery, but there is often a moment when even perfection palls and some variety is called for. Additionally, birds may be old or badly shot (or may have lurked in the freezer a long time) and they are not fit for the simple treatment. In the case of partridges, now becoming rare, it may also be necessary to eke out helpings in a way which isn't possible with roast birds.

If a simple casserole is liked, it can be improved if the game is left in a marinade for any period up to 14 days, and the meat cooked in the liquid. A good marinade is a mixture of ½ breakfastcup vinegar with 1 breakfastcup red wine, a bayleaf, a pinch each of pepper, salt and nutmeg, a sprig of thyme, and 4 chopped onions. This is good for hare, pigeon and venison as well as old tough birds (the tough tissues are broken down by the liquid and cooking time is shortened).

A good game soup can be very comforting on a winter evening. If you haven't old birds to spare, use the trimmings and carcasses of pheasants or partridges, and include onions, carrots, celery, a little lean bacon, a good bunch of herbs, and plenty of seasoning including a clove. The soup will taste best if the bacon is crisped before adding to the stock and if the sliced vegetables are cooked in a little butter until golden. A real family soup can have the vegetables left in; for a more elegant version the stock should be strained off and reheated with a little diced game taken from the breast of the bird.

If you like game pie, it can be made with a mixture of game, even with the addition of rabbit, and perhaps a little pork or veal. A little savoury forcemeat can be added for extra flavour. Hot water pastry is best used, and will be easy to handle if put into the refrigerator for just 30 minutes after making before moulding into shape. Stock for the jelly should be made from the game trimmings with a pig's trotter or calf's foot added.

One of the nicest things about game is that it is so delicious with the other traditional autumn foods such as apples, chestnuts, red cabbage and mushrooms. Venison and hare are included here. Likewise are those spreading vermin, pigeon and rabbit, which afford both sport and good food.

POACHER'S POT

Allow 1 small bird (any bird)　　*1 oz butter*
per person　　*1 teaspoon mixed herbs*
Seasoned flour

Prepare the birds as for roasting. Dip in well-seasoned flour. Have 1 oz butter very hot in a large saucepan, brown the birds in this, add a small teaspoon mixed herbs, put on a close fitting lid, and cook slowly for about 1½ hours. Serve with the liquid in the pan, slightly thickened as gravy, bread sauce and chips.

SALMI OF GAME OR HARE

1 cooked pheasant or *2*
smaller birds or *hare*
1 teaspoon redcurrant jelly
Seasoning
1 pint espagnole sauce

Wineglass of Port Wine
Garnish: glacé cherries,
button mushrooms,
fleurons of puff
pastry

Joint and skin the birds, or hare, and place them in a casserole. Pour over the sauce and jelly. Heat thoroughly in the slowest possible way. Pour the wine over the joints at the last minute and garnish with glacé cherries, button mushrooms which have been cooked in butter, and the fleurons of puff pastry.

HERTFORDSHIRE SALMI OF GAME

1 lightly roasted pheasant or
equivalent in other game
¾ pint espagnole sauce
Shallots
4 tablespoons port wine
1 level tablespoon redcurrant
jelly

12 button mushrooms
6 glacé cherries
Fleurons of puff pastry, cut
from remains of pastry case
baked blind, large enough to
hold salmi when cooked

Put the bird(s), cut into easy joints for dishing-up, into a heavy casserole, sprinkle with finely chopped shallots – a few or many according to taste – cover with espagnole sauce, the wine and reducrrant jelly. Dot the mushroom stalks around, adding a little thin stock if necessary, and cover down well before cooking at a gentle pace for about 1–1½ hours until the birds are really tender.

Have ready the pastry case and arrange the joints in it; pour over the sauce and garnish with the mushroom heads, sweated, and small fleurons of the pastry, and finally a few glacé cherries. Serve with buttered carrots and green peas.

The advantage of this dish is that the 2 stages can be achieved earlier for last-minute dishing while guests drink their sherry.

GROUSE

In Season: August 12 to December 10.

Young birds have pointed wings and rounded spurs. 1 younger bird will feed 2 people, and an older one will do for 3. Grouse is best roast unless very old, or badly shot. Roast for 20–25 minutes at 400°F (Gas Mark 6) with bacon over the breast; serve on pieces of toast spread with the cooked liver mashed in a little stock. Accompany with gravy, bread sauce, buttered crumbs and wafer potatoes, with a garnish of watercress; rowan-berry jelly is delicious with grouse.

ROAST GROUSE

Pluck, singe, draw and truss as a chicken, season inside and out with pepper and salt, put a piece of butter about the size of a walnut inside. Place a few rashers of fat bacon on the bird's breast and roast in a quick oven 20–30 minutes. Baste frequently during cooking, when almost done remove bacon and dredge with flour and return to the oven to brown the breast. Serve with undressed salad and straw potatoes. A piece of toasted or fried bread may be placed under the bird after 15 minutes cooking so the liquid from the bird drains into it, this then can be used when serving.

BRAISED GROUSE (for old birds)

Clean, truss and draw the number of birds you wish to use. Joint them and fry in bacon fat until brown. Put the joints into a casserole with enough stock to cover, with pieces of onion, and sticks of celery, cook gently for 2 hours, draw off the liquid, thicken with a little cornflour; gravy browning will need to be added to give a good colour, pour this over the joints of game.

Serve with creamed potatoes and green vegetables.

DUBLIN ROAST GROUSE

Allow 1 grouse for 2 people. Cook the grouse in a hot oven for about 30 minutes, basting frequently with the dripping in which it is cooked, with the addition of a small wineglass Irish whisky. Pour 1 tablespoon whisky over each bird before serving. Garnish with watercress and game chips and serve on crisp fried bread.

GROUSE ROAST WITH CRANBERRIES

2 grouse   Butter

Leave grouse to hang for at least a fortnight. After plucking, trussing and
dressing, stuff with butter and cranberries. The juicy fruit melts almost
away during cooking (25 minutes at 450°F, Gas Mark 8) but the melted,
spicy, buttery juice is all the gravy requires.

GROUSE IN ASPIC

3 to 4 grouse   Salt and pepper
Faggot of herbs   Gelatine or aspic gelatine

Skin and draw the grouse or pluck and draw. Carefully slice off the meat
from each side of the breastbone in 2 neat portions, using as much meat
from the wing and leg as possible without cutting into the bone. Simmer
rest of the carcass with faggot of herbs for an hour. Strain, season with
salt and pepper and simmer breast joints gently in this stock until tender.
Remove joints and skin. Place in a shallow dish. Strain stock again, and
for each pint of liquid add ½ oz gelatine previously softened in a little
warm water, or use aspic gelatine using the stock instead of water. The
heat of the stock should dissolve gelatine and when clear and cool, pour
gently over joints in dish.

Any remaining jellied stock may be chopped and used as a garnish. A
little sherry added to the stock is an improvement.

SALMIS OF GROUSE

2 small grouse   12 mushrooms
1 oz butter   8 small button onions
½ gill tomato sauce   Seasoning
18 stoned French olives   1 croûte of fried bread
½ pint espagnole sauce   1 small bouquet garni
¼ gill sherry

Pick, draw, singe and truss the grouse. Put them in a baking dish, cover
the breast of each with ½ oz butter, and roast them for about 10 minutes in
a quick oven. Take up, untie, and cut the birds into small joints. Cut up the
carcasses and fry in a baking dish with the butter left over from the birds.
Pour off the fat and put the carcasses in a saucepan, add the wine, cover
and let it reduce quickly. Add the espagnole and tomato sauces, boil up,
season to taste, skim, and cook for 10 minutes. Peel the onions, fry them
in butter, and braise in a little of the sauce. Arrange pieces of grouse in a
clean saucepan, season with pepper and salt, add the olives and mush-

rooms (sliced), and pour the sauce over. Simmer gently for 20 minutes. Lay the bread croûte on an entrée dish and on this lay the pieces of grouse. Garnish with olives, onions and mushrooms. Pour over the sauce. Serve hot, piping hot.

PARTRIDGE

In Season: September 1 to February 1.
First year birds have the first flight feather pointed at the tip, not rounded. The grey partridge is most delicious after only 3–4 days hanging, but the red-legged variety needs 6–7 days. One bird will serve 2 people.

Roast at 350°F (Gas Mark 4) for 25 minutes, with bacon on the breast, basting with butter. Serve split in 2 with clear gravy, watercress, wafer potatoes. A crisp apple and celery salad is a good side dish.

ROAST PARTRIDGE

Prepare the bird, season inside and out by dredging with salt and pepper, stuffing may be used if desired, such as breadcrumbs or parsley. Cover the breast with a little fat bacon and roast in a moderate oven for 30 minutes, basting with its own fat. Try to avoid over-cooking. Serve with straw potatoes and garnish with watercress seasoned and sprinkled with a few drops of vinegar and quarters of lemon.

PARTRIDGE CASSEROLE

2 *old partridges*	1 *savoy cabbage*
2 *onions*	$\frac{1}{2}$ *pint stock*
2 *carrots*	*Thyme and parsley*
4 *oz streaky bacon*	*Salt, pepper*
8 *oz chipolata sausages*	

Cut the vegetables into neat pieces and brown them in a little butter, together with the partridges. Cut the cabbage into quarters and cook in boiling water with the bacon for 5 minutes. Drain well. Cut bacon and cabbage into small pieces. Put half the cabbage into a casserole, season with salt and pepper, and put on the partridges. Cover with bacon and vegetables, chopped herbs, and the rest of the cabbage. Pour in stock, cover with a lid and cook at 300°F (Gas Mark 2) for 3 hours. Grill the sausages lightly and add $\frac{1}{2}$ hour before serving time. The addition of a glass of dry cider, and a little less stock, makes a good dish.

PARTRIDGE WITH GRAPES

Take 2 plump partridges, 1 lb under-ripe grapes, 4 oz finely cut streaky bacon, pepper and salt. Line a casserole with the rashers and put the birds on top. Add the washed grapes, 1 bayleaf, a pinch of thyme, a sprig of rosemary, season highly with pepper and salt. Pour over the juice of an orange. Cook in a low oven until the birds are tender – this will depend entirely on the age of the birds. Serve surrounded with cooked grapes; the liquor in the caserole is all the sauce that is needed.

OCTOBER PARTRIDGE

2 partridges	*1 small red cabbage*
2 rashers bacon	*¼ pint cider*
Juice of ½ lemon	*6 chestnuts*
Salt and pepper	*1 oz butter*
1 small onion	*1 teaspoon vinegar*

Wipe the partridges inside and out, dust with salt and pepper and sprinkle with lemon juice. Melt butter in a pan and brown the birds slowly all over. Cool slightly, then wrap each bird in a slice of bacon. Slice the onion and red cabbage very finely, season with salt and pepper and put into a saucepan with the cider and vinegar. Bring to the boil and simmer for 20 minutes. Put birds on top and put on lid, then simmer for 1½ hours. Peel the chestnuts, toss in butter and add to the dish 10 minutes before cooking is finished.

BROILED PARTRIDGE

When the partridges have been prepared for roasting, cut off the heads and split up the backs, flatten the breastbone, wipe them inside with a damp cloth, season with cayenne and salt, and broil over a clear, gentle fire for 15 minutes. Have ready some good brown gravy, or mushroom sauce, rub the birds over quickly with butter, place on a hot dish, and serve with the sauce in a tureen.

HARE

In Season: Early autumn to end of February.

Young hare can generally be recognised by white pointed teeth and fresh-looking fur; the older animals will have cracked brown teeth and be scruffy-looking. A hare will feed 10 people easily. The saddle can be roasted (best for a young animal) while other parts are good in casserole, as soup or pâté

ROAST HARE

1 hare
4 or 5 rashers of streaky bacon

Cooking fat
Stuffing: sage and onion or sausage meat

Skin and draw then wash the hare in cold water to which a little vinegar has been added to whiten the flesh, dry well and stuff. Heat knob of fat in roasting tin and spoon the hot fat over the hare. Cover the top with bacon and then put a lid on the tin or cover with foil. Cook for about 1½ hours in a moderately hot oven.

Serve with roast potatoes, a green vegetable and redcurrant jelly.

CASSEROLE OF HARE

1 hare
1 onion
3 cloves
Bouquet garni
3 oz butter

1½ pint stock – or equivalent in stock and stout – or cider
1 oz flour
Fat for frying

Prepare hare and cut into pieces suitable for serving. Fry pieces in 2 oz butter until brown, then pack them into a casserole. Slice and fry onions, add to casserole with cloves, bouquet garni and salt and pepper. Cover closely, simmer for about 2½ hours until tender.

Serve with vegetables of choice and redcurrant jelly.

SOMERSET HARE WITH WALNUTS

Drain a jointed hare after it has soaked for 24 hours in a mixture of sweet Somerset cider and water. Brown the pieces in 3 oz butter mixed with 3 tablespoons of olive oil and then add the grated contents of one cored cooking apple (preferably Bramley's Red Seedling) an eggcup of lemon juice and a little brandy. Cover with a weak stock or water, throw in a bay-leaf, seasoning and a little cinnamon, cover and cook very gently until the meat is quite tender (2–4 hours, in 2 intervals if liked). Then add 4 oz double minced shelled walnuts with a good dessertspoon of flour (whole-meal is good). Cook on top, slowly stirring till the flour is cooked and the sauce has thickened, then serve with forcemeat balls. A wineglassful of port added at the last minute before serving makes this a dish fit for a king.

HARE IN WINE

1 *hare*	1 *onion*
1 *bottle claret*	1 *clove garlic*
Onion	*Flour*
Garlic	*Parsley, thyme, bayleaf*
Bouquet garni	2 *lumps sugar*
Pork fat	*Salt and pepper*
2 *rashers bacon*	1 *glass Armagnac*
5 *shallots*	*Croûtons*

Put a glass of claret in the blood of the hare. Joint the hare and marinade it in claret with onion, garlic and herbs. Brown the pieces of hare in the pork fat. Cook the bacon, shallots, onion, garlic in the pork fat. Brown the liver. Reduce the claret and add to casserole. Add the pieces of hare, herbs, sugar. Pound the liver and stir into the blood. Add to casserole. Simmer. Cool. Re-heat. Season. Add Armagnac. Serve garnished with croûtons.

CAMBRIDGE HARE IN BEER

1 *hare*	$1\frac{1}{2}$ *oz plain flour*
2 *large onions*	$\frac{1}{2}$ *pint brown ale or stout*
8 *oz carrots*	$\frac{1}{2}$ *pint stock*

Joint the hare. Slice the onions thinly and the carrots rather thickly. Fry the onions in a little dripping until soft but not coloured and put them into a casserole. Coat the hare joints in a little of the flour seasoned with salt and pepper, and cook them in the dripping until golden. Put on top of the onions and add the carrots. Work the remaining flour into the fat in the pan and cook for 2 minutes. Gradually add the beer and stock and cook until smooth. Pour over the hare, cover the casserole, and cook at 350°F (Gas Mark 4) for $2\frac{1}{2}$ hours. Very good with jacket potatoes.

ROAST SADDLE OF HARE

For this cut the back of the hare in 1 piece. Dredge the meat well with black pepper, wrap some rashers of bacon round it, then wrap in grease-proof paper and put into a covered pan with plenty of dripping. Roast for 20–30 minutes. Take out the meat, add a little flour to the fat in the pan, add stock or water and let it thicken. Carve the meat from the saddle, put it into an ovenware dish, pour over it the thickened gravy, add a little port wine, cover and put the dish back into a hot oven to cook for a further 15 minutes.

TO JUG HARE

1 hare
Bunch of sweet herbs; chervil,
thyme, tarragon
6 allspice
2 onions, each stuck with a
few cloves

½ teaspoon black pepper
Little lemon peel
2 tablespoons ketchup
Wineglass of port wine
1 oz butter, and 1 oz flour, for
thickening

Wash the hare and cut it into small joints, flour each piece with seasoned flour. Put into a pan with the herbs, the onions, cloves, allspice, salt, pepper and lemon peel. Cover with cold water and bring to simmering point. Simmer until tender, this will take about 2 hours.

Take out the joints of hare and lay them neatly in the dish in which you intend to serve them. Heat the butter, add the flour and cook for 2–3 minutes, add the liquid in which you have cooked the hare and allow to thicken. Then add ketchup and wine. Pour the gravy over the joints of meat and let it stand where it may keep hot but not continue cooking, for 10 minutes. Serve with forcemeat balls and redcurrant jelly.

HERTFORDSHIRE JUGGED HARE

Take 1 hare and marinade it in red wine or vinegar and water for 12 hours minimum, or better still 24 hours, having first cut it into neat joints, dipped in olive oil. Take hare out of marinade and when it has drained well fry it in a little bacon fat or olive oil. Into a casserole, or proper clome jug, put 1 onion stuck with 3 or 4 cloves, a sliced large carrot, a few shallots, a bouquet garni, a few black peppercorns, a small bayleaf, a stick or two of sliced-up celery, some powdered allspice, a level teaspoon of salt, and a little orange peel; then the hare joints carefully placed. Cover the whole with stock and finally seal it with a lid of flour and water paste to prevent its drying out. Cook slowly for 3½ hours, starting off at 350°F and after half the cooking reducing the heat to around 300°F. Then remove the paste or lid (the paste is only strictly necessary if the lid is not really heavy and tight-fitting) and take out the hare joints and keep them hot. Meanwhile strain the liquor and make it as thick as you wish (it should be pretty thick) with flour and water mixed to smooth cream. Simmer this gravy-sauce carefully for a few minutes and then take it off the heat. Use a spoonful or two of this to add to the hare's blood, then pour all that back into the sauce. Add a dash of port wine and a tablespoon of redcurrant jelly and put back on to the heat but do not allow it to boil or the blood will coagulate. Arrange the hare in the cleaned and heated casserole and pour the sauce over it. Decorate with twirls of orange peel and garnish with forcemeat balls.

JUGGED HARE

After the hare has been skinned it should be cut up into joints and suitable pieces, then fried in some fresh butter to a golden brown. Put all the portions into a stoneware jar, with a tumbler of port wine or Burgundy, and sufficient water just to cover the meat. Put in also 1 blade of mace, 6 cloves, 3 eschalots (shallots), 1 clove of garlic, 1 small onion, $\frac{1}{2}$ teaspoon each of allspice and peppercorns, the juice of $\frac{1}{2}$ lemon; and salt to taste. Cover the jar securely and place it in a saucepan, with a small plate at the bottom, turned upside down to prevent the jar from touching the bottom of the saucepan. Fill up with water to about 3 inches from the top of the jar and let the water boil for 4 to 5 hours, replenishing the water as it boils away. When done, the gravy will be plentiful and rich, and it may be thickened with a little cornflour if desired. Take out the jar and put all the joints of the hare into an entrée dish. Strain the liquor through a wire sieve over the hare and serve with redcurrant jelly and some forcemeat balls (fried) which may be placed round the dish.

CORNISH JUGGED HARE

Take 1 hare, 1 bunch sweet herbs, 2 onions, each stuck with 3 cloves, 3 whole allspice, $\frac{1}{2}$ teaspoon black pepper, a strip of lemon peel, thickening of butter and flour, 2 tablespoons mushroom ketchup and some small pieces of bacon, 1 tablespoon clotted cream.

Wash the hare and cut it into small useful sized joints, flour and brown them; put them in a stew pan with the herbs, onions, cloves, allspice, pepper and lemon-rind; cover with hot water, and when it boils remove the scum and let it simmer gently till tender (2–3 hours or more). Take out the pieces of hare, thicken the gravy with flour and a little butter; add the ketchup, let it boil for 10 minutes, add the clotted cream, strain the gravy over the hare joints and serve. A few fried forcemeat balls should be added or they may be stewed for last 10 minutes in the gravy. Serve with redcurrant jelly.

ROAST HARE

On the Wiltshire Downs, the Dorset Downs, the Hampshire Downs and the White Horse Hills, hares were very plentiful and did much damage. Yet roast hare was always something to look forward to.

In selecting a hare for roasting, particular care must be taken to get a young one – one that is not more than three-quarters grown. Old and fully grown hares will do very well for stewing or jugging, but on no account may they be roasted, as they would be too tough and dry.

Let the hare hang as long as possible, 10–14 days is average but this can be varied to please individual preference. (This hanging softens and relaxes the 'strings' in this fast running animal.) Skin and paunch and soak in salt water for an hour or so. Truss the hare ready for stuffing (a suitable stuffing recipe follows later). Fill the hare with a good forcemeat, and lay it in a baking tin, making sure that the stuffing is sewn in securely with strong thread or fine string. Pour over 1 pint of milk and cover the hare with butter which should be spread on evenly all over. Water and dripping can be used for this but milk and butter are considered best. Baste the hare at frequent intervals, never letting it get dried up – a well buttered paper helps to keep the mositure in; and have the oven turned as low as will keep the hare gently cooking but not 'baking-up'. When the hare is cooked through, sprinkle it with salt and flour and brown it all over. A very young hare would be nicely roasted in 1¼ hours but much depends on the size and age. Remove all string and skewers and send to table with a tureen of rich gravy and some redcurrant jelly.

PHEASANT

In Season: October 1 to February 1
A young cock bird has round spurs in the first year, short pointed ones in the second year, sharp long ones when older. A young hen bird has soft feet and light feathers, while the older one has hard feet and dark feathers. Hen birds are smaller, but less dry and more tender with good flavour. One good bird should feed 4 people. The pheasant is best hung for about a week in normal temperatures; if badly shot or mauled it is better to use the bird more quickly.

Roast pheasant is best cooked at 400°F (Gas Mark 6) for about 45 minutes, according to the size of the bird. Bacon should be tied on the breast, and the bird seasoned inside and out with salt and pepper. The bird is better for basting with butter, and better still if a little red wine is added to the roasting pan at half time. Serve with clear gravy, bread sauce, fried crumbs, wafer potatoes. Mushrooms are a delicious accompaniment, also chestnuts and braised celery.

PHEASANT WITH APPLES

1 pheasant	*4 tablespoons cream*
4 oz butter	*Salt and pepper*
1½ lb apples	

Season the bird with salt and pepper and cook in butter until golden. Peel and slice the apples and line a casserole with half of them. Pour in some of the butter, put in the bird and surround with remaining apples. Pour in the rest of the butter and the cream, cover tightly and cook at 350°F (Gas

Mark 4) for 45 minutes, though time may be a little longer if the bird is old. A wineglass of Calvados (apple brandy) is a delicious addition.

ROAST PHEASANT

1 pheasant *A little fat bacon*
2 oz butter *Salt and Cayenne pepper*
A few mushrooms

Prepare the pheasant, tie the fat bacon on the breast. Wipe and skin mushrooms and stuff the bird with them adding the 1 oz butter, salt and a few grains of cayenne pepper, truss and cover with a piece of thickly buttered greaseproof paper. Roast for 30 minutes, basting frequently, then take off the paper and roast for a further 10 minutes. Serve with gravy and bread sauce or redcurrant jelly.

PHEASANT SOUP

Take the meat from the breast and wings, put these on one side. Break up the remaining carcass and put all pieces into a pan with onions, leeks, carrots, stick of celery and some herbs. Let this simmer 5–6 hours, put the breast meat through a mincer, then pound it and rub through a coarse sieve, mix with a handful of brown breadcrumbs, and the yolk of an egg until it binds well and can be shaped into small balls. Strain the bones and vegetables from the stock, add the meat balls to it and bring to the boil again. Just before serving add a little fresh cream.

DEVILLED PHEASANT

1 roast pheasant *1 teaspoon Worcester sauce*
1 pint cream *Salt*
1 teaspoon mustard *Optional: mushrooms*
1 teaspoon Harvey's sauce

Roast the pheasant. Whip the cream with the other ingredients. Cut up the pheasant and put it into a flat earthenware dish. Pour over the cream sauce. (If you wish, add the cooked mushrooms at this stage.) Brown but do not boil.

PHEASANT IN CIDER

1 old pheasant *½ pint cider*
1 lb cooking apples *1 clove garlic*
8 oz onions *Bunch of mixed herbs*
2 oz butter *Salt and pepper*

Wipe pheasant thoroughly inside and out. Cut apples in quarters after peeling and put into casserole. Slice onions and cook in butter until soft and transparent. Put pheasant on top of apples and cover with onions. Pour in cider, and put in herbs and crushed garlic clove. Season with salt and pepper. Cover tightly and cook at 325°F (Gas Mark 3) for 2½ hours. This dish may be served immediately, or the sauce sieved and poured over it.

PHEASANT WITH CHESTNUTS

1 *pheasant*	*Grated rind and juice of* ½
1 *oz butter*	*orange*
8 *oz peeled and skinned*	1 *dessertspoon redcurrant*
chestnuts	*jelly*
8 *oz small onions*	1 *teaspoon red wine vinegar*
1 *heaped tablespoon flour*	*Parsley, thyme and bayleaf*
1 *pint stock*	*Salt and pepper*

Brown the pheasant all over in hot butter. Remove from fire and put into casserole. Toss the chestnuts and onions quickly in the fat until they turn colour, and remove from fat, putting round the pheasant. Blend the pan juices with flour, then work in the rest of the ingredients. Bring to the boil and pour over pheasant. Cover tightly and cook at 325°F (Gas Mark 3) for 2 hours. Remove the pheasant and cut in pieces. Put on serving dish with chestnuts and onions. Remove parsley, thyme and bayleaf, skim the liquid and reduce if necessary. Pour over pheasant and scatter with finely chopped parsley.

PHEASANT WITH CELERY SAUCE

1 *large old pheasant*	*Parsley, thyme and bayleaf*
1 *pint stock*	1 *clove*
1 *head celery*	*Salt and pepper*
2 *oz butter*	1 *oz butter with* 1 *oz flour*
1 *onion*	1 *gill cream*

The stock for cooking the pheasant should include a carrot and onion, a couple of cloves, salt and pepper and a good sprig of parsley. Poach the pheasant in this until tender (this will depend on the age of the bird). Cut the bird into neat pieces for serving with the celery sauce. Make this by cooking the chopped celery in butter with the onion, herbs, clove, salt and pepper until tender, then simmering in ½ pint stock until really soft (use some of the pheasant stock). Put the celery through a sieve and thicken with the butter and flour worked together. Finally, stir in the cream and pour over the pheasant. The sauce should be rather thick. If time is short and the celery young and without strings, the pieces may be left whole without sieving. If money is short, use a little top milk instead of cream for the sauce. The same recipe may be used for partridges, and this quantity of sauce will be enough for 2 birds.

PHEASANT WITH CREAM

Truss the bird, cover the breast with strips of bacon, and brown in a casserole with 3 tablespoons of butter, 8 shallots, salt and pepper. (Here you can pour in a little brandy and light it, but this is not strictly necessary.) Add 1½ cups of veal or chicken broth, and cook for ½ hour, basting frequently with the juice. Then add 1 good cup of cream, a ¼ cup of grated horseradish, and cook for another 20 minutes, basting with the sauce. Season to taste, put the bird on a dish, carve, and pour the sauce round.

Miss Barker, Halstead, Essex

LINCOLNSHIRE PHEASANT (for young birds)

1 *pheasant*	2 *tablespoons flour*
1 *onion*	1½ *pints stock or water*
1 *carrot*	4 *tomatoes*
4 *oz dripping*	½ *lb mushrooms, peeled*
Salt and pepper	1 *tablespoon parsley*

Cut up a tender pheasant, peel and shred the onion and a carrot. Melt the dripping in a pan, add the carrot and onion and fry for 5 minutes, stirring with a wooden spoon. Place the pieces of pheasant in this, with a little salt and pepper, and fry for another 5 minutes, stirring all the time. Add the 2 tablespoons of flour and cook for 3 minutes more, gradually adding the stock and stir till it boils. Cut the tomatoes and the peeled mushrooms in quarters, add these to the contents of the pan together with the chopped parsley and simmer for ½ hour. Set the pheasant in the centre of a hot dish, pour over the sauce and garnish with mushrooms. This will only be successful with a young bird; it is a well-known fact that the poacher takes only the best young birds.

PHEASANT AND MUSHROOMS

3 *oz butter*	¾ *pint stock*
8 *oz mushrooms*	½ *wineglass sherry*
1 *pheasant*	*Salt and pepper*
3 *tablespoons flour*	

Melt half the butter and cook the sliced mushrooms gently for 10 minutes. Season lightly and cool. Stuff the pheasant with three-quarters of the mushrooms. Brown the bird in the rest of the butter, and put in a casserole. Blend the flour into the pan juices, and gradually work in the stock and sherry. Season well and pour over pheasant. Cover tightly and cook at 325°F (Gas Mark 3) for 1½ hours but allow an extra 30 minutes for an older bird. Just before serving, add remaining mushrooms, and garnish with watercress. The sauce is rich and delicious.

PHEASANT IN MILK

1 pheasant　　　　　　　　　*½ pint milk*
Seasoning　　　　　　　　　*½ pint stock*
Flour

Prepare the bird for roasting and dust well with seasoned flour; put into a pan and dredge with more flour. Pour the milk into the pan and then add half a pint of good stock – this should be drenched over the body and breast of the bird. Cook for 40–50 minutes in a good oven, 400°F (Gas Mark 6), basting frequently with the milk-stock liquid. Take out and put on to a hot dish. Stir together all the thick liquid on the bottom of the tin, and serve this as gravy; it should need no additions but may be thinned a little if it is too thick.

NORFOLK CASSEROLED PHEASANT

1 pheasant　　　　　　　　　*4 or 5 good cooking apples*
A little cream　　　　　　　　*Salt and pepper*
Butter

Take a pheasant and prepare it in the usual way. When it is clean and dry, melt some nice fresh butter in a largish pan and cook and turn the pheasant in this until it is golden brown all over. Meanwhile slice 4 or 5 good cooking apples and slice them nice and thinly, lay them around the sides of a greased, good-sized casserole dish. Placing if liked a slice of bread under the bird, put the pheasant carefully in the casserole and fill up the spaces with the rest of the apples. Pour over any butter left from the browning operation and add more if necessary; sprinkle well with salt and pepper and cover the bird with a greased paper, before covering tightly. Cook in a moderately hot oven, 350°F (Gas Mark 4), for about an hour (longer if bird is tough). If the bird is then tender uncover it and allow a few minutes longer back in the oven. Serve with forcemeat balls or bread sauce and bacon rolls, mashed potatoes and carrots.

LEDBURY ROAST PHEASANT

Have ready a nice plump pheasant for roasting, wiped inside with clean dry cloth. Dust its breast with salt and pepper and a little flour. Fry some croûtons of bread, white or brown, in butter and stand aside. In the butter in the frying pan, cook a few field mushrooms (if possible). Mix the croûtons and the mushrooms together and place inside the pheasant with a little salt and pepper. Sew up the gap and cover the bird with fat bacon slices or rashers of fat bacon, cover with butter paper and cook in a good oven, reducing the heat after about 20 minutes. After cooking for a further 50 minutes to an hour, remove the paper and bacon and return to the oven to completely brown the breast. Serve on a good hot dish garnished with parsley or watercress. After the first initial hot spell of cooking, it is better to have quite a gentle heat as pheasant can become dry in cooking if care is not taken.

SALMIS OF PHEASANT (1)

Cut up the meat from a pheasant that has been cooked, and is not quite cold. Put the bones and trimmings into a saucepan with 2 glasses of sherry and 1 pint of brown sauce. Let it simmer until reduced by one half. Strain the sauce and put it into a saucepan with the meat from the pheasant, and when it is warm serve.

SALMIS OF PHEASANT (2)

Prepare and joint a pheasant. Stew it in brown sherry sauce, together with some minced ham, and a few mushrooms. Garnish with fried bread croûtons and whole button mushrooms.

PHEASANT WITH APPLES

One lunchtime, soon after we were married, my husband telephoned to say he was bringing two delightful strangers to dinner. With no time for shopping I took two pheasants from the deep-freeze, and prayed that they would thaw, picked some apples and made *Faisan Normande* straight from the cookery book. This was such a success that Theo has slightly adapted it so that he can feel civilised and have a drink when the guests come.

Brown a pheasant in a pan or cast iron casserole in half butter and half oil. Peel, core and chop a couple of Cox's apples and add to the casserole. Add a bouquet garni and some stock and simmer gently till done. Remove pheasant, carve on to serving dish, keep warm but don't let it dry. For the sauce, mash the apples into the stock, remove bouquet, season and add a squeeze of lemon juice. At the last moment add as much cream as you can bear, pour over pheasant, sprinkle with chopped parsley and there you are.

Joan Dampney, Christchurch, Hants

BROILED PHEASANT

After the bird has been prepared for cooking in the usual manner, divide it into neat joints. Place them in a frying pan with a little fat, and fry them until they are browned all over. When they are drained well, sprinkle them with salt and cayenne all over, roll them in egg and breadcrumbs and broil over a clear fire for about 10 minutes. Place on a hot dish, and serve with 'sauce piquante', mushroom sauce, or brown sauce. The remains of any cold pheasant may be treated in the same manner.

NORMANDY PHEASANT

Fry the pheasant in a casserole, then place on a layer of freshly chopped apples (about 4). Add three or four tablespoons of cream and cook for about $\frac{3}{4}$ hour in a moderate oven.

PIGEONS

Pigeons are classed as vermin, but they have the advantage of being in season throughout the year and at their best in late summer and early autumn when stuffed with illicit snacks of ripe corn. Country people affect to despise the birds, but they must still have a soft spot for them, referring fondly to a two-child boy-and-girl family as a 'pigeon pair' with the greatest pride.

Great houses used to breed pigeons for useful food, and the many different species of domesticated pigeons used not only for food but for ornament, sport or messengers rejoice in such names as pouters, carriers, homers, fantails, jacobins, nun, turbits, tumblers and trumpeters. The Star Chamber Accounts constantly carry the price of pigeons, making a difference between the tame or 'house' pigeons and the wild ones. From 1519 to 1535, the usual charge was a penny each or 10d per dozen. By 1590, the price had risen to $2\frac{1}{2}$d each for wild birds and 6d for house birds. In 1602 and 1605 they cost 8d each, and by 1635 were 13s and 14s a dozen. Two and a half centuries later, when they were a favourite on Victorian and Edwardian tables, the price remained at about 1s each. Cassell's Dictionary of Cookery, popular at the beginning of the century, lists no less than forty-three recipes for them, including such delicacies as Pigeon

Cutlets and Pigeons Stewed with Asparagus. Today, the birds are still relatively cheap, and two or three will provide a gourmet meal very cheaply.

Pigeons may be rather dry, and plenty of fat bacon will give them flavour and richness. Fat used in cooking pigeons should not be too hot, as their flesh is delicate, and over-heated fat toughens them and destroys flavour. When the birds are plainly roasted, a slice of crustless toast put under them 10 minutes before serving will absorb gravy and fat and is delicious to eat with the dish.

Pigeons need not be hung, but if they are hung head downwards for an hour immediately after killing, they will bleed freely and the flesh will be paler. Young fat pigeons may be roasted; older birds are close and dry, and need longer cooking. Allow 1 pigeon for 2 people, or 1 each if appetites are hearty.

CIDER PIGEONS

2 pigeons	*1 oz flour*
Butter	*¾ pint stock*
1 small apple	*¼ pint cider*
1 small onion	*Parsley, thyme and bayleaf*

Brown the pigeons in butter, then split them in half. Brown sliced apple and onion in same fat, then sprinkle on flour and cook until golden. Add stock and cider and bring to the boil. Season with salt and pepper, add herbs and halved pigeons. Cover tightly and cook on top of the stove or in a low oven for 2½ hours. Serve pigeons in the gravy with a garnish of fried apple rings and bacon rolls.

PIGEONS WITH CABBAGE

1 large firm cabbage	*2 pigeons*
8 rashers fat bacon	*Parsley, thyme and bayleaf*
Butter	

This is a very good winter dish made with a firm-hearted cabbage and old birds. Blanch a large firm cabbage in boiling water for 10 minutes, drain very well and chop finely. Mix with 4 rashers of chopped bacon and put into a greased fireproof dish. Season with salt and pepper, and put in a sprig each of parsley and thyme, and a bayleaf. Brown pigeons in a little butter and put them into the dish, covering with the remaining rashers of bacon. Add stock just to cover, cover tightly and simmer for 2 hours. Serve the birds (which may be split in half) on a bed of cabbage. A Victorian version of this dish suggests thickening the gravy before serving with a knob of butter and flour and 2 tablespoons of thick cream.

JELLIED PIGEONS

3 or 4 pigeons
Salt and pepper

Mixed herbs
1 oz gelatine

This is a very good way of dealing with old birds. Simmer the birds in just enough water to cover with plenty of seasoning and herbs for about 1½ hours until the meat leaves the bones easily. Remove the meat from the bones, taste the gravy for seasoning, and dissolve the gelatine (which has been softened in a little cold water) in the hot liquid. Pack the meat into a wetted mould and pour over it the stock. Leave to set before turning out to serve with salad.

POT ROAST PIGEONS

1 bird per person
Seasoned flour
Butter

¼ pint stock
1 teaspoon mixed herbs (for
4 birds)

Dip the birds in seasoned flour, then brown them in a little butter. Add herbs and stock, cover tightly and cook very gently on top of the stove or in the oven for 1½ hours. Serve with the pan gravy, bread sauce and game chips. This is a useful recipe if you are not sure of the age of the birds, but don't want to casserole them.

PIGEONS WITH BACON

With a sharp knife make a slit on each side of the breastbone and insert slices of streaky bacon. Pack the birds into a roasting dish, cover with dripping and greaseproof paper and cook slowly in the oven for 2½ to 3 hours. When cooked, the breasts and bacon will lift away from the birds, and the remains are discarded.

SLOW-COOKED PIGEONS

4 pigeons
12 small onions
3 rashers lean bacon
8 oz mushrooms
1 pint stock
1 wineglass wine or cider
(optional)

1 oz butter
¾ oz flour
1 teaspoon sugar
Parsley, thyme and bayleaf
tied in a bunch

Use an oven-to-table dish which will allow the pigeons to fit side by side. A cast-iron one is perfect as it can be started on top of the stove, then put into the oven. Peel the onions, cut the bacon into thin strips and wipe the mushrooms. Heat the butter and lightly fry the bacon. Put on to a dish, and cook onions until lightly golden, sprinkling with sugar. Remove to dish. Cook the mushrooms in the same fat and remove to dish.

Brown the pigeons in the fat, very slowly and carefully, and lift out. Work the flour into the fat, cooking until brown. Gradually add stock and wine, bring to the boil and strain. Rinse out the pan, put back the sauce and bring to the boil. Add all the ingredients, cover with a greased paper and well-fitting lid. Cook at 300°F (Gas Mark 2) for 2½–3 hours. Remove bunch of herbs before serving.

POT ROAST PIGEONS

Prepare the birds as for roasting, dip in well-seasoned flour. Have 1 oz butter very hot in a large saucepan, brown the birds in this, add a small teaspoon of mixed herbs, put on a close fitting lid, and cook slowly for about 1½ hours. Serve with the liquid in the pan, slightly thickened, as gravy; bread sauce and chips.

To marinade pigeons

To marinade meat or game means to cover it with a mixture of wine, herbs, spices, onions and vinegar for any period of up to 14 days. The effect of putting tough meat into this mixture is to break down the tissues and shorten the cooking time.

Allow 1 bird per person	*Vinegar*
½ bottle cheap red wine	*Little sliced onion*

Cut up the birds and put them in a large earthenware jar. Allow half as much vinegar as you have wine, mix the 2, add the sliced onion, pour this over the cut joints. Leave for 12–14 days.

When wanted, remove the meat from the marinade, fry some sliced onion, then lightly fry the joints of meat, pack into a greased fireproof casserole, add a little flour to the fat in which you have cooked the birds, and then enough of the marinade liquid to make a thick sauce, pour this over the joints, and put the casserole in a fairly hot oven for about 2 hours.

WOOD PIGEONS WITH CABBAGE

1 *large green cabbage*	*Salt and pepper*
2 *pigeons*	*Little parsley, thyme and a*
3-4 *rashers fat bacon*	*bayleaf*

Blanch the cabbage in boiling water for 10 minutes. Drain and plunge into cold water, leave for 10 minutes. Drain well and press out as much water as possible. Chop, and line a greased fireproof dish with the chopped vegetable and the rashers of bacon. Season with salt and pepper and add the herbs, all except the bayleaf. Have some fat very hot in a pan and brown the prepared, trussed pigeons in the fat, turning so that they are browned all over. Put the birds into the casserole, with the bayleaf, cover with a few more rashers of bacon and put on a close fitting lid. Bring to the boil and allow to simmer for at least 2 hours. The birds can be cut in half and served straight from the bed of cabbage.

ROAST STUFFED PIGEON

Allow 1 bird per person　　　　　*Fat for roasting*
Sausage meat, 4 oz per person

Prepare the birds and put into a steamer, cook for 2–3 hours and leave to get cold. When cold, make a shallow cut across the breast of each bird and pull the skin gently off, being careful not to pull the flesh as well. Stuff the birds with the well-seasoned sausage meat, brush with dripping and dredge with breadcrumbs. Have some fat very hot in a baking tin, put the birds in this and bake for about an hour, basting frequently. Serve with good gravy made from the water in which the birds were steamed, a green vegetable and mashed potatoes.

SUFFOLK BRAISED PIGEONS

4 pigeons　　　　　　　　　　*¼ pint dry red wine*
2 small oranges　　　　　　　*(optional, but a great*
Streaky bacon　　　　　　　　*improvement)*
Butter　　　　　　　　　　　　*½ pint stock*
A few sliced mushrooms　　　*Bouquet garni*
1 onion, sliced　　　　　　　*Chopped parsley*
1 dessertspoon flour

When the pigeons are prepared, peel the 2 oranges and put one half in each bird; truss the birds then wrap each one in a piece of bacon and fry in butter until they are going brown. Drain them then put them in a casserole. Meanwhile fry the mushrooms and onion in the same butter, but not too much; stir in the flour to make a roux and cook for about 3–4 minutes. Gradually blend in the wine and stock, bring to the boil very gently, season to taste before pouring over the birds. Put in the bunch of sweet, fresh herbs (bouquet garni) or if out of season, use dried mixed herbs, cook in a pretty moderate oven (say 325°F) until really tender, at least 1½ hours. After testing, when the birds are well done, remove them from the gravy and arrange them on a flat dish. The gravy can be strained or left as it is, only removing the bouquet garni, and poured over the pigeon joints. Use some nice chopped fresh parsley to garnish. Enough for 4.

JUGGED PIGEONS

Time 3 hours. Some pigeons, two hard-boiled eggs; a sprig of parsley; the peel of $\frac{1}{2}$ lemon; the weight of the livers in suet; the same of breadcrumbs; pepper; salt; and nutmeg; 1 egg; 1$\frac{1}{2}$ oz butter; 1 head of celery; a glass of white wine; a bunch of sweet herbs; 3 cloves; blade of mace.

Pick and draw 4 or 6 pigeons, wipe them very dry, boil the livers a minute or two, then mince them fine and bruise them with a spoon, or beat them in a mortar; mix with them the yolks of 2 hard-boiled eggs, a sprig of parsley, and the peel of half a lemon all shred fine; the weight of the livers in suet, chopped as fine as possible, the same weight of breadcrumbs, and a little pepper, salt, and grated nutmeg; mix it all together with a well beaten egg, and a little fresh butter.

Stuff the pigeons and the crops with this forcemeat, sew up the vents, and dip the pigeons into warm water; dredge over them some pepper and salt, and put them into a jar with the celery, sweet herbs, cloves and beaten mace with a glassful of white wine. *Cover the jar closely*, and set it in a stew-pan of boiling water for 3 hours, taking care the water does not go up to the top of the jar. When done, strain the gravy into a stewpan, stir in a little butter rolled in flour, boil it up again till it is thick, and pour it over the pigeons. Garnish with lemon.

TO FRICASSEE PIGEONS BROWN

Time 1 hour. 5 or 6 pigeons; $\frac{1}{2}$ blade of beaten mace; pepper and salt; 1 pint of gravy or broth; a glass of port wine; a bunch of sweet herbs; peel of $\frac{1}{2}$ lemon; 3 onions or shallots; 2 oz of butter; 1 tablespoon of flour; juice of $\frac{1}{2}$ lemon; and a few pickled mushrooms.

Cut the pigeons into quarters, season them with a blade of mace, well beaten, pepper and salt. Fry them a light brown in butter, and lay them on a sieve to drain, then put them into a stewpan with a pint of gravy or broth, a glass of port wine, a bunch of sweet herbs, the peel of $\frac{1}{2}$ lemon, and 3 shallots choped fine. Cover them closely and stew them for $\frac{1}{2}$ hour, then stir in a piece of butter rolled in flour, season with pepper and salt, add a few pickled mushrooms (or fresh if available) squeeze in the juice of lemon, and add a few forcemeat balls. Let all stew together until both the birds and the forcemeat balls are cooked, skim the gravy if necesasry, put the fricassée on a hot dish and garnish with lemon.

RABBIT

A good rabbit should feed 6 people. If you have a very young one, the legs are excellent if boned, beaten flat, and fried in egg and breadcrumbs, served with slices of lemon. Rabbit casseroles are best with plenty of herbs and seasonings, onions and bacon; leftover rabbit may be minced and potted with butter.

HAMPSHIRE RABBIT

1 *rabbit*	4 *oz streaky bacon rashers*
Seasoned flour	*Dripping*
Poultry stuffing	*Stock*
8 *oz onions*	*Salt and pepper*
8 *oz tomatoes*	

Joint the rabbit and soak in salt and water until blanched. Dry joints and toss in seasoned flour. Put joints in a fireproof dish and surround with balls of poultry stuffing. Cover the rabbit with sliced onions and tomatoes and top with bacon rashers. Dot with dripping, and brown in a hot oven for 20 minutes. Add stock to come half way up the dish, season well with salt and pepper, and cover with a lid. Cook at 325°F (Gas Mark 3) for 2 hours.

BAKED RABBIT

1 *rabbit*	*Seasoning*
1 *lb onions*	2 *oz dripping*
1 *large carrot*	*Sage*

Wash the jointed rabbit in salted water and dry thoroughly. Chop the onions and carrot, and put with the rabbit into a saucepan. Cover with water and simmer until almost cooked. Strain, keeping the stock. Put the rabbit and the vegetables into a baking-tin. Season, and add the dripping and a sprinkling of sage. Bake until browned, basting occasionally. Remove the rabbit joints and keep warm. Make gravy, using the pan juices and stock. Serve separately, or poured over the rabbit.

CURRIED RABBIT

2 *fresh young rabbits*	1 *dessertspoon good curry*
½ *lb bacon*	*powder*
2 *teaspoons butter, or good*	1 *dessertspoon flour*
dripping	1½ *breakfastcups water*
1 *large sour apple*	*Salt to taste*

Cut the rabbits into pieces sufficient for serving, wash well in salted water and dry; put the butter in a stewpan, and allow it to become hot. Have the bacon cut into small pieces and fry it. Remove cooked bacon to a plate, then fry the pieces of rabbit, which also remove when browned. Have the onions and apple finely chopped then fry these next. When soft crush into a pulp with the back of a wooden spoon, and carefully mix into this the curry powder and flour. Return the rabbit and bacon to the stewpan, and over them pour water, simmer gently for 2 hours, add a little lemon juice, and serve with boiled rice.

Rabbits were once upon a time the standby of many a farmhouse in midweek before the butcher's weekly call on a Friday. Some farmers were so up against it in the hard times before World War II that rabbits, which were thick upon the ground, had to be eaten more than once a week. The farmer's wife would be hard put to it to serve the meat in an acceptable fashion, after a while, as her family would be heartily sick of rabbit in any shape or form. Farmers don't take kindly to 'foreign' dishes but if she didn't overdo the curry powder, she might get away with this dish, for a change.

FRICASSEE OF RABBIT (1)

1 *rabbit*	1 *or 2 strips celery*
½ *pint milk*	1½ *oz flour*
6 *white peppercorns*	1 *blade of mace*
1 *carrot*	*Salt and pepper*
2 *onions*	*White stock*
2 *oz butter*	*Bouquet garni*

Cut the rabbit into neat joints, rinse in warm water, place in a saucepan, and add enough white stock to cover. Bring to the boil and add the washed, prepared vegetables, sliced, the peppercorns and a little salt. Simmer for about 1¼ hours, or until the rabbit is tender, adding a little milk from time to time to replace reduced stock. Melt the butter, add the flour, and stir to a smooth paste. Take out the rabbit and keep hot; strain ¾ pint of the stock on to the flour, stir until boiling, and boil 3 or 4 minutes. Rub the vegetables through a fine sieve, and stir the purée into the sauce. Season to taste, replace the rabbit, and heat through thoroughly. Serve at once.

FRICASSEE OF RABBIT (2)

1 *rabbit*	½ *pint white stock*
1 *onion*	*Bouquet garni*
2 *oz butter*	*Seasoning*
½ *pint milk*	1 *teaspoon lemon juice*
4 *mushrooms*	*Bacon rolls*
2 *oz flour*	

Cut the rabbit into neat pieces. Put into a pan with the onion, mushrooms, seasoning and stock and the bouquet garni. Bring to boiling point, cover and cook gently on the simmering side for 10 minutes, then continue cooking for a further 2–2½ hours either gently simmering on top of the stove, or transfer to a gentle oven. Put the meat in a hot dish and keep hot; strain the liquor, melt the butter in the pan, add the flour and cook for a few minutes. Add the strained liquor and milk and stir until the sauce is thickened and boiled. Add the lemon juice and pour over the meat. Garnish with the bacon rolls, lemon, parsley and fried croûtons.

TO FRICASSEE RABBITS BROWN

2 *young rabbits*	½ *pint fresh mushrooms if*
Pepper and salt	*you have them*
Flour and butter	3 *shallots*
1 *pint gravy*	*Spoon of ketchup*
Bunch of sweet herbs	1 *lemon*

Take 2 young rabbits, cut them in small pieces, slit the heads in two, season them with pepper and salt, dip them in flour, and fry them a nice brown in fresh butter. Pour out the fat from the pan, and put in 1 pint of gravy, a bunch of sweet herbs, ½ pint of fresh mushrooms if you have them, and 3 shallots chopped fine, season with pepper and salt, cover them close, and let them stew for ½ hour. Then skim the gravy clean, add a spoonful of ketchup, and the juice of ½ lemon. Take out the herbs and stir in a piece of butter rolled in flour, boil it up till it thickens and is smooth, skim off the fat, and serve the rabbits garnished with lemon.

RABBIT STEWED IN MILK

Select a nice rabbit, thoroughly wash and dry it, cut it into small joints, place in a stewpan with about 1½ lb of pickled pork, a large onion stuck with cloves, a blade of mace, a bunch of savoury herbs. Cover it with milk, let it boil, then draw the saucepan to the side and let it simmer gently for 1½ hours. When done, place on a hot dish, strain the liquid, thicken it with flour, and add some finely chopped parsley. Pour over the rabbit and send to table.

Mrs Thorne, 1911

IRISH ROAST RABBIT

1 rabbit	*½ pint scalded milk*
4 rashers bacon	*Pepper*
2 medium onions	*1 dessertspoon chopped*
1 tablespoon flour	*parsley*
2 oz butter	

Cut up rabbit and soak in vinegar and water. Dry pieces well and coat in flour seasoned with pepper. Brown in the butter and put into a casserole. Add chopped bacon, onions and parsley and pour over milk. Cover and bake at 375°F (Gas Mark 5) for 1 hour. Serve with plenty of floury potatoes. Parsley sauce is also good with this.

RABBIT BRAWN

1 rabbit	*Pinch of ground cloves*
2 carrots	*Sprig of thyme*
2 onions	*2 hard-boiled eggs*
Salt and pepper	*2 oz gelatine*
Pinch of nutmeg	

Cut up rabbit and simmer until tender in 3 pints of water with diced carrots and onions, seasoning, spices and thyme. Rinse a mould with cold water and decorate the bottom with slices of hard-boiled egg. Cool the cooked rabbit and cut meat into small pieces. Dissolve the gelatine in a little water, then add it to the rabbit stock and boil. Strain over the rabbit meat and leave in a cold place to set. This is much improved if a little cooked ham, bacon or stewing beef is added.

RABBIT WITH ONION SAUCE

1 rabbit	*3 oz butter*
3 lb onions	*Some thick cream*

Rabbit and onions have an affinity for each other. This dish goes very well with jacket potatoes. Joint and soak rabbit, then cook in boiling water with seasoning, reducing to simmering heat and cooking for about 1½ hours until tender, depending on the age of the rabbit. Cut rabbit in pieces and serve covered with onion sauce. Make this by cutting onions very finely and stewing gently in butter until they are very soft but not brown, keeping lid on the pan and stirring frequently. Add ¾ pint rabbit stock, season again to taste, and stir in some thick, hot cream before pouring over rabbit.

HUNTER'S RABBIT

1 *rabbit*	*Salt and pepper*
1 *small hard cabbage*	1 *small onion*
1 *lb chipolata sausages*	¼ *pint stock (made with a*
4 *bacon rashers*	*beef cube)*
Thyme, parsley and bayleaf	½ *pint dry cider*

Cut rabbit in pieces and soak, then dry thoroughly. Cut cabbage lengthways into 6 or 8 pieces, and boil in very little water for 5 minutes, draining well. Fry sausages and sliced onion. Put cabbage in a casserole, then put in rabbit pieces, followed by sausages and onion, and the chopped, uncooked bacon. Add herbs and seasoning, pour in stock and cider, and cover tightly. Cook at 325°F (Gas Mark 3) for 2½ hours.

JUGGED RABBIT

1 *rabbit*	*Pinch of nutmeg*
1 *onion*	1 *teaspoon sugar*
1 *bayleaf*	½ *pint dry cider*
Salt and pepper	

Soak rabbit joints overnight in 1 pint water with 2 tablespoons vinegar, together with chopped onion, bayleaf, salt and pepper and nutmeg. Drain joints, keeping the liquid, and dry joints well. Fry rabbit in dripping or bacon fat until golden, then cover with liquid and simmer gently until tender (about 1 hour). Add sugar and cider to pan and continue cooking for 15 minutes. Thicken gravy with a little flour or cornflour, and serve with forcemeat balls and redcurrant jelly.

MOCK HARE

Soak rabbit joints overnight in equal parts of vinegar and water, with 1 bayleaf, a chopped onion, salt and pepper and a pinch of grated nutmeg. Take out the joints, drain and dry, and fry till golden. Pour on the liquid and stew slowly till tender. 30 minutes before serving time, add ½ pint cider, and just before serving thicken the gravy with flour or cornflour. Serve with redcurrant jelly and forcemeat balls.

RABBIT WITH LENTILS

Soak ¼ lb lentils in water overnight. Put 1 oz finely chopped bacon into a saucepan and fry till the fat runs; add 1 small chopped onion, and soften without browning. Stir in the lentils and any water remaining, and simmer gently till soft, adding a little more water if necessary to prevent burning. Put through a sieve. Pour ¼ pint cider over the rabbit, add a bunch of mixed herbs, salt and pepper, and simmer with the lid on till it is tender. Add the rabbit liquid to the sieved lentils, simmer till thick, then add the pieces of bacon and rabbit. Serve very hot, accompanied by a green vegetable or a salad.

RABBIT IN CIDER

Joint and soak the rabbit with a good squeeze of lemon juice in the water for an hour, then dry well. Fry the rabbit till brown in bacon fat, and add 4 large sliced onions. Cook till the onions are soft, and add 1 bayleaf, a sprig of thyme, 2 oz chopped bacon and ½ lb peeled sliced tomatoes. Simmer for 10 minutes, then pour on ¼ pint of dry cider. Simmer with the lid on till the rabbit is tender, and season with salt and pepper just before serving, removing the bayleaf.

GLOUCESTER RABBIT

Though this is one of the most simple ways of cooking rabbit, it is extremely tasty because of the preliminary frying of the onions. Joint and soak the rabbit, then dry very well and roll in flour. Melt plenty of butter, and brown the rabbit all over. Put rabbit pieces in a casserole and use the butter for frying 2 lb thinly sliced onions. When the onions are golden, pour in a little stock or water, stir well, pour over the rabbit pieces and cover the casserole tightly. Put in a slow oven for 2½ hours.

RABBIT BRAWN

Cover 2 pig's feet with water and gently cook for 1½ hours. Then put in a jointed rabbit, previously soaked for an hour. Boil together for 2 hours till the meat is tender, adding a little more water if required. Remove all bones, cut meat into neat pieces, and season with salt, pepper and nutmeg. Boil together again for 15 minutes, then pour into moulds or basins well rinsed with cold water. Leave overnight before turning out and serve with salad, or in sandwiches.

A NEW CURRIED RABBIT

1 *young rabbit*
1 *onion chopped*
1 *tablespoon each lemon*
juice and curry powder
3 *tablespoons chopped*
coconut

1 *teaspoon each sugar and*
salt
1 *cup white stock or water*
½ *cup milk*
Boiled rice

Joint rabbit, wash thoroughly and dry each piece upon a clean cloth. Fry a light brown in butter if possible, remove from pan, fry onion, add curry powder, coconut, sugar, salt, milk and stock or water, put in the rabbit and simmer 1 hour; add lemon juice and serve surrounded with rice.

Mary Bull, 1914

TO ROAST A SWAN (1)

Take 2 lb rump steak – chop it fine and season it well with spice, and add a slice of butter; then stuff with the above, taking care to sew the bird up carefully, and let it be tied tightly on the spit so that the gravy may not escape. Enclose the breast of the swan in a meal paste. Afterwards cover the whole bird with paper, well greased with butter. A ¼ hour before it is taken up, remove the paper and paste. Baste well with butter and flour till it is brown and frothy. A swan of 15 lb weight will require 2¼ hours roasting, with a fire not too fierce. To be served up with gravy and redcurrant jelly. *The swan is not to be skinned.*

Mrs Garden, 1847

TO ROAST A SWAN (2)

Take three pounds of beef, beat fine in a mortar.
Put it into the swan (that is when you've caught her).
Some pepper, salt, mace, some nutmeg, an onion,
Will heighten the flavour in gourman'd opinion.
Then tie it up tight with a small piece of tape,
That the gravy and other things may not escape.
A meal paste, rather stiff, should be laid on the breast,
And some whited brown paper should cover the rest.
Fifteen minutes, at least, ere the swan you take down,
Put the paste off the bird, that the breast may get brown.

Mrs Garden, 1847

In Norfolk there is a book recording the 'swan marks' of the peerage and gentry and the Public Record Office has records of marks from other countries. These were intricate patterns made on the beaks of the birds to indicate ownership. Swan was certainly eaten from the middle of the fifteenth century, and always formed part of the feasting in great houses, or for special events. As late as 1931, the Master, Great Hospital, Norwich, was offering cygnets (young swans) dressed for dinner and banquets, or alive for ornamental waters, through an advertisement in *The Times*. The great cook Francatelli gave a recipe in the 1850s for a Norwich-fed cygnet, so it would seem these were certainly superior birds. Cygnets were usually used, and in best condition in September. They were often cooked in the same way as geese.

TRUSSED WOODCOCK

In trussing the woodcock great care must be taken not to tear the tender skin. It must be well plucked, and the head and neck also. Do not draw the bird; cut off the ends of the toes after singeing the hairs. Bring the feet upon the thighs by twisting the legs at the joints. Press the wings to the sides, and the head under one wing, with the beak forward. The legs and breast must have a string tied round them, and also round the head and tip of bill. The bird must hang from the spit feet downwards.

ROAST WOODCOCK

These birds require little time for cooking, as all dark fleshed game is digestible when almost raw, therefore they must not be left from the time they are put down till the time they are taken up. The legs require more cooking than the breast, and this latter should be underdone – very underdone. To obviate this inequality in the cooking, the spit should be stopped while the legs are turned to the fire, constant attention being given to the roasting, when the woodcock are plucked, necks and heads also, they must not be opened but trussed securely. Cover the woodcocks with slices of bacon, put them before a clear fire, nicely bright, feet downwards, fastened to the spit; sprinkle them with flour and baste them continually. Prepare some buttered toast without crust, and when the birds have been down about 5 minutes, place this under them to catch the drippings. When basting hold a dish under them, and they will be sufficiently cooked when the steam draws to the fire. Serve with a piece of the toast under each, garnish with watercress and send to the table with some melted butter.

DEVILLED WOODCOCK

Take a brace of woodcocks that are underdone, and divide them up into joints. Make a savoury powder with $1\frac{1}{2}$ teaspoons of curry powder, $1\frac{1}{2}$

teaspoons salt, 1½ teaspoons of cayenne, and 1½ dessertspoons of mush-room powder. Mix all thoroughly together and well cover the joints with this. Take the brains after splitting the heads, and put them in a basin with the grated rind of a lemon, the yolk of a hardboiled egg, the trail, a pinch of pounded mace, and a tablespoon of soy. Rub the mixture with a spoon until it is quite smooth, and add two dessertspoons of ketchup, the juice of 1½ Seville oranges, and a glass of Madeira. Put the sauce with the birds into a fireproof dish over a gentle fire, and let it simmer very closely until the flesh is thoroughly impregnated with the sauce, stir in 2 tea-spoons of salad oil, and serve.

ROAST WOODCOCK

1 woodcock (per person)   *½ lb butter*
1 piece of toast

Do not clean out the inside of the woodcock. Skewer its beak through its body. Tie over its breast a piece of fat bacon. Fill it with butter. Heat some butter in a baking dish. Put in a piece of toast. On that put the wood-cock and cook it for 10 minutes. Cut off the bacon and string. Cook for another 5 minutes. Pour the juices of the pan over the bird.

WILD DUCK

Under the provision of the Protection of Birds Act 1954, some wild duck are protected by special penalties during the close season, i.e. common scoter, gargany teal, golden eye, long tailed duck, scaup-duck and velvet scoter. Wild duck that may be killed or taken outside the season are the common pochard, gadwall, mallard, pintail, shoveller, teal, tufted duck and widgeon.

ROAST WILD DUCK

Wipe and dry bird. If so desired they can be stuffed with skinned quarter oranges. Season with salt and pepper and place a knob of butter inside. Truss and place on a rack in a baking tin. Roast in hot oven for 30 minutes. Don't overcook. Baste frequently. Dredge with flour then baste again. Serve with orange salad.

    If fishy taste is disliked, cover a deep roasting tin to a depth of ½ inch with boiling salted water, put the bird in and bake it for 10 minutes, basting frequently with the salt water.

SALMI OF DUCK, TEAL OR MALLARD

1 *mallard*	1 *oz flour*
4 *oz bacon*	½ *pint stock*
1 *onion*	*Glass of red wine*
Bouquet garni and 1 *bayleaf*	*Few black olives*
Walnut of butter	

Wild duck can carry an unmistakable taste of fish if it has been feeding on salt marshes, so cook it slowly with bay leaves and a glass of red wine.

Dice the bacon and fry lightly, add a bayleaf and the herbs, then transfer half the contents of the pan to a fireproof dish and the rest to a baking tin. Put the bird in the baking tin on the chopped bacon and slice into the tin a large onion. Cover the bird with fat or lard, seeing that the breast particularly is protected so that it does not dry out while cooking. Bake for 20 minutes in a medium oven, 350°F (Gas Mark 4) then remove the bird and slice off all the meat. Have ready the fireproof dish with the rest of the bacon, add the fillets. Make a sauce with the fat, flour, stock and claret, pour this over the meat in the casserole, adding the stoned olives at the same time. Put into a slow oven to cook for a further 30 minutes. Serve just as it is from the dish, with plain boiled potatoes and mixed vegetables.

ROAST SNIPE

2 *snipe*	2 *slices toast*
2 *pieces bacon*	1½ *oz butter*

Snipe, plover and woodcock are dressed without being drawn, truss for roasting, but skin head and leave it on. Wipe dry and place in a baking tin. Cover with bacon. Stand them on a rack in the tin with pieces of toast underneath. Roast for 25-30 minutes, in very moderate oven. Serve on the toast garnished with watercress.

POACHED SNIPE

4 *snipe*	4 *thick slices bread*
½ *lb butter*	

Poach the snipe for 12 minutes in water. Drain and put on the toasted bread. Pour over foaming hot butter.

ROAST TEAL

These birds should be plucked, drawn and trussed like wild duck. Dredge them with flour liberally, put them down to a brisk fire, but do not baste them for the first 3 or 4 minutes, as this will help to keep the gravy in;

after this baste continually. When they are nicely browned, which should be in about 15 minutes, and when the steam draws to the fire, place them in a hot dish with some good brown gravy round them, but not over them, and send some gravy to the table in a tureen. Also send a cut lemon to table, and at the moment of serving sprinkle a little cayenne on the breast, and a squeeze of lemon juice.

ROAST QUAILS

When the birds are firmly trussed a slice of fat bacon should be tied over each, and a vine leaf underneath, if procurable, to correct its deficiency of flavour. If the birds are not drawn they should be served on pieces of toast, which have been placed in the pan 5 minutes after the cooking has commenced. Roast before a clear fire for about 15 minutes, basting continually. Place the quails on the toasts in the centre of a hot dish, pour some good brown gravy round, not over, the quails, and garnish with watercress.

GUINEA FOWL

The guinea fowl forms a convenient substitute for game (says an early Victorian cookbook) as it is in season from February to June. It is rather like pheasant when well-kept, in appearance and taste, and the flesh digestible and savoury.

ROAST GUINEA FOWL

The guinea fowl may be trussed like a young turkey, with the head left on, or like a pheasant, then larded and filled with a good forcemeat. Put it before a clear fire, and to prevent it becoming dry it must be continually basted. Let it cook for about 1 hour, dredge a little flour over it a few minutes before it is taken up, let it froth nicely, and send it to table with bread sauce and gravy.

GUINEA FOWL BOILED WITH OYSTERS

Empty the fowl in the usual way, and dredge 2 dozen oysters with flour; add 2 oz butter, some salt and pepper, and place inside the fowl. Put it into a close fitting jar, and cover with a strong stock or gravy. Place the jar in a saucepan of boiling water, and let it boil very fast for about 2 hours. When the fowl is tender remove it from the jar, drain the liquor and cover it with white sauce or parsley and butter sauce.

VENISON

In Season: Late June to January

The meat should be hung 8–10 days, and is best larded or put into a marinade of wine and herbs before roasting, as there is little fat (a larding needle costs about 5p and is used to thread the meat with strips of fat bacon or pork). Large joints are best roasted; smaller and unidentifiable pieces are best stewed. Chops and fillet may be grilled, and cutlets can be jugged. Cold venison makes excellent cottage pie, or a good galantine if pressed in a mould with plenty of seasoning. Traditional accompaniments are redcurrant, rowan or cranberry jelly.

ROAST VENISON

1 joint venison
½ pint red wine
½ pint vinegar

1 sliced onion
Parsley, thyme and bayleaf

Mix together the wine, vinegar, onion and herbs, and put the venison in it to soak for 2 days, turning the meat from time to time. When ready to cook the meat, put the joint on a rack in a baking tin, with the marinade in the tin. Cook at 375°F (Gas Mark 5) until meat is tender, basting frequently. Strain the pan juices through a sieve, thicken with a little flour, and, if liked, a gill of sour cream or yoghurt.

ROAST VENISON (ROE DEER)

Depending on the weather and whether the beast has been shot that day or bought from a butcher, hang it for 4 days at least in an airy place. We used to have a 'Game Larder' made of perforated zinc, like a bird cage, hanging on the wall outside with a solid roof to keep out the rain and lots of hooks on a beam across the ceiling. If the weather is sultry don't hang it longer than 4 days, but if frosty it is perfectly all right to leave it for 3 weeks – but do watch it and unless you like it strong, 2 weeks is enough, even when the temperature is low. Don't worry about grey mould; it doesn't harm the meat.

When you decide it is time to cook it, take a leg or a saddle for roasting. Wipe it all over with a cloth wrung out in a mixture of permanganate of potash and water, ½ teaspoon to a pint, or salt and water with 1 dessertspoon to a pint. Either spread the joint with butter or wrap it in bacon, wrap it in greaseproof/foil or put it in a self-basting roasting tin – a lid with dimples in. Venison is a very dry meat and care must be taken or it will be uneatable. Roast at a temperature of between 350° and 450°F. If young and well hung at 450°F at 20 minutes per lb., if old and not hung for long at 350°F for 30 minutes per lb. ½ hour before the end of roasting time take the wrappings off the meat to let it get brown on the outside.

Take it out of the tin and lay on a hot dish and to the juices in the pan add 1 glass port, a pinch of mace, 6 peppercorns, a bayleaf and a teaspoon of redcurrant jelly or rowan jelly which has a more bitter flavour. Leave to simmer – add a little stock if necessary. Venison gravy should not be thick.

Mrs Chaplin, Finsthwaite, Lancs

NEW FOREST VENISON ROLL

2 lb venison *6 oz breadcrumbs*
½ lb fat bacon *1 tablespoon chopped parsley*
Salt and pepper *2 eggs*
Stock or water (to mix)

Mince the venison and bacon, add the onion finely chopped, seasonings, breadcrumbs and chopped parsley. Beat the eggs and add to the former ingredients. Add sufficient stock to bind. Flour a pudding cloth and place the mixture on it in a long roll, wrap up, tie the ends with string and boil for 2½ hours. Serve with brown gravy and cranberry or redcurrant jelly. Rowanberry jelly is also good with this dish.

NORMANDY VENISON

Venison is always better if it is marinaded before cooking. This dish should be made with the haunch.

Make a marinade with 1 pint cider, 1 gill wine vinegar, a sprig of parsley and thyme, 1 bayleaf, 2 crushed cloves of garlic, 2 carrots and 2 onions cut in rounds and fried in olive oil until golden, salt and pepper. Mix the marinade and leave the venison in it for at least 4 days.

Drain the joint, cover it with a few rashers of fat bacon and roast it in a hot oven, allowing 10–15 minutes per lb. Halfway through cooking-time, baste with a wine glass of Calvados or brandy, mixed with the juice of ½ lemon and 6 tablespoons of the marinade. While the meat is cooking make a purée of cooking apples with a little of the marinade (add no sugar). Make a gravy with the juices from the meat, a little of the marinade and ½ gill fresh cream. Serve surrounded with apple purée.

VENISON ROAST IN FOIL

Joint of venison *A little flour*
Dripping

Rub the meat all over with clarified fat or dripping and wrap in grease-proof paper. Then wrap in foil. Roast by the slow roast method in a moderate oven, 350°F (Gas Mark 4) for 3–4 hours according to the size of joint (40 minutes to the pound) basting often. ½ hour before serving, take off all coverings, dredge with flour, raise the heat of the oven and baste.

VENISON STEWED IN ALE

Venison—stewing cuts   **2 tablespoons black treacle**
½ lb demerara sugar   *1 pint beer*

Dissolve the sugar and treacle in the beer. Put the well-hung meat into a stewpan or casserole, cover with the liquid, put on the lid and bring to the boil. Simmer gently until tender, the time of the cooking being approximately 30 minutes to the pound and 30 minutes over.

ROAST HAUNCH OF VENISON (1)

The joint is best if kept as long as possible before cooking, and to ensure it being in a good condition it must be examined every day. The kernel of the fat should be removed and the parts from which it is taken then wiped dry, and this as well as the whole haunch should be dusted with pepper and powdered ginger. The fatter the meat the better, and to preserve the fat the haunch should be covered with white cartridge paper, well-greased and then with a stiff paste of flour and water rolled out to the thickness of ¾ inch. Tie securely over this with a string or tape 2 additional sheets of greased paper. Put the haunch down to a clear fire, near at first to harden the paste, draw it back after a minute or two, and gradually bring it nearer again. Baste it continually to prevent the outer paper from burning, until the meat is done sufficiently. Remove the paper and paste, sprinkle a little salt on the meat, dredge it with a little flour, and then baste with a table-spoon of dissolved butter. Make a little brown gravy with the fat etc. from the dripping tin, season with salt and pepper and a squeeze of lemon, and strain it over the venison on the dish. Send redcurrant jelly to table with it. The dish and all the plates must be very hot, as the fat of venison hardens very quickly. The time required to roast is from 10 to 15 minutes for each pound in weight.

ROAST HAUNCH OF VENISON (2)

Time – 3 to 4 hours. Haunch from 20 to 25 lb.
This joint is trimmed by cutting off part of the knuckle and sawing off the chine bone, then the flap is folded over, and it is covered in a paste made of flour and water. This paste should be about an inch thick. Stand the

haunch in a suitable roasting dish and cover the paste with dripping. Place in a hot oven to cook the paste but reduce the heat immediately the paste hardens. Baste frequently as venison has very little fat of its own. After 3 to 4 hours, according to the size, test the venison with a thin skewer, running it well in to see if it is done enough, if not, return it to the oven for further cooking. When it is 'dressed' glaze the top and sala-mander it. Put a frill round the knuckle and serve very hot with strong gravy. Redcurrant jelly in a glass dish or a tureen. Vegetables: French beans.

NECK OF VENISON

Time – $\frac{1}{4}$ hour per lb.

Cover it with paste and paper as for the haunch, fix it on a spit and roast. To hash venison: some cold roast venison; wineglass port wine, a little mutton broth; half a shallot; a pinch of cayenne pepper; $1\frac{1}{2}$ oz of butter; a spoonful flour; and salt to taste.

Cut some slices of cold roast venison, nicely, and season them lightly with salt; put the bones, trimmings, any cold gravy from the venison, the shallot etc. and as much broth as you may require into a stewpan, and let it simmer for quite an hour, but slowly, then strain it off. Stir the butter and flour over the fire until sufficiently brown to colour the gravy, taking care it does not burn. Pour the gravy from the bones and the port wine onto it, and let it simmer until it boils. Then draw the stewpan to the side of the fire and put in the slices of venison, and when thoroughly *hot* serve it up, with redcurrant jelly in a glass dish. Garnish with forcemeat balls about the size of a marble.

BRAISED SHOULDER OF VENISON

Remove the bone from a well-hung shoulder of venison, and marinade the meat in equal parts of vinegar and water, with a bunch of savoury herbs. Let it remain in this 3 or 4 days, then chop up 1 large onion, 1 shallot, $\frac{1}{2}$ lb fat bacon, 3 cloves and 3 oz of butter. Let this fry in an earthenware brazing pan; lay the venison on top, squeeze over it the juice of $\frac{1}{2}$ lemon, cover closely, place it in a moderate oven for 3 hours. Just before serving, add a glass of sherry and a teacup of cream. Let it cook a further 10 minutes, and place on a very hot dish, strain the gravy over it, and serve.

STEWED VENISON

Take the remains of a roast haunch of venison, cut it up into small pieces, place it in an earthenware pan with 2 glasses of port wine, a small bayleaf, and the gravy that was left over. Let it stew gently for 15 minutes, and serve it with croûtons of toast and with redcurrant jelly.

VENISON RISSOLES (from the Scottish Highlands)

Roll out some puff paste or shortcrust paste, stamp out in circular pieces, put a teaspoon of minced venison in the centre, brush the edges with beaten egg, fold over to form a half-circle, and press the edges firmly together. Brush over with egg, dip in breadcrumbs and fry in smoking fat to a light golden brown. Drain and garnish with parsley, fried for 1 minute in the fat and then well-drained.

CHESTNUT PURÉE

2 lb chestnuts	*Butter*
½ onion	*Cream*

Slit the chestnuts on the flat side and boil them for 15–20 minutes. Chop the onion finely and cook it in butter. Add the peeled chestnuts and mash them with a fork. Put through a sieve or mill. Melt some butter in a saucepan and add the purée. Season. Add some cream.

BREADCRUMBS

6 slices stale white bread with the crust on.
Leave the slices of bread in a slow oven or the plate drawer to make them hard. Crush them with a rolling pin. Brown in butter. Dry on blotting paper. Keep warm in oven.

FRIED CRUMBS

Some people like to serve fried crumbs with game. Simply melt a lump of butter, about the size of a pigeon's egg, in the heavy frying pan then stir in a cupful of breadcrumbs until evenly blended and cook gently until golden brown all over.

BREAD SAUCE

Take 3 or 4 nice firm onions and cut them with the sign of the cross without scoring right through to their base. In 1 onion, stick 6, 8 or more cloves and remember to account for each one later! In a suitable saucepan pour a little hot water and add 1 oz butter, 1 level teaspoon salt and a good shake of pepper. Place the onions in this and then pour in sufficient milk to nearly cover the onions – the saucepan should be as small as possible in order that too much liquid is not necessary. Cook the onions slowly and carefully – this takes some time according to the texture of the onions. Meanwhile, remove all crust from 4–6 oz of white bread and soak it in a little hot water; when this is all absorbed add a little milk and leave to continue soaking until the onions are really soft and well-cooked, then pour off the onion milk on to the soaking bread. Remove the exact number of cloves and mash the onion with a fork. Add the bread and milk and if liked another knob of butter. Beat well with the electric beater until smooth and creamy and season to taste. Serve in a hot sauce boat.

Mrs Rene Woodhouse

BREAD SAUCE (2)

1 *onion*
Salt, pepper and nutmeg
1 *pint milk*

1 *cup dried breadcrumbs*
Cream

Chop the onion and cook it in milk till it is soft, adding salt, pepper and nutmeg. Add the breadcrumbs and more milk. Just before serving, add some cream.

TO MAKE GAME GRAVY

Take the giblets, bones and any trimmings and just cover with cold water. Add salt and pepper, onions, a bayleaf, any available fresh herbs such as thyme, parsley etc. a clove or two, and a pinch of allspice. Bring carefully to the boil and then simmer well until quantity is reduced. Pour off the fat from the roasting tin, then rinse the tin with a little of the game stock and add to the gravy. Boil again and skim if necessary.

FORCEMEAT STUFFING

For hares and rabbits. Soak some bread, from which all crust has been cut, in a little milk or milk and water. Chop up 1 small onion quite finely and fry in hot pan in which has been cooked small, cut-up pieces of left-over rashers of bacon. Pour off fat if too plentiful, retaining about 2 table-spoons in pan with bacon, now nicely browned, and onion softened but not browned. Beat up an egg, if liked, and add to the mashed-up, lump-free bread, which has been squeezed free of surplus liquid, of milk, or milk and water. To the egg and bread add the onions and bacon with the dripping in which they were fried, season well with salt and pepper and add fresh chopped thyme and parsley, or mixed dried herbs, as required for personal preference, and as available; add a little grated lemon rind or pure lemon juice. Mix all together very thoroughly. If mixture is too soft, a little flour or a few more breadcrumbs may be added to make a better texture for stuffing. Season according to taste. Leave to soak in together, for a while before using, but cover with plate to keep 'bouquet' from evaporating into thin air.

8 Pies

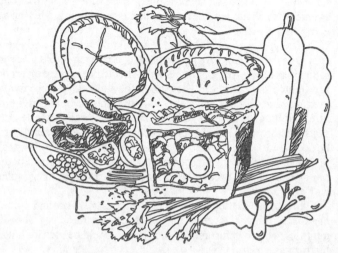

Simple Simon met a pieman going to the Fair
                              Nursery Rhyme

Little Jack Horner
Sat in a corner
Eating his Christmas pie

                              Nursery Rhyme

Sing a song of sixpence,
A pocketful of rye,
Four-and-twenty blackbirds
Baked in a pie.
When the pie was opened,
The birds began to sing.
Wasn't that a dainty dish
To set before a King?

                              Nursery Rhyme

Who can doubt the popularity of the British pie, when we have been singing about it for hundreds of years? All farming families love pastry, and every farm wife knows that a lid or case of melting pastry can transform the dullest meat or the plainest fruit into a luxury dish which is also filling.

For *Shortcrust Pastry*, half as much fat as flour is needed, and the flour rubbed in with the fingertips. For the richer types, *Rough Puff* and *Flaky*,

143

the fat is rolled in, and lemon juice is added (for rough puff, use 4–6 oz fat to 8 oz flour and 2 teaspoons lemon juice; for flaky pastry, use 6 oz fat to the same amount of flour and lemon juice). *Hot Water Pastry* uses one-third as much fat as flour, and the fat is melted before adding, while an egg yolk is an optional extra.

Basically, a good quality plain flour should be used, and everything kept as cool as possible. Rich pastry needs 'resting' in a cold place between rollings, or before use. Dry ingredients should be sieved to incorporate air and lighten the mixture. Water should be added all at once to make the mixture bind without being sticky. Pastry should be rolled lightly, but firmly, rolling on one side only. A hot oven is necessary, the richer the pastry the hotter the oven being a good general rule; the temperature can be decreased as soon as the pastry is firm and brown. A professional finish makes all the difference to savoury pies. For meat pies and patties and sausage rolls, brush over before baking with beaten egg, or egg yolk mixed with a little water.

Fillings can be varied endlessly to suit the family taste and purse. Small pies for the lunch-box can be filled with leftover meat, egg, cheese or fish mixtures; a thick white sauce or good gravy should be used for binding the mixtures.

For supper-time, the favourite bacon and egg pie can be improved with the addition of a few mushrooms or with slices of pork sausage. Again, cooked bacon and hard-boiled egg may be combined in a creamy sauce to give variety.

For more formal occasions, the traditional steak pie can appear in many disguises. Pieces of pigeon or game can be included, hard-boiled eggs, diced vegetables, mushrooms, forcemeat balls, kidneys, or even a few canned oysters. This type of pie is delicious if the meat is rolled round a forcemeat filling and packed firmly into the pie-dish with some onions and a quantity of strong beef stock.

Chicken pies are a useful way of using the odd old boiler, or of eking out the remains of a roast bird. One mixture can be a combination of chopped, cooked chicken and ham, onion and hard-boiled eggs and small forcemeat balls, with plenty of herbs and good chicken stock, and a topping of flaky pastry. This use of good stock and plenty of herbs is always important in a chicken pie.

INSTRUCTIONS FOR PASTRY MAKERS, 1870

We believe it is utterly impossible to teach verbally how to make good paste or pie-crust; a lesson from a good cook would be worth whole volumes on this subject. Some general directions, however, may be given on this important art. First, the cook should have smooth *cold* hands – very clean – for making paste or crust. She should wash them well, and plunge them in cold water for a minute or two in hot weather, drying them well afterwards before beginning her paste.

The pastry slab, if possible, should be made of marble; if it is a wooden paste-board, it should be kept scrupulously clean.

The crust used for homely pies need not be as delicate as that used for company; it may be made of clarified beef dripping or lard instead of butter.

Be very careful about the proper heat of the oven for baking pies, as if it be too cold the paste will be heavy, and have a dull look; if too hot, the crust will burn before the pie is done.

Try if the oven is hot enough by holding your hand inside it for a few seconds; if you can do so without snatching it out again quickly, it is too cold; it is best, however, to try it by baking a little piece of the crust in it first.

Always make a small hole with a knife at the top of the pie to allow the gases generated in it by the cooking to escape. This aperture is also useful for pouring gravy into the pie when it is done, if more is required. The hand of a pastrycook should be light, and the paste should not be worked more than is absolutely required for mixing it.

We give first three plain receipts for pie crust, such as people of small means can use, and will find good, and also instructions for clarifying dripping, so as to render it fit for making pie-crusts.

To Clarify Beef Dripping

Put the dripping into a basin, pour over it some boiling water, and stir it round with a silver spoon; set it cool, and then remove the dripping from the sediment, and put it into basins or jars for use in a cool place. Clarified dripping may be used for frying and basting, everything except game or poultry, as well as for pies etc.

To Make a Short Crust with Dripping

1 *lb flour*	1 *wineglass of very cold water*
¾ *lb clarified beef dripping*	*Pinch of salt*

Take care that the water you use is cold, especially in summer. Cut the flour, well dried, into a large basin (which should be kept for the purpose) with a pinch of salt; break up the clarified beef dripping into pieces, and mix them *well* with the flour, rubbing both together till you have a fine powder. Then make a hole in the middle of the flour, and pour in water enough to make a smooth and flexible paste. Sprinkle the pasteboard with flour, and your hands also, take out the lump of paste, roll it out, fold it together again, and roll it out – i.e. roll it 3 times; the last time it should be

the thickness required for your crust, that is, about ¼ inch or even thinner.
It is then ready for use.

Or, a still Plainer Crust for Children

1 *lb flour*	*Cup of water*
5-6 oz clarified beef dripping	

Put the flour into a bowl, and work it into a smooth paste with about a
cupful of water. Divide the clarified dripping into 3 parts, roll out the
paste, and put over it, in rows, one portion of the dripping broken into
pieces the size of a bean; flour it, fold over the edges, and again roll it;
repeat this folding, spreading and rolling 3 times, dredging a very little
flour over the paste and rolling-pin each time. It will be fit for any common purpose, or for children.

Common Puff Paste

1 *lb sifted flour*	½ *teaspoon salt*
¼ *lb lard*	½ *lb butter*

Put 1 lb of sifted flour on the slab, or in an earthen basin, make a hollow in
the centre, work into it a ¼ lb of lard and ½ a teaspoon of salt. When it is
mixed through the flour, add as much cold water as will bind it together,
then strew a little flour over the pasteboard or table; flour the rolling-pin,
and roll out the paste to ½ inch in thickness; divide ½ lb of butter in 3
parts; spread evenly over the paste, fold it up, dredge a little flour over it
and the paste-slab or table; roll it out again, spread another portion of the
butter over, and fold and roll again; so continue until all the butter is
used; roll it out to ¼ inch in thickness for use.

Mrs Giles, Shaftesbury, Dorset

BEEF AND BACON PIE

This is good hot or cold. Make it with cheap bacon pieces.

1 *onion*	¼ *pint water*
8 oz bacon pieces	*Pinch of fresh mixed herbs*
8 oz minced raw beef	*Salt and pepper*
1 tablespoon plain flour	*8 oz short pastry*

Chop the onion and bacon in small pieces, put in a heavy pan, and cook
gently until the fat runs from the bacon, and the onion and bacon are soft
and golden. Add the mince and cook until mince browns. Stir in flour
mixed with a little water, and the rest of the water, herbs and seasonings

146

and cook until mixture is thick and well blended. Roll pastry into 2 rounds and line an 8 inch pie plate. Put in filling, and cover with second round of pastry. Bake at 400°F (Gas Mark 6) for 30 minutes.

CHESHIRE PORK PIE (1)

Take the skin off the loin of pork, and cut it into steaks. Season them with pepper, salt and nutmeg, and make a good crust. Put into your dish a layer of pork, then a layer of pippins, pared and cored, and sugar sufficient to sweeten it. Then place another layer of pork, and put in a ½ pint of white wine. Lay some butter on the top, close your pie, and send it to the oven. If your pie is large, you must put in a pint of red wine.

Thomas Train, Gateshead, 1812

CHESHIRE PORK PIE [1870] (2)

Time to bake – 1½ hours

2 *lb pork*	*Pepper, salt and nutmeg*
3 *oz butter*	½ *pint white wine*
6-8 *pippins (sweet apples)*	*Enough puff paste*
2 *oz sugar*	

Take the skin and fat from a loin of pork, and cut it into thin steaks; season them with pepper, salt and nutmeg; line a pie-dish with puff paste, put in a layer of pork, then of pippins pared and cored, and about 2 oz sugar; then place in another layer of pork and a ½ pint of white wine, and lay some butter on top; cover it with puff paste, pass a knife through the top to leave an opening, cut the paste even with the dish, egg it once and bake it.

Mrs Giles, Shaftesbury, Dorset

ROMAN PIE

¾ *lb pastry*	I *egg*
2 *oz fine spaghetti or*	¼ *teaspoon grated lemon rind*
vermicelli	¼ *pint white sauce*
I *lb cooking veal*	*Salt, pepper and nutmeg*
¼ *lb ham*	*(grated)*

Well butter a dish and line it with the pastry right through. Throw the vermicelli into a pan of fast boiling salted water, and let it boil for 5 to 10 minutes, until it is tender; then drain well. Put a layer of vermicelli in the dish, pressing well round on the sides, so that it lines the pastry. Next put in the meat cut into neat cubes, add the grated lemon rind, add a seasoning of pepper, salt and nutmeg. When the dish is full, pour in the sauce, cover the top with pastry as you would any pie, bake it for $\frac{3}{4}$ hour, loosen the edges, turn out the pie, brush over with beaten egg and return to the oven for a few minutes to set. Mutton or beef can be used instead of veal. It is delicious eaten hot or cold.

POTATO PIE

Allow as much meat per person as possible (4 oz per person is ample). Cook together stewing steak, onions (as required), potatoes, in water to cover, adding salt and pepper to taste. When meat is tender ($1\frac{1}{2}$–2 hours according to cut of meat used) take the dish out of oven (or turn into dish if stewed on top). Cover with a thickish crust of pastry and cook again until golden brown and cooked through. This is best cooked in oven from the start.

DORSET LAMBS' TAIL PIE

For those fortunate enough to find a good supply, put tails in bucket and sprinkle over a handful of salt. Cover completely with boiling water and leave to steep for 20 minutes or so. Then using very sharp pointed knife, cut sharply down length of tail to peel off outer skin and wool. Drop into cold salted water each tail as it is cleaned and finally drain all tails and cook immediately.

Take 2 lb (say) lambs' tails, 3 or 4 hard boiled eggs, 5 slices streaky bacon, salt and pepper and sweet herbs – thyme, parsley and marjoram. Place lambs' tails in sufficient water to cover and cook till tender, on a slow simmering heat. Onions may be added at this stage if liked.

Meanwhile make pastry using $\frac{1}{2}$ lb lard to 1 lb self-raising flour with $\frac{1}{4}$ teaspoon salt dissolved in sufficient ice-cold water to make a firm paste. The secret is to rub fat into flour as little as possible leaving lumps of lard the size of marbles to be rolled into the paste to make air-flakes. This quantity is for a deeper dish, for a shallow flatter one use $\frac{3}{4}$ lb lard to $1\frac{1}{2}$ lb flour. Put pastry aside to 'rest' in a cool place.

Remove cooked tails from liquor and arrange one layer in dish then cover with sliced hard-boiled eggs and bacon. Continue in this fashion until dish is full, then pour over liquor to which has been added salt and pepper to taste and chopped mixed sweet herbs. Cover whole with pastry rolled to required thickness and brush with egg yolk or milk. Cook in hot oven until pastry is beginning to turn colour, then reduce heat until pastry is golden brown. Cool slowly and preferably leave overnight. Serve cold with new potatoes and salad.

STEAK AND KIDNEY PIE (1)

1½ lb skirt of beef	¼ pint dry red wine
6 oz ox kidney	¼ pint stock
1 oz seasoned flour	½ teaspoon dried thyme
1 oz dripping	1 bayleaf, crumbled
2 large onions or 8 pickling onions	½ lb flaky pastry

Trim the meat and cut into approximately 1 inch pieces. Cut the kidney into pieces of about the same size. Discard the core. Dust the meat and kidney with well-seasoned flour. Heat the fat and brown the meat very slowly. Remove from the heat, pour over the red wine and the stock (or omit the wine and make up the total amount of liquid in stock). Add the thyme and the crushed bayleaf and additional salt and pepper if necessary. Allow to cool, and if possible stand for 2 to 3 hours (covered). Transfer to a pie dish. Cover with the pastry supported in the centre and sealed around the edges of the dish. Cut slits in the pastry cover. Decorate if wished and brush with a little milk or beaten egg to glaze. Place on a low shelf in the oven at 400°F (Gas Mark 6) and cook for about 20 minutes or until the pastry is golden brown. Cover the pie completely with grease-proof paper then reduce the oven heat to 300°F (Gas Mark 2) and continue cooking for a further 3 hours or until the meat is tender. If necessary additional stock may be added through the slits in the pastry during cooking.

STEAK AND KIDNEY PIE (2)

1½ lb steak and kidney (for 4)	Stock
1 small onion	Seasoned flour

Dice meat and roll in seasoned flour. Brown in hot dripping, add onion and cook all slowly until tender – approximately 1½ hours.

Pastry

8 oz flour (mix plain and wholemeal)	6 oz margarine and lard mixed
1 teaspoon baking powder	Salt

Rub in fats. Little water needed as fat proportion is high. Put meat in pie-dish and cover with pastry. Decorate top with leaves and 'flowers'; brush with egg or milk. Cook in hot oven for 1 hour or until pastry is well browned.

STEAK AND KIDNEY PLATE PIE

1 lb stewing steak
¼ lb kidney
1 rounded tablespoon
well-seasoned flour

1 oz fat
1 smallish onion
½ pint water
1 teaspoon made mustard

Cut meat into small pieces and toss in seasoned flour. Fry the sliced onion slowly until brown. Move to one side and brown the meat lightly in the fat. Add the water; cover and simmer very gently for 1½ to 2 hours. Stir in mustard and correct seasoning to taste.

Take 6 oz plain flour, ¼ teaspoon salt, 2 oz butter or margarine, 2 oz lard or vegetable fat, squeeze of lemon juice and water to mix.

Sift flour and salt. Cut the fat into almond-size pieces and drop into the flour. Add the lemon juice to about 5 tablespoons water and mix the flour and fat to a stiff dry dough, handling quickly and lightly. Turn on to a floured board, roll to an oblong. Fold in 3 and give a half turn so folds are on the side. Stand in cool place for a few minutes. Repeat the rolling and folding 3 or 4 times to flake the fat into the flour.

Roll to a thin sheet, about ½ inch thick. Cut a strip and line moistened edge of 9 inch pie plate, and moisten top of strip.

Turn hot filling into the plate. Cover with pastry, trim and cut up edges, using flat of finger along edge of pastry while slitting into pastry with the flat knife blade. Decorate with pastry leaves and slit centre. Brush top with beaten egg or milk. Bake in a hot oven at 450°F (Gas Mark 8) for 10 to 15 minutes. Reduce heat to moderate and bake a further 10 minutes until the pie is golden and flaky. Serve hot, with hot greens, jacket potatoes and mustard.

EGG AND PARSLEY PIE

8 oz short pastry
4 eggs
1 teacup chopped parsley

1 tablespoon dripping
Salt and pepper
Pinch of Cayenne pepper

Roll out the pastry and cut into 2 rounds the size of a pie plate. Wash and dry the parsley thoroughly, and remove sprigs from stalks. Chop the parsley finely. Line the pie plate with one round of pastry. Put a thick 'cross' of pastry on the bottom. In each space, put an egg. Season with salt, pepper and cayenne pepper, and pour over melted dripping. Sprinkle remaining parsley over the eggs. Cover with pastry, and mark lid lightly with a knife between the eggs. Bake at 400°F (Gas Mark 4) for 40 minutes. Cut the pie along the marked lines so each portion contains an egg. Serve with sauce, gravy or chutney.

SAUSAGE AND ONION PIE

8 oz short pastry
8 oz sausage meat
1 onion

1 egg
Mixed herbs

Roll out the pastry and cut into 2 circles to fit a pie plate. Line the plate with 1 round of pastry. Mix the sausage meat, chopped onion, beaten egg and plenty of chopped fresh herbs. Cover with a pastry lid. Bake at 425°F (Gas Mark 7) for 30 minutes.

Gillian Tetlow, Debden, Essex

PORK AND KIDNEY PIE

1 lb pork shoulder or hand
of pork
3 pigs' kidneys
2 teaspoons basil
½ pint stock

Pinch of nutmeg
1 medium onion
2 medium carrots
6 oz short pastry

Cut pork and kidneys in pieces and put into a pie dish with basil, stock, nutmeg, chopped onion and carrots. Cover with a lid or piece of foil and cook at 325°F (Gas Mark 3) for 1 hour. Cover with pastry lid and bake at 400°F (Gas Mark 6) for 30 minutes.

LAMB AND MUSHROOM PIE

1 lb shoulder lamb
2 lambs' kidneys
Seasoned flour
1 onion

½ pint stock
4 oz mushrooms
Salt and pepper
8 oz short pastry

Cut the meat into cubes and cut the kidneys into small pieces. Toss in a little seasoned flour and brown in a little fat with the sliced onion. Add stock and mushrooms. Bring to the boil and simmer until tender. Season with salt and pepper to taste and put into a pie dish to cool. Cover with pastry, glaze with a little beaten egg and bake at 400°F (Gas Mark 6) for 40 minutes.

BEEF AND COW HEEL PIE

13 oz shin beef
½ cow heel
1 onion stuck with cloves

Salt and pepper
6 oz self-raising flour
3 oz shredded suet

Cut up the beef and cow heel, cover with water and add the onion, salt and pepper. Simmer for 3 hours. Strain, and keep the liquid. Remove bones and onion and cut the meat into neat pieces. Put into a greased pie dish, moisten with cooking liquid, and taste for seasoning. Mix the flour and suet with a pinch of salt, and mix to a soft dough with cold water. Roll out and put on top of the meat. Bake at 400°F (Gas Mark 6) for 1 hour. Make gravy with the remaining cooking liquid, and serve the pie with gravy, mashed potatoes and a green vegetable.

CHICHESTER CHICKEN PIE

1 chicken or boiling hen (cooked until entirely tender – preferably in a clay casserole) using water or stock with salt, pepper, one bayleaf, an onion stuck with cloves (4–6). Allow this to cool sufficiently for any fat to form on top. Remove all fat carefully.

½ *lb sausage meat made into*	1 *large onion*
small balls	*4-6 oz bacon 'bits'*

Take all (cooked) meat off chicken bones and cut up into neat smallish pieces. Fry bacon and if available field mushrooms; dip sausage balls in flour and fry them in bacon fat with the onion sliced and chopped. Mix all ingredients together with a few peas if liked. Make a white sauce well seasoned and add to other ingredients. Cover with pastry made in the following way: ½ fat to flour rubbed in very roughly; pinch salt; sufficient iced water to mix to neat dough which should then be left in very cool place to 'rest' for as long as possible. Cover ingredients with the pastry and cook until golden brown in a pretty brisk oven.

CHICKEN PIE (1)

Remains of cold fowl cut into neat joints; remove skin, pack it in a pie dish alternately with forcemeat balls, slices of hard-boiled eggs, and thin slices of bacon or ham. Sprinkle well with pepper and salt, half-fill the pie dish with chicken stock (made from boiling skin, bones, giblets etc. with an onion, salt and pepper). Allow to cool, wet the edges of pie dish with water and cover with pastry. Brush round the edge with water, make hole in middle and brush all over with egg yolk. Cook quickly 20 minutes and slowly for another ½ hour.

1870 CHICKEN PIE (2)

Time to bake – $1\frac{1}{4}$ hours.

2 small chickens	*Cup of good gravy*
Some forcemeat	*A little flour and butter*
A sweetbread	*4 eggs*
Few fresh mushrooms	*Some puff paste*

Cover the bottom of a pie-dish with some puff paste, upon that round the side lay a thin layer of forcemeat; cut 2 small chickens into pieces, season them highly with pepper and salt; put some of the pieces into the dish, then some sweetbread cut into pieces well seasoned, a few fresh mushrooms, and the yolks of 4 or 5 hard-boiled eggs cut into pieces of 4, and strewed over the top. Put in a little water and cover the pie with a piece of puff paste; glaze it, ornament the edges and bake it. When done, pour in through the top a cupful of good gravy, thickened with a little flour and butter.

Mrs Giles, Shaftesbury, Dorset

INDIVIDUAL CHICKEN PIES

8 oz rough puff pastry	*I teaspoon parsley*
I small chicken	*½ teaspoon salt*
4 oz mushrooms	*½ teaspoon Worcester sauce*
4 hard-boiled egg yolks	*Stock made from chicken*
I medium onion	*carcass*
I tablespoon vinegar	*4 rashers streaky bacon*

Make rough puff pastry. Remove flesh in neat pieces from an uncooked chicken, and simmer carcass in water for an hour to make stock. In a bowl mix pieces of light and dark flesh, sliced mushrooms, mashed egg yolks, finely chopped onion, vinegar, parsley, salt, sauce and chopped bacon, and divide mixture between four individual pie dishes. Half-fill each dish with stock, and cover with pastry. Brush tops with beaten egg, make an air vent in each, and cook at 375°F (Gas Mark 4) for I hour.

CHICKEN PIE

I lb cooked chicken	*Salt and pepper*
I lb potatoes	*Chopped parsley*
½ pint chicken stock	*12 oz puff pastry*
½ pint evaporated milk	

Cut the chicken and the peeled potatoes into small cubes. The chicken stock should be made from the broken carcass and should be rich and strongly flavoured with plenty of herbs. Mix the stock and milk and pour over the chicken and potato in a pie dish. Season well with salt and pepper, and add plenty of freshly chopped parsley. Cover with a pastry lid and bake at 425°F (Gas Mark 7) for 40 minutes.

Harold C. Palmer, Great Bardfield, Essex

NEW YEAR CHICKEN PIE

Line a pie dish with bacon rashers, top with cooked chicken, and then with sausage meat. Just cover with some chicken stock. Bake at 325°F (Gas Mark 3) for 30 minutes. Top with breadcrumb stuffing well flavoured with herbs. Bake for 30 minutes more. Turn out when cold. Quantities can be as variable as you like, and as suits your numbers. This is a useful dish to make in the post-Christmas season when there is cold poultry around (turkey can be used instead of chicken); it is a sort of elementary terrine, and very delicious.

AUTUMN CHICKEN PIE

8 oz *plain flour*
1 *teaspoon salt*
2 oz *lard*
2 oz *margarine*
2 *eggs*
½ *pint milk*

1 *teaspoon tarragon or*
parsley
Grated rind ½ lemon
Salt and pepper
1 *lb cold cooked chicken*

Sift together flour and salt, rub in lard and margarine, and add about 6 teaspoons cold water to make stiff dough. Leave to rest for 10 minutes, then line a 7 inch flan ring or sponge tin with ⅔ of the pastry. Blend eggs and milk, add tarragon or chopped parsley, lemon rind, salt and pepper, and chicken cut in ½ inch strips. Put mixture into pastry case, cover with remaining pastry, seal and flute edges. Cut slits in the top, and bake at 425°F (Gas Mark 7) for 20 minutes. Remove flan ring and continue baking at 350°F (Gas Mark 4) for 40 minutes. Serve cold with salad. This is a good evening meal to follow soup, but is excellent for a packed lunch with whole tomatoes.

GIBLET PIE (1)

Scald the giblets, clean them, place in a saucepan, cover with cold water, and let it come to the boil; skim well, add pepper and salt, simmer gently about 2 hours. When soft, cut the giblets into small pieces, place in a pie dish, and dredge with flour. Cut up $\frac{1}{2}$ lb of beef steak and mix with it, also a large onion cut in thin rings, 2 or 3 cloves, and 2 hard-boiled eggs cut in quarters. Fill up the dish with stock from the giblets, cover with a good short crust (give 2 little cuts on the top to let out the steam), decorate according to taste. Bake in a moderate oven for $\frac{3}{4}$ hour. Serve hot.

Mrs Thorne, 1911

GIBLET PIE (2)

This is real old-fashioned pie and if no blood is available with the giblets, add 8 oz chopped black pudding to the ingredients. Clean the giblets, cut the neck into neat pieces, cut the liver in pieces, and slice the flesh from the gizzard. Put into a pan with 1 lb chuck steak cut into cubes, a small onion stuck with three cloves, salt and pepper. Cover with water and simmer $1\frac{1}{2}$ hours until tender but not broken up. Put meat into a pie-dish, with any blood from the bird, and remove the onion. Cover with short pastry and bake at 375°F (Gas Mark 5) for 1 hour, covering the top if it browns too quickly. Serve with jacket or mashed potatoes, and swedes, carrots or parsnips.

EXMOOR MUTTON PATTIES

$\frac{1}{2}$ *lb cold mutton*	*dried mixed herbs*
2 *oz cold boiled bacon or ham*	*Salt and black pepper to taste*
1 *rounded teaspoon plain flour*	$\frac{1}{2}$ *lb flaky pastry*
1 *level teaspoon chopped*	1 *teacup thickened mutton*
parsley	*gravy*
$\frac{1}{2}$ *teaspoon crushed herbs or*	*Cold water*

Chop mutton and bacon or ham. Mix with the flour, parsley, herbs and seasoning to taste. If liked, stir in 1 rounded teaspoon of finely chopped onion. Roll out pastry fairly thinly. Cut 6 rounds for lids. Pile trimmings together, roll out a little thinner and cut out rounds for lining patty tins. Then line them smoothly. Fill with mixture. Srpinkle a tablespoon of gravy over each filling. Brush edge of lining with cold water. Cover with pastry lids. Press edges lightly together and notch. Make a slit in the centre. Decorate centre of each patty with leaves made from trimmings of pastry. Bake in moderately hot oven, 400°F (Gas Mark 5), for about 20 minutes. Heat remainder of gravy. When patties are ready, lift up leaves and add a little gravy.

1870 MUTTON PIE

Time to bake – 1½–2 hours.

2 lb loin of mutton	*3 mutton kidneys*
Pepper and salt	*Gravy made from the bones*
A little forcemeat	*Pastry*

Strip off the meat from the bones of a loin of mutton without dividing it, and cut it into nice thin slices, and season them with pepper and salt; put a pie-crust round the edge of a piedish, place in it a layer of mutton, then one of forcemeat, and again the slices of mutton with 3 or 4 halves of kidneys at equal distances; then pour in a gravy made from the bones seasoned and well cleared from fat. Moisten the edge with water. Cover with a paste ½ inch thick, press round with your thumbs, make a hole in the centre, and cut the edges close to the dish, ornament the top and border according to your taste, and bake it.

Mrs Giles, Shaftesbury, Dorset

HOT MUTTON PIES

Pie made on a 2 lb jamjar:

4½ oz plain flour	*3 tablespoons water*
1½ oz lard	*⅛ teaspoon salt*

Pie made on a 1 lb jamjar:

3 oz plain flour	*2 tablespoons water*
1 oz lard	*⅛ teaspoon salt*

Filling (sufficient for larger pie):

¾ lb lean mutton	*Salt, pepper and nutmeg*

If smaller pies are required, a larger quantity of pastry can be made and then moulded on tumblers.

Sieve the flour and salt into a bowl. Put the water and lard into a pan and bring to the boil. Pour into the flour and mix well with a knife. Grease and flour an upturned 2 lb jam jar. Mould ⅔ of the pastry over the jar and leave to go cold. Carefully take away the jar and fill the pastry case with the meat cut into small pieces and seasoned with salt, pepper and nutmeg. Roll out the remaining pastry for the lid. Seal the edges well, decorate with leaves. Make a hole in the centre to allow the steam to escape.

Tie a piece of greaseproof round the pie so that it will keep a good shape. Bake approximately 30 minutes at 375°F (Gas Mark 5). Remove the paper, brush over the whole pie with egg wash and return to the oven for a further 30 minutes. Serve very hot with gravy poured into the hole.

MUTTON PIES

Have a pan containing ½ pint of boiling water. Add 4 oz beef dripping and 1 teaspoon salt. Pour it on to 1 lb of flour. Mix. When cool, form it into a lump. Knead this on a floured board. Divide ⅔ of the dough into 6 to 9 small straight-sided tins. Fill these with ¾ lb lean lamb or mutton, chopped small. Add salt, pepper, and nutmeg and then moisten with gravy. Make the rest of the pastry into lids. Damp the edges, put them on, make a little hole in each, brush with milk. Bake in a moderate oven, 350°F (Gas Mark 4), for 40 minutes. Fill up each pie with gravy before serving.

BACON PASTIES

12 oz short pastry	*1 large onion*
8 oz minced raw steak	*Salt and pepper*
6 oz streaky bacon	*½ teaspoon Worcester sauce*
4 oz lambs' kidneys	*Egg for glazing*

Roll out pastry and cut out 6 7-inch rounds. Chop the bacon, kidney and onion, and mix with the steak, seasoning and sauce. Put mixture on half of each round and fold over pastry. Pinch edges together. Put on to a wet baking sheet. Bake at 425°F (Gas Mark 7) for 15 minutes; then at 350°F (Gas Mark 4) for 45 minutes. Serve hot or cold.

SAUSAGE AND EGG ROLL

Cheese Pastry:	*1 egg yolk*
3 oz butter	*Water to mix*
6 oz plain flour	**Filling:**
Pinch of salt	*1 lb pork sausage meat*
Pinch of ucayenne pepper	*4 hard-boiled eggs*
3 oz cheese (grated)	*Milk or beaten egg to glaze*

To make pastry, rub butter into sieved flour, and seasoning. Add cheese, and mix to a stiff dough with egg yolk and water. Roll to a rectangle approx. 11 × 8 inches. Flatten sausage meat on a floured board to approx. 11 × 5 inches. Place sausage meat on pastry and arrange eggs in a line along centre. Fold sausage meat over eggs. Wet edges of pastry and fold over to enclose sausage meat. Seal edges. Use pastry scraps for decoration. Glaze with milk or beaten egg. Bake in a fairly hot oven, 400°F (Gas Mark 6), for 30 minutes, then reduce heat to 375°F (Gas Mark 5) for a further 30 minutes. Leave until cold. Wrap in foil or greaseproof paper.

BEEF PATTIES

1 *lb self-raising flour*
6 *oz lard or dripping*
¼ *pint water*
6 *oz beef*

1 *minced onion*
2 *tablespoons thick brown*
gravy
Seasoning

Make the pastry, cut into rounds, and line some patty tins with it. Cut the meat into small pieces, or mince finely with the onion, mix with the gravy, onion and seasoning. Place a spoonful in each pastry case, put on pastry lids and press the edges together. Bake in a good oven till brown. Reduce heat and leave in oven for a few more minutes to finish. Serve on a hot dish, garnished with parsley.

MUTTON PASTIES

Cut ½ lb cooked lamb or mutton into small pieces, add ½ lb peeled and sliced potatoes, 1 chopped onion, 1 teaspoon chopped parsley, ½ teaspoon salt, ¼ teaspoon pepper, 2 tablespoons water. Roll 1 lb plain pastry into ¼ inch thickness, stamp into rounds, using small teaplate as guide, and place a heap of mixture in centre of each round. Wet the edges of pastry, fold over meat and press edges together. Brush with beaten egg and bake in hot oven for 15 minutes, or until pastry is lightly browned, then reduce heat and continue cooking for a further 15 minutes. Cover with a greased paper and leave 10 minutes before serving.

CORNISH PASTIES (1)

Allow 3–4 oz pastry per pasty according to age and capacity of appetite. Have ready sufficient peeled and 'shripped' potatoes (i.e. potato which has been cut up in fine small wafers by constantly turning the potato in order that the corners can be 'shripped' off – a worndown potato peeler sometimes makes a good 'shripper') allowing one potato per person.
1½ lb of best raw chuck steak – the better the meat the better the pasty is. Onions as desired, and/or swede.
Make pastry well in advance using the usual shortcrust recipe and having consistency pliable but not too wet. Have clean dishcloth or rag handy. Keep shripped potatoes in bowl of water to cover, to prevent their going brown. Take 3–4 oz pastry (about a good handful) and roll out until pastry is smooth and firm trying to keep it as near circular as possible. Use 6 inch plate to cut round if possible. On this circle of pastry place about 2 table-spoons of shripped potato and sprinkle with salt. If onion is desired, arrange on top of this.

Now take 3–4 oz meat and place carefully on top of onion – the meat can be rolled on a floured paper if liked in order to keep pieces of meat separate from one another. Wet around edge of pastry then sprinkle top of meat with pepper. Now dry fingers in clean cloth and then start to 'crimp' edges of pasty by first bringing front half-moon up to meet back half-moon in centre. Press wetted edges together then move fingers down to righthand corner and pinch, roll and crimp altogether in one movement. This takes practice! But don't despair – 'patches' of pastry can always be added both before and during cooking to repair those splits in the pastry cover. Make sure there are no gaps anywhere in the pasty and then brush with milk and stand on piece of butter or lard paper, place on baking sheet and just before popping in good oven, 425°F (Gas Mark 7), make cut up near crimped edge for steam to escape. Settle the pasty slightly back on itself and bake for about 15 minutes or until pastry is golden brown, then reduce heat to finish cooking until meat, tested through steam-hole, is tender. Keep hot by covering with thickish clean cloth in very low oven.

When Cornish men worked down in the lead mines, the usual Cornish 'docky' of bread and fish or meat was not practicable because of the danger of lead poisoning. Eventually the traditional 'docky' became the hot Cornish pasty which could be eaten by holding the pointed end in paper and eating through from the other pointed end. To this day it is customary for a man working away from home to take his pasty with him and many a farmer's wife is asked if 'the missus will warm me pasty for I? If you be so kaind'.

CORNISH PASTIES (2)

Shortcrust Pastry	Filling
4 oz plain flour	*Potato, finely sliced (not*
2 oz fat	*diced)*
Pinch salt	*Onion and/or turnip, finely*
Water to mix to a firm dough	*cut*
	4 oz steak (Chuck or Skirt)
	Seasoning

Roll pastry into round or rounds. Pile up sliced potato on about half the pastry. Put onion and/or turnip on potato. Cut meat in small pieces and spread over. Season with salt and pepper. Put a few thin pieces of potato on top to save the meat drying. Damp edges of pastry. Fold over to semi-circle and crimp edges. (Crimp by pinching the pastry with the left hand and fold over with right hand, forming a rope-like effect on the side of the pastry.) Place on unfloured baking sheet and bake at 425°F (Gas Mark 7) for 10–15 minutes, reducing to 350°F (Gas Mark 4) for a further 30 minutes.

Mrs Thomas, Truro, Cornwall

SAVOURY BEEF ROLL

1 lb minced beef
1 teacup breadcrumbs
½ egg
1 onion
¼ teaspoon spice or ground ginger
½ teaspoon mixed herbs
Seasoning

Pastry
6 oz flour
2 oz butter or margarine
½ teaspoon baking powder
1 teaspoon salt
A little milk

Put mince (uncooked meat is best for making the roll) into a basin, add breadcrumbs, onion very finely chopped, the herbs and the spice. Mix thoroughly with hand, then form into roll. Place in a well-greased tin, cover well with greased paper, bake 20 minutes in a good oven. Meanwhile prepare pastry. Sieve dry ingredients into a basin, rub in butter till free from lumps, then add enough milk to make a stiffish paste. Turn this on to floured board and roll into an oblong. Remove the roll from the oven and taking off paper, wrap it quickly in the pastry. Put a few pastry leaves on top, brush over with milk or beaten egg, and return to oven. Cook about ½ hour longer, until the pastry is brown and thoroughly cooked. Serve with brown or tomato sauce.

CURRIED EGG PIE

8 oz short pastry (8 oz plain flour, 4 oz mixed butter and lard)
6 hard-boiled eggs
1 oz butter
1 small onion
2 tablespoons plain flour

1 tablespoon curry powder
Juice of 1 lemon
1 medium apple
1 tablespoon tomato purée or 2 ripe tomatoes
Salt and pepper

Make pastry and roll out 2 10-inch circles to fit pie plate. Melt fat, add chopped onion and fry until pale gold. Stir in flour and curry powder and cook until mixture bubbles. Add ¼ pint plus 3 tablespoons water, and stir until smooth. Add lemon juice, peeled and chopped apple and either tomato purée or peeled and quartered tomatoes. Season to taste and simmer with lid on for 30 minutes. Cool. Line pie plate with one round of pastry. Cut eggs in half and put cut side down on pastry. Spread curry sauce over eggs. Cover with second piece of pastry, seal, and glaze with beaten egg or milk. Bake at 425°F (Gas Mark 7) for 30 minutes. Serve with crisp lettuce and tomatoes.

COTTAGE CHEESE PIE

8 oz plain flour
6 oz lard
3 eggs
8 oz cottage cheese

2 tablespoons cooked peas
2 tablespoons chopped
parsley
½ teaspoon mixed herbs

Sieve flour with a pinch of salt and add cut-up lard. Mix with a squeeze of lemon juice and enough iced water to make a stiff dough, using a knife to avoid breaking up fat. Form into an oblong and roll lightly into a long strip. Fold into 3, enclosing as much air as possible, close and seal ends. Give pastry a half turn and repeat rolling and folding twice more. Leave pastry for 20 minutes, then roll out 2 6-inch rounds to fit deep pie plate or flan ring. This rough puff pastry is good for savoury pies. Whisk eggs and mix with sieved cottage cheese. Add peas, parsley, herbs and plenty of salt and pepper. Pour into lined pie plate or flan ring. Cover with remaining pastry and seal edges. Make a cut to allow steam to escape and glaze with beaten egg. Bake at 425°F (Gas Mark 7) for 10 minutes, then reduce heat to 350°F (Gas Mark 4) for 35 minutes.

FISH ENVELOPE

8 oz cooked cod or haddock
fillet
1 hard-boiled egg
1 tablespoon capers

¼ pint white sauce
Salt and pepper
8 oz short pastry

Flake fish and chop egg, and add fish, egg and capers to sauce, seasoning with salt and pepper. Roll out pastry thinly to form a square, put fish filling in the centre, brush edges of pastry with beaten egg or milk and draw sides up over the centre to form an envelope. Seal edges well, decorate with trimmings and brush with beaten egg or milk. Bake at 400°F (Gas Mark 6) for 30 minutes, and serve hot or cold. This filling can be varied by using canned salmon instead of the fish, or by adding a few mushrooms or shrimps to the mixture.

CURRIED LAMB PIES

½ lb flaky pastry
1 dessertspoon lard
1 teaspoon minced onion
1 dessertspoon plain flour
½ pint stock
1 teaspoon curry powder

Salt and pepper
½ lb cubed cooked lamb
½ diced apple
2 talespoons coconut
2 tablespoons sultanas

Line individual patty cases with pastry. Melt lard and brown onion lightly. Stir in flour, then stock, curry powder, salt and pepper to taste, and stir until the mixture thickens and boils. Add meat, apple, coconut and sultanas, heat through and leave to cool. Put a spoonful of the mixture into each patty case, top with rounds of pastry and seal edges; make a small hole with a skewer in the top of each, and bake at 450°F (Gas Mark 8) for 20 minutes. Serve hot or cold. These pies are excellent for the lunch-box.

FRIED MEAT PIES

½ lb short pastry
1 medium onion
1 tablespoon lard
1 lb minced raw beef
½ pint stock

2 teaspoons chopped parsley
Salt and pepper
2 tablespoons flour
2 chopped hard-boiled eggs

Chop onion finely and soften in melted lard. Add minced beef, stock, parsley, salt and pepper to taste, and simmer with a lid on for 30 miuntes. Stir in flour, heat and stir until thick, then add egg and leave to cool. Roll out pastry thinly and cut in circles the size of a saucer; this quantity should make 6 circles. Put 3 tablespoons of meat mixture on one side of each circle, fold over the other side, damp and pinch edges to seal them. Fry in hot deep fat for about 3 minutes until golden. If there is any meat mixture over, add a little water and simmer until the mixture is like a sauce, then use to pour over the pies at serving time. These pies are a variation of a favourite South American recipe, and make a very pleasant change when served really hot with a crisp salad. The filling may be varied by using corned beef flavoured with a little tomato purée or table sauce; a little chopped green pepper is also good cooked with the onion.

HAND-RAISED PORK PIES (1)

This is for 2 pies over large and small moulds (large: 5¼ inches diam. × 3¾ inches depth; small: 3½ inch diam. × 3 inches depth).

2 lb plain flour	2½ lb seasoned pork
12½ oz lard	1 egg
2 teaspoons salt	Stock
½ pint water	Gelatine if necessary

Bring fat and water to the boil and simmer for 5 minutes. Make well in sifted flour, pour in quickly and work up with wooden spoon. Put in refrigerator for 30 minutes. Knead with hands and turn on to floured board. Cut off enough paste for the tops. When you are not using paste, cover with cloth to keep it warm, for it is more pliable when hot. Flour the moulds well, and also the paste on the side going over the moulds. Roll out and mould paste over moulds upside down. Tie a double band of greaseproof paper round paste (2½-inch for large mould; 2-inch for small mould). Turn right way up and cut round edge level with moulds. Make tops as large as pie. Fill with pork 1 inch from top, moisten the inside rims of pies with beaten egg, press lids in position and nip round with fingers. Cut 3 air holes in lid with scissors. Bake in middle of the oven at 375°F (Gas Mark 5). The top may be glazed with beaten egg. If you want to glaze the sides, take pies out of oven and remove paper and brush over with egg 30 minutes before cooking time is finished. Allow 1½ hours for large pie; 1 hour for small pie. Simmer bones and trimmings for 3 to 4 hours. Let pies cool 1 hour, then pour just warm stock through small funnel at intervals so stock has time to soak through.

HAND-RAISED PORK PIE (2)

Pastry	½ teaspoon powdered sage
12 oz self-raising flour	Salt and pepper
½ teaspoon salt	
4 oz lard	**Jelly**
¼ pint water	Pork bones or a trotter
1 egg	2 pints water
	1 onion
Filling	Seasoning
1¼ lb shoulder pork	1 teaspoon gelatine

Sieve the flour and salt into a bowl. Boil the lard and the water in a pan. When dissolved, pour into the centre of the flour. Work all together until a smooth dough is obtained. Cut ⅓ off dough and reserve for lid. Work the remainder on a floured board, gradually moulding to form bowl shape. (A cake tin can be used as a guide.) Put on to a greased baking sheet and fill the centre with the diced pork, sage and seasoning. Roll out the reserved ⅓ for lid, brush edges of the pie with beaten egg and seal on the lid. Use trimmings to form leaves for decoration. Make a hole in the top and brush all over pie with the egg. Bake in oven 400°F (Gas Mark 6) for 30 minutes, then reduce heat to 350°F (Gas Mark 4) for further 1½ hours. Make a jelly from the bones, water, onion, and seasoning by boiling for about 2 hours. Strain and add the dissolved gelatine. Allow to cool. Pour some of this into the hole in the lid when the pie is cool and leave to set before cutting.

RAISED PORK PIE (3)

1 *lb flour*
¼ *lb butter*
1 *egg*

½ *pint water*
Pinch salt

Rub butter into flour, beat egg and water together, and mix all into a dry dough. Grease cake-tin well and line with pastry. Cut stewing pork into dice removing any fat, and cook partly; drain quite free from liquor, put layer of pork into pie, sprinkle well with salt and pepper, layer of finely minced onion and sage leaves; continue until tin is full; brush round edge with egg, and lay pastry cover on, rolled out not too thinly. Brush top over with yolk of egg, and ornament with leaves. Make a slit in centre. Before the pie is covered put in 2 or 3 tablespoons of stock. Stand on another tin and bake in steady oven for 2 hours. Turn carefully out of tin and brush around sides with egg yolk, and put back in oven to glaze.

ECONOMY PORK PIE

Pastry
5 *oz lard*
1 *teaspoon salt*

⅓ *pint milk*
1 *lb flour*

Filling
1 *lb pork pieces or meat from the blade*
½ *lb pork sausage meat*
¼ *teaspoon mixed herbs*
Pinch of mace
1 *bayleaf*

1 *tablespoon breadcrumbs*
Salt and pepper
4-5 *hard-boiled eggs*
A little beaten egg
¼ *oz gelatine*
¼ *pint stock or water*

Heat the lard with salt and milk and when boiling beat into the flour which has been sieved into a warm bowl. When smooth, cover with a cloth and prepare the filling.

Chop or mince the meat and sausage meat, add herbs and spices and breadcrumbs. Season well with salt and freshly ground pepper. Use the warm pastry to line a cake tin or pie mould, taking care to seal all the joins by wetting the edges. Place a little of the mixture in the pie case, add the hard-boiled eggs and pack the remaining mixture into the pie together with a spoonful of water. Cover the pie and decorate the edge. Brush with beaten egg. Make a few leaves and a rose or tassel from the scraps of pastry.

Bake at 425°F (Gas Mark 7) for ½ hour. Cover with greaseproof paper and reduce to 325°F (Gas Mark 3) for a further 1½ hours. Cool and remove from the tin. Dissolve the gelatine in the stock and pour into the pie (under the rose) and serve cold with a crisp green salad. Endive can be used with tomato, vegetable and potato salads.

VENISON PASTY

8 oz shortcrust pastry	*6 peppercorns*
12 oz cold cooked venison	*¼ teaspoon mace*
½ pint stock	*1 dessertspoon redcurrant*
1 bayleaf	*or 1 teaspoon rowan jelly*

Line a pasty dish with half the pastry. Mince the meat – not too fine. Simmer the stock with the rest of the ingredients for 20 minutes and strain enough over the minced meat to make it moist but not sloppy. Mix it well and leave for a minute or two for the meat to absorb the stock. Put it into the prepared pastry case. Roll out the rest of the pastry and make a lid, moistening the edges. Make a few slits in the pastry to let out the steam and cut out leaves and put them on, moistening the underside first to make them stick. Paint the whole thing over with egg yolk and water and put fairly near the bottom of a brisk oven for 15–20 minutes. If it is overcooked it becomes dry and crumbly and impossible to eat tidily. Like Haggis it is best with vegetables with a high percentage of water in them – turnips, swedes, marrows, carrots. Mashed potatoes with a *lot* of butter.

Mrs Chaplin, Finsthwaite, Lancs

GAME PIE

Pastry	*6 tablespoons milk*
12 oz plain flour	*4 oz lard*
2 level teaspoons salt	*2 egg yolks*
Filling	*1 pheasant, drawn*
12 oz sausage meat	*Salt and pepper*
4 oz raw lean ham	*¼-½ pint jellied stock*
6 oz lean chuck steak	*Gelatine*

Assemble a $7\frac{1}{2}$-inch raised game pie mould with a hinged side. Grease. Place on a baking sheet. Sieve the flour and salt together. Make a well in the centre. Warm together the milk and lard, and when lard has melted, pour into the flour with beaten egg yolks. Gradually work in the flour with a wooden spoon to give a smooth pliable dough. Knead lightly on a floured board until smooth. Leave to cool slightly. Line the mould with $\frac{3}{4}$ of the prepared pastry, rolled out to $\frac{1}{8}$–$\frac{1}{4}$ inch thickness. Press the pastry to the sides of the tin, so that there are no cracks or wrinkles. Line the pastry with sausage meat, reserving a little to make small balls. Cut the ham and steak into small cubes. Cut the flesh away from the carcass of the pheasant. Cut in small pieces. Mix the prepared meats with the seasoning and fill up the pie mould. Add a little stock. Cover with remaining pastry. Decorate as desired. Make a hole in the centre for the steam to escape.

Bake at 425°F (Gas Mark 7) for $\frac{1}{2}$ hour. Reduce the heat 375°F (Gas Mark 5) for a further $\frac{1}{2}$ hour. Finally reduce to 350°F (Gas Mark 4) for a further 30–35 minutes. If pastry shows signs of over-browning, cover with greaseproof paper. Remove the pie from the oven, fill up with hot stock, leave to cool. Remove tin mould when the pie is cold. Fill with more jellied stock. Serve when set, garnished with watercress and sausage balls.

Cook some tiny sausage meat balls in the oven until golden brown. Cool and glaze in jellied stock.

REV. R. W. PEDDER'S GAME PIE

Small pie dish holding about 2 pints. Cut lean raw game into large dice and fill pie dish almost full. Have ready some *jellied* stock in saucepan with $\frac{1}{2}$ saltspoon mixed herbs, $\frac{1}{2}$ inch cinnamon stick, $\frac{1}{2}$ inch square of bayleaf, 2 cloves, 2 saltspoons salt, sprinkling of pepper or 3 peppercorns. Let it infuse and then strain it over the meat in the dish. Cook in slow oven for 3 hours (or 2 if the game is young). Eat cold – tomorrow – not before. Keep lid on pie dish in oven.

He always made this with roe deer venison but any game will do – varying in richness. I made one with only pheasants and mallard in equal numbers and added a glass of port for richness.

Mrs Chaplin's father was a sporting, farming parson, once a traditional character in English life, but now alas rare. She is always the person to turn to when a delicious recipe for game or salmon is needed. Like many old game 'pie' recipes, this contains no pastry. Occasionally one finds beautiful unglazed oven dishes, decorated with elaborate modelling of game, and used for this kind of pie.

Mrs Chaplin, Finsthwaite, Lancs

GAME PIE

If venison is used for this, the delicacy of its flavour will entirely depend on its having been hung long enough. Trim the best end of the neck, and rub it with cayenne pepper, nutmeg, mace and salt. Boil down the trimmings of the venison, and the inferior joints of hare or any other game used, and make a rich gravy. Make a forcemeat of the raw liver of the hare and shallots all finely minced together. Remove the bones from the principal parts and fill with forcemeat. Line a dish with shortcrust, place the venison and hare in it and fill in the spaces with forcemeat; add a little of the gravy, cover the top of the pie with pastry, ornament the top with leaves or whatever, and bake in a hot oven for 10 minutes. Then reduce the heat and let it cook in a slower oven for 1½ hours, and when the oven is quite cooled down, it can remain in it to finish cooking. If venison is not obtainable or is not liked, another hare, a rabbit or whatever is available may be used instead.

Farmers on the edge of Savernake Forest had the right to kill deer if they became a menace to their crops – and one or two deer grazing on a field of growing wheat or oats can do irreparable damage to that year's crop – consequently venison was on the menu in this part of Wiltshire. Also in the New Forest regular shoots were arranged to thin out the deer population for the sake of its own survival. These were properly undertaken with a minimum of chosen game at a certain time of year, by the verderers and those in charge.

This is a very old recipe from the Wiltshire/Hampshire border.

GROUSE PIE

Make a farce of 1½ lb calf's liver and ½ lb fat bacon. Cut it up and put in stewpan with a shallot and a little chopped parsley. Let it heat gently on the fire, skimming occasionally. When the meat is tolerably done, turn all into a mortar and pound thoroughly. Have ready the meat cut from bones of 3 grouse and ½ lb veal cut in thin slices. Put layer of thin fat bacon at bottom of the pie, then a layer of the farce, then one of the grouse, then the veal and so on till the dish is full and a slice fat bacon over the top and 2 bayleaves. When nearly cold, fill in with the gravy drawn from the bones and set with a little gelatine. Run it through a sieve, let it get cold and skim off all fat. Heat it again and then put over the pie. Cover with paste of flour and water and bake 4 hours.

Mrs Garden, 1847

GROUSE PIE

2 grouse	*Salt, pepper and herbs*
½ lb pie-crust pastry	*Few yolks hard-boiled eggs*
Game forcemeat	*Few slices raw ham*

Cut up a brace of grouse, each of them in 5 parts, and season with pepper and salt. Mask the bottom of a pie dish with a layer of game forcemeat, in which place the pieces of grouse; sprinkle over a little cooked fine herbs; fill the cavities between the pieces with a few yolks of hard-boiled eggs, and place on top of the grouse a few slices of raw ham; pour in good gravy, to half the height, cover the pie with paste, egg it, and put it in a moderate oven, 350°F (Gas Mark 4) for 1½ hours.

GROUSE AND STEAK PIE

2 casserole grouse	*Parsley*
1 lb steak	*Pastry*
2 onions	

Cut the flesh of two 'casserole' grouse. Make a stock with the carcasses. Fry some finely chopped onion golden in butter. Add the steak cut in cubes and brown. Cut an onion and parsley into a pie dish, add some stock and cover with pastry. Cook for about 2 hours.

1870 PLAIN PIGEON PIE

Time to bake – 1¼ hours.

2-3 pigeons	*A little gravy*
1 rump steak	*2 oz butter*
Pepper and salt	*Puff paste*

Lay a rim of paste round the edge and sides of a pie-dish, sprinkle a little pepper and salt over the bottom, and put in a thin beefsteak; pick and draw the pigeons, wash them clean and cut off the feet, press the legs into the sides; put a bit of butter, and a seasoning of pepper and salt into the inside of each one, and lay them in the dish with their breasts upwards, and their necks and gizzards between them; sprinkle some pepper and salt over them, and put in a wineglass of water; lay a thin sheet of paste over the top, and with a brush wet it all over; then put a puff paste ½ inch thick over that, cut it close to the dish, brush it over with egg, ornament the top, and stick 4 of the feet out of it, and bake it. When done, pour in a little good gravy. You may put in the yolks of 6 hard boiled eggs, or leave out the beefsteak, if you think proper.

Mrs Giles, Shaftesbury, Dorset

PIGEON PIE (1)

Take 2 or more dressed pigeons and stew them until tender – this should be done the night before. If you have a pressure cooker, a great deal of cooking-time is saved by cooking the pigeons in this, following makers' instructions. When the birds are properly cooked, and cooled, pull them apart using fingers and a sharp pointed knife, and place the joints or pieces in a dish. Meanwhile boil up the liquor in which they were cooked until it is reduced by half. Over the meat sprinkle some fresh sweet herbs chopped (parsley and thyme or marjoram) or 2 teaspoons of dried mixed herbs, some finely chopped onion or shallot, some grated lemon peel ($\frac{1}{2}$ lemon to 2 birds) salt and pepper to taste; then place 1 layer of cut up rashers of bacon, and 1 layer of sliced hard-boiled eggs. Pour over the liquor now cooled, and cover the whole with a good pastry. Bake in a good oven until the pastry is nicely browned and cooked right through. Reduce heat, cover pastry with a butter-paper and leave in oven for a further 10 minutes. Remove from oven and stand to cool leaving butter-paper undisturbed for about 15 minutes.

Pigeons are more numerous than they have ever been in living memory and do tremendous harm to standing crops such as brussel sprouts, cabbages etc. which of course makes the loss of income reflect in the market prices, because of depleting the supply. Pigeons are on sale in many well-known chain suppliers these days and are an economical and welcome addition to the menu. Pigeon pie eaten cold, with dressed lettuce, spring onions and cold new potatoes, cooked with a nice sprig or two of mint, is a banquet fit for even your richest relations. This is a version which came from a Dorset grandmother.

PIGEON PIE (2)

Prepare $\frac{3}{4}$ lb shin of beef and $\frac{1}{4}$ lb ox kidney, by cutting them up into small pieces and stewing them with $\frac{1}{2}$ pint of stock or water until quite tender, in a pie-dish. Take 2 pigeons, each cut into 4 pieces. Cut up 2 onions, 4 shallots, very finely, and 3 teaspoons chopped parsley, and cut up into slices 2 hard-boiled eggs.

Put a layer of meat in the bottom of the pie-dish, sprinkle a layer of onion, shallot, parsley, salt and pepper and hard-boiled egg, and then a layer of pigeon, and so on until the pie-dish is filled. Melt a little gelatine into $\frac{1}{2}$ pint of stock, put this to the gravy in the pie, and cover with a good puff pastry. Ornament top and edges, brush over with the yolk of an egg. Bake in a moderate oven for $\frac{3}{4}$–1 hour or until pigeon is cooked. If the birds are tough, cover the pastry with greased paper and reduce heat, so that the prolonged cooking will not dry up the pastry.

PIGEON PIE (3)

4 pigeons, take the livers, gizzards, and chop them up fine, add to them pepper, salt and Cayenne to taste, fry them lightly in butter, then add 2 tablespoons of breadcrumbs, then divide the whole into 4 portions. To

each portion put a small knob of butter about as big as a blackbird's egg, and place in the body of each pigeon for seasoning. Truss the birds neatly, and place them breast down in a deep dish; fill the dish half full with water, lay on top a piece of steak peppered, cover with good pie crust and bake for $\frac{3}{4}$ hour.

PIGEON PIE (4)

6 pigeons   Salt, pepper and mace
8 oz chuck steak   8 oz pastry

The nicest pie is made with breasts only, in which case the remains of the birds should be simmered in a little water to produce a rich gravy. Small mushrooms and/or hard-boiled eggs are a good addition to the pie. Remove the breasts from the pigeons with a sharp knife, and put into a pie-dish with the steak cut into small pieces. Just cover with water, season well with salt, pepper and a pinch of mace, cover with a lid, and simmer in a medium oven for an hour. Cover with pastry, brush with beaten egg and bake in a hot oven, 425°F (Gas Mark 7) until golden.

PIGEON PIE (5)

5-6 pigeons   Seasoning
8 oz medium quality steak   Little good gravy
8 oz pastry crust

Joint the birds so that each one yields 4 joints, 2 breast joints and 2 leg joints, put the rest of the carcasses to stew in a little water, for the gravy. Cut the steak into small thin pieces each about the size of a tablespoon, line a pie dish with these slices, then lay the pigeons on top, cover with water, add plenty of seasoning, cover with greased paper and put into a medium oven, allow to simmer for 1 hour. Take out the dish, have ready a good pie crust pastry, cover the pie with this. Brush the top with beaten egg, and put back into the oven, bake until the pastry is a golden brown. Mix a dessertspoon of cornflour with a little cold milk, add a cupful of the hot bone stock, and allow to thicken, season to taste, and when the pie is done, lift up the crust and add the thickened gravy.

COMPANY PIGEON PIE (6)

Use only the pigeons' breasts. To save plucking and drawing, slit the skin over the breast, fold back skin and feathers, and cut out the breasts. Put into a dish with an equal quantity of steak (veal or pork will do). Season well and fill dish with stock. Cover with a lid and cook at 350°F (Gas Mark

4) for 1 hour. Take off the lid and add a little more stock and a layer of hard-boiled egg slices. Cover with short or flaky pastry and bake at 400°F (Gas Mark 6) for 30 minutes.

PARTRIDGE PIE (1)

2 partridges	2 oz butter
½ lb veal	2 hard-boiled eggs
½ lb fat bacon	Parsley
6 mushrooms	¼ pint of stock
Salt and pepper	Shortcrust pastry

Cut each partridge into 4 pieces. Melt the butter in a pan, put in the joints and fry lightly. Cut the veal and bacon into thin slices, line the pie dish with the sliced meat, cover with the joints of partridge and season well, adding the parsley and mushrooms, finishing with a layer of bacon and veal. Cover the pie with short pastry and bake for 1 hour in a hot oven. When cooked fill with a good stock and serve hot or cold.

Game is excellent in pies, and an economical way of serving. You can vary the above recipe by using the game you have available.

PARTRIDGE PIE (2)

2 partridges	1 tablespoon chopped parsley
8 oz lean veal	4 oz mushrooms
8 oz boiled bacon or ham	Salt and pepper
¼ pint onion sauce	Pinch of nutmeg
1 oz butter	Puff pastry
2 hard-boiled eggs	Rich stock or gravy

Cut the birds in halves and cook them lightly with butter until just coloured. In a pie-dish put a layer of mixed chopped veal and bacon. Put in partridges. Add parsley, mushrooms and seasoning, and put on a second layer of veal and bacon. Pour on the onion sauce and cover with slices of egg. Cover with pastry, glaze with beaten egg and bake at 400°F (Gas Mark 6) for 1 hour. When the pie is removed from the oven, pour in a little rich hot stock or gravy. Serve hot or cold.

HARE PIE (1)

Cut hare meat into small pieces and roll them in a little flour seasoned with salt and pepper and a pinch of mixed spice. Put into an oven dish with half the meat weight in butter. Cover tightly and stand the dish in a tin of hot water. Cook at 350°F (Gas Mark 4) for 1½ hours. In a large pie dish, put a layer of sausage meat. Cover with the hare and its gravy, and add a wineglass of red wine or port and some fried forcemeat balls. Cover with a good short crust and brush with egg or milk. Bake at 400°F (Gas Mark 6) for 30 minutes. As the pie cools, pour some melted stock or consommé (jellying consistency) through a hole in the pastry. Leave until completely cold.

HARE PIE (2)

3 joints hare	8 oz plain flour
1 teaspoon fresh herbs	Pinch of salt
Salt and pepper	2 oz lard
3 tablespoons cider or red wine	½ gill milk and water
	Stock

Chop or mince the hare finely, season with herbs, salt and pepper, and leave to stand overnight in cider or wine. Sieve flour and salt in a warm bowl. Bring lard, milk and water to boil together and pour into the middle of the flour, stirring until cool enough to handle. Knead until smooth, adding more hot milk and water if necessary. Cover with a tea towel damped in hot water and wrung out, and stand bowl in warm water for 15 minutes, keeping dough only just warm. Roll out ¾ of pastry and line a pie mould or cake tin with removable bottom. Mix hare meat well and stir in a spoonful of stock, and put filling into pastry case to within 1 inch of the top. Brush top edge with egg, cover with pastry lid, and glaze with beaten egg. Make a hole in the centre of the lid. Bake at 400°F (Gas Mark 6) for 20 minutes, then reduce heat to 350°F (Gas Mark 4) for another hour, covering the pastry with thick paper to prevent its burning. When pie is cool, pour in a little cold jellied stock almost at setting point, using a funnel in the hole. Leave in tin until completely cold. This is a very useful way of using hare, and is particularly good for a harvest supper table.

1870 PLAIN RABBIT PIE

Time to bake – 1¼ hours.

1 large rabbit	Pepper and salt
12 oz rather fat bacon	1 shallot
Sprig of parsley	Puff paste

Skin and wash a fine large rabbit; cut it into joints, and divide the head. Then place it into warm water to soak until thoroughly clean; drain it on a sieve, or wipe it with a clean cloth. Season it with salt and pepper, a sprig of parsley chopped fine, and 1 shallot if the flavour is liked (but it is equally good without it). Cut the bacon into small pieces, dredge with flour the rabbit, and place it in the pie-dish with the bacon, commencing with the inferior parts of the rabbit. Pour in a small cupful of water, or stock if you have it; put a paste border round the edges of the dish, and cover it with puff paste about ½ inch thick. Ornament the top and glaze it, make a hole in the centre, and bake it.

Mrs Giles, Shaftesbury, Dorset

SUSSEX RABBIT PIE

Cut up a young wild rabbit into 12 or 14 pieces. Do not use the head. Wash the pieces and place them in a pie-dish with 1 lb pickled pork or suitable pieces of rashers of cold boiled bacon, cut up into suitably-sized pieces; sprinkle over pepper and a little salt to taste, add a blade of mace, 2 cloves, and 1 shallot or small onion minced. Barely cover the meat with some good veal or other white stock. Cover the pie with a tin or plate and cover with a good paste. Brush over with egg to which has been added salt, and bake in a brisk oven until the pastry is done. This pie may be served hot or cold. If you are short on bacon or pickled pork, 1 or 2 hard-boiled eggs are a great addition to the protein content and the flavour.

RABBIT PIES

1 rabbit
½ pint thick white sauce
½ lb cooked ham or corned beef
4 tablespoons breadcrumbs

½ teaspoon grated lemon rind
1 teaspoon chopped parsley
Pepper and salt
Short or puff pastry

Simmer the rabbit pieces gently until tender, cool, and mince the flesh with the ham or corned beef. Add breadcrumbs, lemon rind, parsley and seasoning and bind with white sauce. Roll out pastry thinly and cut into 4 inch rounds. Cover half the rounds with rabbit mixture and top with the other half, pressing edges together. Brush tops with milk and bake at 450°F (Gas Mark 8) for 20 minutes. These little pies are delicious for a packed meal.

RABBIT PIE

Joint a rabbit and soak in cold salted water for 2 hours, then dry thoroughly. Cut ½ lb steak into cubes, and form ¼ lb pork sausage meat into small round balls. Arrange layers of rabbit, steak and sausage meat balls in a pie-dish, sprinkling thickly with salt, pepper, grated nutmeg and chopped parsley. Cover with stock or water, put on a pastry lid, and bake at 450°F (Gas Mark 6) for 20 minutes, then reduce to 350°F (Gas Mark 4) for another 1¼ hours.

ROYAL RABBIT PIE FROM HUNTINGDON

1 *nice rabbit*
About ½ *lb stewing steak*
(or shin, well cooked)
Chicken stock (if possible)
½ *lb bacon*
Salt and pepper

¾ *pint water*
1 *level tablespoon cornflour*
Onion or mushroom if liked
1 *lb pastry (puff for*
preference)
Egg for glazing

Make the pastry and put to 'rest' in a cool place. Meanwhile skin, wipe and dry the rabbit. Cut up the beef and bacon and arrange in pie-dish. Add onion or mushroom if desired. Blend the cornflour with a little cold water and add to the chicken stock; bring carefully to the boil, stirring all the time, and cook for a further minute or so. Place the joints of rabbit in the pie-dish on top of the other ingredients and pour the 'gravy' over all adding more stock or water if necessary. Bring to the boil, gently, then cover the pie-dish and place in a medium oven, 350°F (Gas Mark 3) until all the meat is cooked but not falling apart – about 1 hour. Take out of oven and cool the pie-dish and its contents, then cover with the prepared pastry. Decorate the pie as required and brush with beaten egg before returning to a good oven for the best part of ½ hour. Garnish with parsley, and serve with brussels sprouts or kidney beans, if in season, and mashed potatoes. This pie is also delicious eaten cold with beetroot and green salad, says Mrs R., who sent the recipe.

ESSEX RABBIT PIE

In one Essex family about fifty years ago, rabbit pie was served regularly for Monday morning breakfast. During the month of May (and May only) the pies contained a mixture of rook and rabbit. At other times, the mixture could be moorhen and rabbit.

ROOK PIE (1)

6 *rooks*
4 oz *stewing beef or mutton*
Salt and pepper

Powdered mace
2 *cloves*
Short pastry

Skin and clean the rooks and cut away the backs and ribs, leaving the breasts with the two upper wing bones attached, also the two legs without the fat. Wash and dry. Dip in flour and arrange in a pie-dish with meat cut in cubes. Season with salt and pepper, a pinch of mace, and cloves. Cover with water and put on a lid, and simmer very slowly until the meat leaves the bones. Cool and add some hard-boiled eggs if liked. Cover with short pastry, brush with egg, and bake at 400°F (Gas Mark 6) for 45 minutes.

1870 ROOK PIE (2)

Rooks must be skinned and stewed in milk and water before being put into the pie-dish; they may then be treated as pigeons. Epicures assert that only the breast must be used, but if when the rook is drawn and skinned it is laid on its breast and an incision made on each side of the spine of about a finger width, and that piece removed, the whole of the bird is wholesome food, that being the really bitter part.

4 rooks	*3 hard-boiled eggs*
½ lb puff paste	*About 2 oz butter*
Pepper and salt	*Small piece of rump steak*

Lay the rump steak in the pie-dish, cut the rooks as directed, and lay them in the dish well seasoned, add the butter in knobs and some hard-boiled eggs. Bake as you would a pigeon pie.

Mrs Giles, Shaftesbury, Dorset

YORKSHIRE ROOK PIE

After skinning and cleaning the rooks, cut away the backs and ribs, leaving the breasts with the two upper wing bones attached, also the two legs without the feet. Wash, dry, dip in flour and arrange in pie dish. If the dish is small, cut the breast in two down the breastbone. Season with salt and pepper, a large pinch of mace and 2 cloves for every 6 rooks. Cover with water and a lid, and stew very slowly until the meat leaves the bones, filling up with cold water if necessary. When cold, cover with pastry and bake in usual way until pastry is golden brown. If a little stewing beef or lamb is available, cut it up and add to the pie allowing ¼ lb to 6 rooks. Hard-boiled eggs are also an improvement.

1870 VEAL AND HAM PATTIES

6 oz ready dressed lean veal	*lemon peel*
3 oz ham	*Some Cayenne pepper and salt*
1 oz butter rolled in flour	*1 spoon essence of ham*
1 tablespoon cream	*1 spoon lemon juice*
1 tablespoon veal stock	*Puff paste*
A little grated nutmeg and	

Chop about 6 ozs ready-dressed lean veal, and 3 ozs of ham, very small and put into a stewpan with 1 oz of butter rolled in flour, a tablespoon of cream, the same of veal stock, a little nutmeg and lemon peel, some cayenne pepper and salt, a spoonful of essence of ham and lemon juice. Mix well together and stir it over the fire until quite hot, taking care it does not burn. Prepare the patty-pans as for oyster patties, and bake them in a hot oven for $\frac{1}{4}$ hour; fill the mixture and serve.

Mrs Giles, Shaftesbury, Dorset

1870 OYSTER PATTIES

Light puff paste
2 dozen large oysters
1 oz butter rolled in flour
½ gill good cream

A little grated lemon peel
A little Cayenne pepper
Salt
1 teaspoon lemon juice

Roll out puff paste less than $\frac{1}{4}$ inch thick, cut it into squares with a knife, cover with it 8 or 10 patty pans, and put upon each a bit of bread the size of a walnut; roll out another layer of paste of same thickness, cut it as above, wet the edge of the bottom paste and put on the top, pare them round and notch them about a dozen times with the back of the knife, rub them lightly with yolk of egg, and bake them in hot oven about $\frac{1}{4}$ hour. When done, take a thin slice off the top, and with a small knife or spoon take out the bread and the inside paste, leaving the outside quite entire. Parboil 2 dozen large oysters, strain them from their liquor, wash, beard, and cut them into four, put them into a saucepan with 1 oz of butter rolled in flour, $\frac{1}{2}$ gill of good cream, a little grated lemon peel, the oyster liquor strained and reduced by boiling to one half, a little Cayenne pepper and salt, and a teaspoon of lemon juice; stir it over the fire for 5 minutes, fill the patties, put the cover on the top, and serve.

Mrs Giles, Shaftesbury, Dorset

1870 VEAL AND OYSTER PIE

Time to bake – $1\frac{1}{2}$ hours.

$1\frac{1}{2}$ lb veal cutlets
$\frac{3}{4}$ lb ham
50 oysters
A cup of weak gravy or broth

Peel of $\frac{1}{2}$ lemon
Pepper and salt
Puff paste

Cut $1\frac{1}{2}$ lb of veal into small neat cutlets, and spread over each a thin layer of minced or pounded ham, season them with pepper, salt and grated lemon peel, and roll each cutlet round. Line the pie-dish edge with a good paste, put a layer of rolled veal at the bottom over the veal a layer of oysters then of veal, and the oysters on top; make a gravy with a cupful of weak gravy or broth, the peel of $\frac{1}{2}$ a lemon, the oyster liquor strained and a seasoning of salt and pepper; cover a crust over the top. Ornament it in any way approved, egg it over, and bake it in a moderate oven. When done, more gravy may be added by pouring in through a funnel into the hole in the top, and replacing the ornament on it after the gravy has been added.

Mrs Giles, Shaftesbury, Dorset

1870 LOBSTER PATTIES

Time – 20 minutes

Some puff paste
A hen lobster
1 oz butter
$\frac{1}{2}$ tablespoon veal gravy
1 teaspoon essence of anchovy

1 teaspoon lemon juice
1 tablespoon flour and water
A little Cayenne pepper and
salt

Roll out the puff paste about $\frac{1}{4}$ inch thick, and prepare the patty pans as for oyster patties; take a hen lobster already boiled, pick the meat from the tail and claws, and chop it fine, put it into a stewpan with a little of the inside spawn pounded in a mortar until quite smooth, with 1 oz of butter, the $\frac{1}{2}$ teaspoon of cream, the same of veal gravy, essence of anchovy, lemon juice, Cayenne pepper, and salt, and a tablespoon of flour and water. Let it stew 5 minutes, fill the patties, and serve.

Mrs Giles, Shaftesbury, Dorset

1870 CONGER-EEL PIE

Time to bake—rather more than 1 hour

A piece of conger-eel
A quart of water
$\frac{1}{4}$ onion
A bunch of sweet herbs
Pepper, salt and spice

A sprig of parsley
4 sage leaves
15 oysters
$\frac{1}{2}$ lb puff paste

Cut a piece of a moderate-sized conger into pieces of convenient size; take out the bone, and put it on the fire with any odd bit of the fish there may be to spare, with a quart of water, a quarter of an onion, a bunch of sweet herbs, pepper, salt, and a little spice, and let it simmer to make the gravy. Season the pieces of conger with pepper and salt, and boil them with parsley and sage minced finely. Arrange them in a pie-dish, pour in the gravy (which should be strong enough to jelly when cold), put the oysters on the top, and pour in their liquor, cover the pie with a good puff paste, and bake it in a moderate oven.

Mrs Giles, Shaftesbury, Dorset

BACON AND EGG FLAN

8 oz short pastry
3 oz streaky bacon
1 small onion
2 eggs

¼ pint creamy milk
1 oz butter
Pepper and salt
1 oz grated cheese

Line sponge tin or flan ring with pastry. Chop bacon and onion in small pieces and soften in butter. Put into flan case. Beat eggs and milk lightly together, season with salt and pepper, and pour on top of bacon and onion. Sprinkle on grated cheese. Bake at 375°F (Gas Mark 5) for 30 minutes. Serve hot or cold.

BACON AND MUSHROOM FLAN

6 oz short pastry
4 oz back bacon
4 oz mushrooms
1 oz butter

2 large eggs
½ pint milk
Salt and pepper

Line a pie plate or flan ring with the pastry. Chop the bacon and mushrooms and cook in the butter until the mushrooms are just soft. Put into the pastry case. Whisk the eggs with the milk and seasoning (the bacon may be a bit salt already). Pour into the pastry case and bake at 425°F (Gas Mark 7) for 35 minutes. Scatter a few chopped chives or a little parsley on the top and serve hot or cold.

CHEESE AND MUSHROOM FLAN

6 oz short pastry
8 oz mushrooms
1 oz butter
¼ pint cream

2 eggs and 1 egg yolk
2 oz grated Cheddar cheese
Salt and pepper

Line an 8-inch flan ring with pastry. Fry sliced or chopped mushrooms in butter. Beat up cream, eggs and egg yolk, and add drained mushrooms and cheese. Season with salt and pepper, and pour into pastry case. Sprinkle with a little cheese, and bake at 375°F (Gas Mark 5) for 40 minutes.

MUSHROOM FLAN

4 oz short pastry	2 eggs
1 small onion	¼ pint milk
2 oz bacon	2 oz grated cheese
1½ oz butter	Salt and pepper
8 oz mushrooms	

Line 7-inch flan ring with pastry. Chop onion finely and dice bacon and cook in butter until soft. Add sliced mushrooms and cook until just tender. Season well with salt and pepper and put into flan case. Beat together eggs and milk and add most of the cheese, and pour over mushroom mixture. Sprinkle with cheese and bake at 350°F (Gas Mark 4) for 40 minutes.

MRS HIBBERD'S PASTRY

Take 1½ lb self-raising flour, ½ teaspoon salt and ¾ lb lard, or lard and butter or margarine. Rub the fat into the flour but *not* too finely, leave lumps of fat but not too big. Add sufficient, very cold water (iced if possible) to bind together into a pastry nice to handle and *leave* for an hour or 2 in the cool before rolling out.

This method is so quick to do that the pastry can be made in an odd moment and put aside.

INSTANT PASTRY MIX

3 lb self-raising flour	1½ lb lard and/or margarine

Rub fat into flour, but stop before the mixture reaches the breadcrumb stage. It should be lumpy. Store in a very cool place up to 2 to 3 weeks. Just add ice-cold water to make flaky-type pastry. You can make instant crumbles, rockbuns, puddings, etc. by adding sugar and more elbow grease. This is a useful standby in the Honey household.

9 *Savoury Puddings*

*'Goose and dumplings,' observed Trumper; 'goose and dumplings: suppose
you can dine off them?'*
'Nothing better,' said Scott; 'nothing better.'
'Lots of onions!' added Trumper; 'lots of onions!'
'That's your ticket,' replied Scott; 'that's your ticket.'

'Hawbuck Grange'
R. S. Surtees

Suet-based pastry has always been a favourite in country kitchens. Steak,
pork, minced meat, offal, poultry, game and bacon have formed the fillings
of delicious gravy-soaked puddings and roly-polys for centuries. The
thick suet crust has helped to make scarce meat go a long way. In many
cases, there has been no meat at all, and some of these puddings have been
simply flavoured with herbs and oatmeal, to serve with a gravy and take
the place of meat. Similar puddings, sometimes made with a batter, were
often devised to eke out expensive roasts (Yorkshire pudding is the classic
example), and were usually cooked under the meat, but served first with
gravy to curb the appetite. Dumplings have also been traditionally used
to extend stewed meats for large families, or to make the best of small
pieces of bacon or offal.

In some of the recipes there are individual measurements for the suet
pastry.

If you want to make up your own recipe to suit the amount of filling you have available, allow 1 oz flour to ½ oz shredded suet for 1 helping of pudding. For a 4- or 5-person family, a suet crust of 8 oz flour and 4 oz suet will give enough for a good-sized pudding which will allow for some second helpings.

Flour can be self-raising, or plain with the addition of baking powder (a teaspoon to 8 oz flour). Black treacle (about 1 teaspoon to 8 oz flour) gives a rich-tasting and well-coloured crust. 6 tablespoons of cold water will be enough to mix this proportion of suet pastry.

Some people prefer to line the basin before putting in the filling, but others say this takes up too much of the meat juices and prefer all the crust on top. Some 'dry' puddings are better cooked as savoury roly-polys, to be served with gravy or a knob of butter, and this is a good method for the various types of bacon and onion pudding.

To cover a pudding, use kitchen foil or double greaseproof paper, brushed with melted fat, or use a pudding cloth. Make sure the water is at boiling point when the basin is put into the steamer or saucepan. A ½ pint of water will evaporate in 30 minutes when boiled, so puddings which are to be left to steam on their own for 2 or 3 hours should be put in a pan containing not less than 3 pints of boiling water. 'Topping up' should always be with boiling water.

STEAK AND KIDNEY PUDDING

8 oz self-raising flour
4 oz shredded suet
Salt and pepper
6 tablespoons water

1 lb stewing steak
3 lambs' kidneys or 4 oz ox
kidney

Cut steak into thin pieces and chop kidney in small pieces. If liked, wrap a piece of meat round each piece of kidney, but otherwise just mix the 2 meats. Mix flour, suet, salt and pepper to a firm paste with water. Line a greased basin with ⅔ of the pastry. Put in the meat, and season well with salt and pepper and add a sprinkling of flour. Add water or stock almost to the top of the basin. Cover with remaining pastry and seal edges. Cover and steam for 4 hours.

Variations: Either add 1 small chopped onion or substitute 3 sliced onions for kidney. 2 oz chopped mushrooms may be added and/or 8 oysters for a special occasion (tinned ones can be used). 1 lb minced steak mixed with 4 oz mushrooms and a small chopped onion also make a good pudding, with a pinch of thyme mixed with the seasoning.

RABBIT OR HARE PUDDING

8 oz self-raising flour
4 oz shredded suet
Salt and pepper
6 tablespoons water
1 small rabbit

½ teaspoon sage
2 sliced onions
2 sliced tomatoes
2 oz chopped mushrooms

Make in the same way as for steak-and-kidney, using rabbit joints and stock or water.

HARE PUDDING

1½ lb meat cut from hare
2 sliced onions
1 sliced apple

1 tablespoon red wine or redcurrant jelly

Make as for steak-and-kidney, adding red wine or redcurrant jelly to stock or water, and using plenty of seasoning. As hare joints are so large it is better to strip the meat from them before using.

KENTISH PORK AND APPLE PUDDING

8 oz self-raising flour
4 oz shredded suet
8 oz fresh lean pork
Medium-sized cooking apple

Salt and pepper
Sage
Stock or water

Prepare pastry with flour and suet and enough water to make a firm paste. Line basin with pastry, and put in pork cut in squares, chopped apple, salt and pepper, a good pinch of chopped sage and stock to cover. Put on pastry lid, cover and boil for 4 hours.

NORTHAMPTONSHIRE BACON ROLL

8 oz self-raising flour
3 oz suet
Salt and pepper

6 oz chopped mixed bacon and onion

Make suet pastry, using just enough water to make a firm dough. Roll into a rectangle and put on bacon and onion, and plenty of seasoning. A little chopped sage may be added. Roll in a floured cloth and boil for 1½ hours. Serve with gravy.

ESSEX PORK PLUGGA

This is made in the same way as Northamptonshire Bacon Roll but using diced streaky pork instead of bacon.

SUSSEX BACON PUDDING

The bacon, onion and some chopped herbs are added to the suet mixture, together with a beaten egg and a little milk (instead of the usual water to make the pastry). The mixture is steamed in a basin for 1½ hours and served with gravy.

SUFFOLK LAYER PUDDING

6 oz self-raising flour
6 oz plain flour
¼ teaspoon salt
4 oz suet

1 lb cooked minced meat
1 medium onion
Salt and pepper

Mix suet pastry with the two kinds of flour, salt, suet and milk to moisten. Line a pudding basin with half the mixture. Use meat left from the joint, or fresh mince which has been cooked, and use a little stock or gravy to moisten. Mix meat with chopped onion and seasoning. Put a layer of meat mixture into basin, then a thin layer of suet pastry, then more meat and pastry until basin is full, ending with pastry layer. Cover and steam for 2 hours. Serve with gravy or parsley sauce.

SUFFOLK ONION PUDDING

4 oz plain flour
2 oz suet

8 oz onions
Salt and pepper

Mix flour and suet with water to a stiff dough – and roll out. Cut up onions, salt and pepper them, and put on to dough. Roll up into a cloth. Boil for 1¼ hours. Serve with a slice of butter. This is very good with boiled bacon or a piece of beef.

CHICKEN PUDDING

12 oz self-raising flour
6 oz suet
1 old chicken
1 chopped onion
1 chopped garlic clove
(optional)

Bayleaf
Salt and pepper
1 dessertspoon chopped
parsley

Make up suet pastry with enough water to give a firm paste. Cut flesh from legs, wings and breast of bird. Line a basin with suet pastry. Fill with alternate layers of meat and onion, with garlic, seasoning and parsley. Put bayleaf in the centre. Just cover meat with stock or water, and top with pastry. Steam for 4 hours. Serve with gravy made from chicken stock, using carcass of bird, or with parsley sauce.

STAFFORDSHIRE LIVER PUDDING

8 oz self-raising flour	2 large onions
4 oz suet	Salt and pepper
2 lb ox liver	

Make suet pastry with enough water to give a firm paste. Put diced liver and onions in a basin, mixing well, and season with salt and pepper. Cover with stock and put on pastry lid. Steam for 3 hours.

PIGEON PUDDING (1)

8 oz self-raising flour	8 oz shin beef
4 oz suet	1 kidney
2 pigeons	

Make up suet pastry and line a pudding basin. Cut pigeons in quarters and put in basin with diced beef and kidney. Season well and cover with stock. Put on pastry lid and steam for 2½ hours.

PIGEON PUDDING (2)

8 oz self-raising flour	8 oz chuck steak
½ teaspoon salt	3 hard-boiled eggs
4 oz shredded suet	Salt, pepper and mace
3 pigeons	

Make a suet pastry by mixing flour, salt, suet and ¼ pint cold water. Line a pudding basin with pastry, leaving enough for a lid. In the basin put the breasts of the pigeons, the steak cut in small pieces, the egg yolks, salt, pepper, and a pinch of mace. Pour in stock from the bones and trimmings, to just cover the meat. Cover with suet crust, tie on a pudding cloth, and cook in a saucepan of boiling water for 3 hours.

GAME PUDDING (1)

1 old grouse or partridge
1 oz butter
1 onion
1 lb stewing steak

Salt and pepper
Mace
Suet pastry

Line a basin with half the suet pastry, made with 8 oz flour. Cut the bird into quarters and brown them in the butter. Cut steak in cubes and roll it in flour. Put game and steak into basin, add chopped onion, salt and pepper and a pinch of mace. Fill up with stock. Cover with remaining suet pastry and steam for 3 hours. Chopped parsley or other herbs may be added, and so can mushrooms and/or ham or bacon. Stock can be made from game livers and carcasses and used as extra gravy.

GAME PUDDING (2)

8 oz suet pastry
4 pigeons or 2 partridges
8 oz stewing steak
Yolks of 3 hard-boiled eggs

Salt, pepper and nutmeg
Stock made from game
trimmings

If pigeons are used, the breasts only can go into the pudding, and the rest be simmered for stock. If partridges are used, they can be split in half. I like the addition of a little bacon and a chopped onion, and sometimes a few mushrooms to this pudding, but they are optional. If appetites are very hearty, the quantity of suet pastry may be increased so that the bowl can be lined as well.

Line the bowl with $\frac{1}{2}$ inch thick pastry if liked. Put in pigeon breasts or halved partridges, chopped steak, egg yolks, seasoning, and gravy to come half way up the bowl. Put on pastry lid and cover with cloth. Cook for 3 hours.

BACON LAYER PUDDING

8 oz suet pastry
8 oz chopped bacon

2 onions
2 carrots

Roll out the pastry thinly and cut out a round to fit the bottom of a greased 2-pint basin. Put in a layer of bacon pieces. Grate the onions and carrots, and put a little of the mixture on top of the bacon. Put on another layer of pastry, then bacon and vegetables. Continue until basin is full, topping with pastry. Cover and steam for 2 hours. Serve with gravy.

NORFOLK BEEF PUDDING

8 oz self-raising flour
3 oz shredded suet
Pinch of salt

12 oz stewing steak
1 shallot
Salt and pepper

Make up a suet crust with flour, suet, salt and water. Roll it out and put on to a piece of greased greaseproof paper. Cut up the meat and shallot finely and put on to the suet pastry. Sprinkle with water and season with salt and pepper. Tie up in a cloth and steam for 3½ hours.

NORFOLK MUSSEL PUDDING

8 oz self-raising flour
3 oz shredded suet
Pinch of salt

2 pints mussels
Salt and pepper

Make the suet crust with flour, suet, salt and water, and roll out. Put on to a piece of greased greaseproof paper. Wash the mussels well and remove their beards. Put them in a pan on a very low heat and they will open quickly. Put them on to the dough, season with salt and pepper. Tie up in a cloth and steam for 1½ hours.

PARTRIDGE PUDDING

1½ lb flour
½ lb suet
¼ lb rump steak
Brace of old partridges
½ teaspoon pepper
1 teaspoon salt

¼ lb mushrooms
1 teaspoon each freshly
chopped parsley, thyme and
tarragon
¾ pint brown stock
¼ pint sweet stout

Line a 2-pint pudding basin with a suet crust made with the flour, suet and enough cold water to make a stiff dough, leaving enough crust for a cover. Cut the rump steak in thin slices and put on the bottom, cut the partridges into neat joints and season with pepper and salt, and put into the basin mixed with sliced mushrooms and herbs. Pour in stock mixed with stout, cover with suet crust and pinch the edges together. Tie a pudding cloth or foil over the basin, place in boiling water, and keep boiling for 3 hours.

GROUSE PUDDING

8 oz *plain flour*
1 *teaspoon baking powder*
½ *teaspoon salt*
4 *oz suet*
1 *old grouse*

1 *lb stewing steak*
1 *onion*
1 *oz butter*
Salt, pepper and nutmeg

Sift together flour, baking powder and salt, and add the grated or chopped suet. Stir in enough cold water to make a pliable dough, and line a pudding basin with two-thirds of the pastry. Cut the flesh of the grouse into neat chunks, stewing the bones and trimmings in water to make a good stock. Brown the grouse and cubes of steak in the butter and put into the basin with salt, pepper and a pinch of nutmeg, chopped onion, and enough stock or water to half fill the basin. Cover with the top crust, put on paper and a cloth, and steam for 3 hours, adding boiling water to the saucepan to keep it almost to the top of the basin. Make a hole in the top crust before serving and pour in hot stock or gravy.

1870 PORK PUDDING
Time to boil – 2½ hours.

1½ *lb pork*
¾ *lb sausage meat*
A few leaves of sage

1 *onion*
Pepper and salt
Suet crust

Line the pudding basin and lay in the slices of pork, add the sausage meat, season highly, cover with the crust, and boil in a floured cloth.

Puddings may also be made in a similar way from ox-kidney slices, and mutton kidneys.

Mrs Giles, Shaftesbury, Dorset

KIDNEY PUDDING

3 *sheeps' kidneys*
2 *teacups breadcrumbs*
1 *teacup milk*
1 *egg*

1 *teaspoon suet*
Nutmeg, parsley and mixed herbs
Salt and pepper

Skin the kidneys, mince them and mix with the suet. Put into a basin with the breadcrumbs. Add a little chopped parsley, some mixed herbs, grated nutmeg, salt and pepper. Beat the egg, mix with the milk, then stir both into the pudding mixture. Pour into a buttered basin and steam for 1½ hours. Turn out and serve with green vegetables and thick gravy.

VENISON PUDDING

1 lb thin fillet of venison
2 oz diced bacon
4 oz mushrooms

8 oz suet crust pastry
½ pint stock
A little red wine if available

Thoroughly grease a pie dish. Flour a thin fillet of venison and lay it at the bottom. Season, and add diced bacon and small mushrooms. Set it in the oven, dry, to cook for about 20 minutes, while you make a light suet crust. Season the crust lightly and roll it out to fit the pie dish. By now the floured meat in the dish should have browned slightly and the bacon be crisp. Fill up the dish with stock and a little red wine if available. Put on the paste and cook until the crust is well risen, about 1¼ hours at 350°F (Gas Mark 4)

After putting on the crust, but before baking, score the top fairly deeply into squares, this gives the dough a better appearance. Suet is advised for the crust as the pie needs long baking. If the steak is cut in small pieces and well fried in the dish first, it should be tender by the time the crust is done.

RABBIT PUDDING

Cut a young rabbit into joints, soak and dry well. Line a pudding basin with suet pastry, and put in alternate layers of rabbit, chopped onion, sage and chopped mushrooms. The layers should be well-floured, and strips of fat bacon inserted at intervals, with a good sprinkling of salt and pepper. Fill the basin with water, cover with a suet crust, and tie on greaseproof paper. Steam for 3 hours. The pudding will make its own rich thick gravy.

MRS CHAPMAN'S BACON ROLL

Mix well together 12 oz flour, 4 oz suet (or dripping), 1 teaspoon of baking powder, ¼ teaspoon salt. Add enough water to make a stiff paste, then roll out ¼ inch thick. Cut ½ lb thin, streaky rashers into pieces, peel and chop 3 large onions. Put the bacon and onions in alternate layers on the pastry. Sprinkle with pepper and a cautious quantity of salt, then roll up. Tie securely in a pudding cloth, and boil for 3 hours. Serve with a good brown gravy, carrots and cabbage cooked in very little water for a minimum of time.

This comes from a very happy Oxfordshire family of 10 children – 5 boys, 5 girls. Their mother was a past master (or should it be mistress?) at making her slender housekeeping allowance stretch to its limit; this recipe was one of her standbys and one will never forget the atmosphere as they all sat round the big kitchen table after just such a delicious dish, which, with home-grown vegetables, cost so little yet fed so many so well.

BUCKS DUMPLING

8 oz liver
8 oz streaky bacon
1 lb flour
6 oz shredded suet

2 large onions
1 dessertspoon chopped sage
Salt and pepper

Cut liver and bacon very small. Mix flour and suet to a stiff dough with a little water and a pinch of salt. Roll out to a rectangle. Cover dough with liver and bacon. Grate onions over the top, together with chopped sage and plenty of pepper and salt. Roll up tightly in a floured cloth and boil 2½ hours. Serve with a good gravy.

KIDNEY DUMPLINGS

Put a well-seasoned lamb's kidney into the scooped-out centre of a large onion, and wrapping the onion in suet pastry, bake at 350°F (Gas Mark 4) for 1¼ hours, and serve with good rich gravy.

SUFFOLK DUMPLINGS

¾ lb flour
6 oz suet
1½ gills water
2 lb lean pork

1½ lb onions
½ teaspoon salt
Seasoning to taste

Grease a pudding basin and find a pudding cloth big enough to tie over the basin and a disc of greased paper which will cover the top. Make a crust from flour, suet and a little water mixed to a thick pastry consistency. Line the basin with the crust, keeping back enough to cover the top. Cut the pork into pieces and mix with the chopped onions. Put into basin in layers with seasoning between. Add remaining water until basin is full. Cover with top crust, which should not be too thin. Cover with paper, wrap in the cloth, and steam for 4 hours.

A TASTY BATTER PUDDING

1 oz shredded suet
4 oz flour
2 eggs

1 pint milk
Pinch of salt

Mix suet and flour with salt. Beat eggs, and add to the mixture, and make into a batter with the milk. Put into a greased pie dish and bake for 1½ hours in a moderate oven. Serve with meat, or by adding 2 tablespoons of sugar and a few currants, make it into a sweet pudding.

SAVOURY PUDDING

2 oz shredded suet	3 eggs
6 oz stale bread	Salt and pepper
½ pint milk	Cayenne pepper
2 oz fine oatmeal	Thyme, sage and marjoram

Soak bread in hot milk and leave it to get cold. Mix dry ingredients with bread. Beat eggs and mix well in. Melt some dripping in a tin to boiling point. Spread in mixture with a fork. Bake for 30 to 40 minutes in oven with joint. Serve like Yorkshire pudding.

YORKSHIRE SAVOURY PUDDING

4 large onions	1 oz oatmeal
2 teaspoons chopped sage	3 oz shredded suet
8 oz bread without crust	Salt and pepper

Pour some boiling water over the bread and leave to stand for 30 minutes. Drain well but do not squeeze out moisture. Chop the onions finely and mix with bread and other ingredients. Put into greased oven tin and bake at 375°F (Gas Mark 5) for 1 hour until well browned. Cut into slices to serve with thick gravy and vegetables.

DUCK PUDDING

3 oz bread without crust	1 teaspoon flour
1½ gills milk	1 onion
1 egg	½ teaspoon chopped sage
2 oz shredded suet	Salt and pepper

Pour the milk over the bread and leave for 10 minutes, then beat well with a spoon. Stir in the egg, suet, flour, finely-chopped onion, sage and seasoning. Grease and warm some small patty tins, and put in the mixture. Bake for 15 minutes at 450°F (Gas Mark 7). Take out and put under roasting duck or pork for the last 15 minutes' cooking time. The mixture can also be baked in an oven tin in a hot oven for 25 minutes until risen, and then be put underneath the duck or pork. Cut into slices to serve.

OATMEAL PUDDING

Mix 2 oz fine Scotch oatmeal in ¼ pint of milk. Add to it a pint of boiling milk and stir over the fire for 10 minutes. Then put in 2 oz sifted breadcrumbs, or as much as will make the mixture rather stiff. Take it off the fire and mix with it 2 oz suet, two eggs and a teaspoonful chopped mar-joram and sage. Butter a Yorkshire pudding pan, put in the pudding and bake for an hour in a moderate oven. Turn out on a hot dish and have a little good gravy in a boat.

Mrs Garden, 1847

LINCOLNSHIRE PUDDING

A Yorkshire pudding with sultanas in.
   Served before meal with a good gravy.

NORFOLK DUMPLINGS

A yeast dumpling.
   Served before meal with gravy.
Make a dough as for bread, but mix with milk, plunge into boiling water and boil for 20 minutes. Serve at once with gravy or sugar and butter. Do not touch with a knife, but tear apart with 2 forks.

SUFFOLK OR LARD DUMPLINGS

1 lb flour   *½ pint water*
½ saltspoon salt

Mix and form into round dumplings, put into boiling water and boil ½ to ¾ of an hour. Serve with roast or boiled meat, sometimes boiled with the meat.

Empire Marketing Board, 1929

MRS CROWFORT'S DUMPLINGS

2 eggs   *8 tablespoons milk*
8 tablespoons flour

Made into two dumplings and boiled ¾ of an hour. The thick gravy is made by dredging the meat well with flour and adding a little water.

Mrs Garden, 1863

SUSSEX DRIP PUDDING

Serve this instead of Yorkshire pudding. Make a suet pudding and cook it the same time as you roast a joint of beef. (By tradition all Sussex pud-dings are cooked in a cloth but if you steam it in a basin, the effect is the same.) When the roast is ready, remove it from the pan, cut the pudding into slices and soak well in the hot dripping. Place the slices on a hot dish and brown in the oven while making the gravy.

MEALY PUDDINGS

Long pudding skins
1 lb oatmeal
½ lb suet

2 large onions (parboiled)
¼ teaspoon salt
¼ teaspoon pepper

Wash pudding skins in warm water and leave to soak in cold water and salt. Chop onions, mix with oatmeal, suet and seasonings. Tie end of pudding skin with thread, put in enough mixture to make length of a sausage. Tie skin again, leaving enough room for pudding to swell. Continue until mixture is finished. Put into pan with boiling water and salt, pricking puddings first to prevent their bursting, and simmer for 20–30 minutes.

Mrs Biggan, Kirkcudbrightshire

LEEK (OR ONION) PUDDING

4 oz self-raising flour
2 oz suet
2 leeks or onions

Water to mix
Seasoning

Sieve flour, add suet and seasoning. Mix to a stiff dough with water. Roll out ⅔ thinly to line greased pudding basin. Chop leeks and fill up centre; cover with ⅓ suet pastry rolled out to form lid. Alternatively, the chopped leeks may be mixed in with the suet pastry, and all turned into the basin. Cover with foil and boil in pan of water for 2 hours. Serve in slices with meat dishes instead of dumplings.

Mrs Biggan, Kircudbrightshire

PEASE PUDDING

½ pint split peas
½ oz butter

1 mashed potato
Salt, pepper and sugar

Tie peas in a pudding cloth (loosely to allow for swelling) and boil for 3 to 4 hours until soft. Drain well, pass through a wire sieve, beat in butter, potato and seasonings. Turn out into a dish and serve with boiled salt pork and baked or boiled ham.

Mrs Biggan, Kircudbrightshire

SAVOURY PUDDING

6 oz stale bread	4 oz suet or dripping
½ pint milk	1 or 2 eggs
6 oz oatmeal	Salt and pepper
½ lb boiled onions (optional)	1 teaspoonful baking powder

Break bread into small pieces, soak in milk and mash well with fork. Add the oatmeal, salt, sage, onion and suet or dripping and stir well. Stir in the beaten eggs, dust well with pepper and add the baking powder. Place in a greased baking tin and bake in a moderate oven, 375°F, for ½ hour.

This dish can be eaten with sizzling sausages for supper or with pork, as a change from sage and onion stuffing. It is delicious eaten with fried or grilled trout which has been dipped in wholemeal flour, served with horseradish sauce.

SAVOURY BAKE

Peel 3 large onions and cook them until tender, then drain well and chop finely. Chop 4 oz suet, crumble 4 oz bread, rub ½ oz thyme and ½ oz sage to a fine powder, or if fresh herbs used, chop them finely; and beat up with 1 egg. Put all these ingredients into a basin, season with pepper and salt, and mix well together, adding a little milk if necessary to moisten. Melt a little dripping (1 oz) in a tin, pour in the pudding and cook for an hour in a moderately hot oven. Serve with good brown gravy. Sausages or odd scraps of bacon chopped and fried could be served with this, with vegetables added to make a main meal.

CHEESE AND ONION ROLY-POLY

8 oz plain flour	4 oz thinly sliced onions
½ level teaspoon salt	8 oz thinly sliced Cheddar
½ level teaspoon baking	cheese
powder	Pinch each pepper, salt and
4 oz suet	nutmeg
Cold water to bind	A little milk

Sieve the flour, salt and baking powder, mix in the suet and sufficient cold water to make a soft dough. Knead lightly and roll out to an oblong strip. Scatter the onions and cheese over the surface with pepper, salt and nutmeg, damp the edges and roll up like a Swiss roll. Brush with milk, bake in fairly hot oven at 400°F (Gas Mark 6) for 40–45 minutes until browned, or roll in greased greaseproof paper and steam for 1½ hours. Serve hot with tomato sauce.

CHEESE AND LEEK PUDDING

$8\frac{1}{2}$ oz plain flour
$\frac{1}{2}$ level teaspoon salt
2 level teaspoons baking
powder
3 oz suet
10 oz grated Cheddar cheese

Cold water to bind
1 lb leeks
$\frac{1}{2}$ oz butter
$\frac{1}{2}$ pint milk (or milk and
water)

Sieve 8 oz flour, salt and baking powder, mix in the suet and 2 oz cheese, and bind with cold water. Use $\frac{2}{3}$ of this dough to line a greased pint-size pudding basin and reserve $\frac{1}{3}$ for the 'lid'. Wash the leeks thoroughly and cut into rounds. Make cheese sauce with the remaining $\frac{1}{2}$ oz flour, cheese, butter and milk, or milk and water. Fill the pudding with alternate layers of leeks and cheese sauce, ending with leeks. Put on the 'lid' and seal the edges. Cover with greased greaseproof paper or foil and steam for $1\frac{1}{2}$ hours. Turn out and serve hot.

10 Egg and Cheese Dishes

When fish is scant, and fruit of trees,
supply that want, with butter and cheese.

Thomas Tusser

An egg boiled soft is not unwholesome
'Emma', Jane Austen

Farm wives like to use a lot of eggs and cheese in their cooking. Tradition-ally, they have been easily available and quick to use on busy days, and a lot of favourite farm dishes combine the two ingredients into tasty snacks.

Most of us know the pleasure of a good hunk of Cheshire or Cheddar with a corner of new bread, creamy butter, and perhaps a crisp radish or onion. Not so many have enjoyed experimenting with Wensleydale, Stilton, Double Gloucester, Derby, Lancashire, Leicester and Caerphilly, with the rare Dorset Blue Vinney, and the more difficult to find Dunlop and Orkney. All of them repay searching out, as do the increasing variety of interesting cream cheeses which appear regionally.

Price for price, these cheeses represent excellent nutritional value com-pared with meat, but what most of us care about is the taste. To get the best cheeses, in perfect condition, with full flavour, seek out a grocer who really knows his business, and there are still quite a lot of them about. When you can see large pieces of cheese side by side, it's so much easier to compare texture and flavour (no good cheese merchant will begrudge you a small 'taster' when you are comparing and buying). Today the trend is towards neat even slices tightly wrapped in plastic; excellent for the bedsitter or the occasional picnic when you can't be bothered with leftovers, but useless for the normal family.

Buy only enough cheese for a week's supply at a time, because cheese will deteriorate after cutting. Keep cheese away from draughts or too much air circulation which will dry it out. Keep the cheese in a polythene bag, foil, or greaseproof paper and store it in a cool place. It can be kept in the refrigerator away from the ice-making compartment, and should be taken out at least an hour before eating to regain temperature and full flavour.

If you find a really good big piece of cheese, it can be frozen, wrapped in polythene (if it has a strong flavour, wrap it in freezer paper or foil, then in polythene, to prevent cross-flavouring in the freezer). Don't try to store the cheese longer than 2 months, and don't expect perfect texture (many cheeses crumble when cut after freezing), but the flavour will still be good.

If you get a lot of cheese ends, grate them finely (easier if the cheese is dried out naturally in a cool airy place), and store the grated cheese in a loosely covered jar in a cool place. This makes an excellent standby for quick and easy cooking, and for adding extra flavour to soups, salads and pasta.

Perhaps most of us tend to forget, or never know, how good these British cheeses can be for cooking. Most of us basically use Cheddar, but Double Gloucester, Wensleydale and Cheshire also give excellent results, and best of all is Lancashire, known to so many as the only cheese for toasting. Orkney, recently introduced, is rather like a mild Cheddar, and though it is too soft for grating well, it is creamy and delicious for Welsh Rarebit. Here are their characteristics:

Cheshire: A mellow, open-textured cheese with the salty tang of the Cheshire pastures. There are red, white and blue varieties, 'Old Blue' being the richest – and rarest. It has been produced in the county since the twelfth century.

Cheddar: The 'prodigious cheese . . . of delicate taste' of which William Camden wrote in the days of the first Elizabeth. Made under the shadow of the Mendip Hills, close by Cheddar Gorge, genuine Cheddar is coveted for its unique 'nutty' flavour.

Wensleydale: 'An apple pie wi owt tha Cheese is like a kiss wi owt a squeeze.' That is what they say in Yorkshire, where this subtle flavoured and flaky textured cheese comes from. The recipe has come down from the abbots of Jervaulx Abbey. Its special peculiarity is the delicious honeyed after-taste, redolent of the lush dale pastureland.

Stilton: A connoisseur's cheese. Rich, mellow Blue Stilton comes from

Melton Mowbray, from Hartingdon in the Dove Valley and from the Vale of Belvoir. A creamy young White Stilton is popular in the North Country.

Double Gloucester: A pungent, smooth-textured, cheese somewhat similar to Cheddar, but fuller in flavour. It was once carried round in the old Gloucestershire May Day processions, garlanded with flowers. Charles Lamb's favourite supper cheese.

Derby: A mild, close-textured, creamy cheese with a pale honey colour that develops a fuller flavour in four to six months. Sage Derby, flavoured with sage leaves, is a traditional Christmas delicacy.

Lancashire: 'Many's the night I've dreamed of cheese – toasted mostly', said Ben Gunn in Stevenson's *Treasure Island*. He probably meant the famous old toaster from north of the Ribble, the original 'Leigh Toaster'. Although possessing a mild flavour when young, this cheese develops a full and rather pungent flavour as it matures. Its loose texture makes it ideal for crumbling over soups and hot-pots. Also obtainable as 'Sage Lancashire' – this contains chopped sage leaves mixed in with the curd during cheesemaking.

Leicester: A fine dessert cheese of mild flavour, becoming more piquant with maturity. Millstone in shape, and with a rich russet colour that looks particularly well on the board.

Caerphilly: The small creamy white cheese that nowadays comes from the West of England as well as from the small Glamorgan village that gave it birth. Gentle and milky in flavour – a cheese for those who like buttermilk and yoghurt. A delicacy in Wales, where it is served for tea, together with celery and thin slices of bread and butter. A great favourite with children.

Hints on separating eggs

There are many ways of separating eggs without the use of a separator:

1. Break an egg on a saucer, invert an eggcup over the yolk and drain off the white.

2. Break the egg in 2, and hold the half-shells like 2 cups. Gently tip the yolk from one half-shell to the other, and the white will gradually drop into a bowl placed beneath.

3. Set a small, wide-stemmed funnel in a glass. Break the egg in the funnel and the white will slip through to the glass.

4. With a needle, prick a smallish hole in the round end of an egg. Gradually enlarge it until the white runs out. Take care not to prick the yolk with the needle.

Never attempt to whip egg whites that contain even the tiniest speck of yolk. The yolk contains fat and this will prevent the whites beating stiffly. So will any smear of grease on whisk, basin or other utensil used.

Egg yolks

They are better if used immediately, but they can be kept for 2 or 3 days if placed, whole, in a screw-topped jar, covered with cold water and put in the refrigerator.

Add an egg yolk to the mixing of pastry, scones and batters, to cream sauces and soups (but do not let the liquid boil after adding the yolk). Add an extra yolk or 2 to scrambled eggs. Or make this dish with yolks alone, adding 2 tablespoons of milk for each yolk when mixing; cook in a greased basin set in a pan of water. Poach them hard (this can be done in an eggcup standing for 15 minutes in simmering water), rub through a sieve and use the resulting Mimosa balls to garnish soups, salads and rice dishes.

Egg whites

They will keep for several days in a covered bowl in the refrigerator (away from the freezer).

Add an extra white or 2 to soufflés, or to any sweets or savouries of the mousse type. Or whisk a white into a just-setting jelly. Give a meringue top to plain milk puddings – jut a few minutes in a hot oven is sufficient cooking. Egg whites can be used in place of egg and breadcrumbs in coating meat cakes and vegetables. Whisked stiffly, they can be added to fruit purée and cream to make a delicious dessert.

WENDOVER EGGS

A plate of cold boiled ham. Chop up 1 or 2 soft-boiled eggs (7 minutes) on top. Whites will be set, yolks creamy. Add butter, pepper, salt.

EGG AND TOMATO SCRAMBLE

Heat some butter in a small saucepan. In this soften a tomato cut into 8. Pour in 1 or 2 well-beaten eggs, stir over gentle heat, until the eggs are set.

EGG AND VEGETABLE SCRAMBLE

Heat any leftover vegetables, bacon pieces, and/or sliced sausage pieces, in fry-pan. Stir in egg and water and scramble.

EGGS IN A NEST

There are many ways of making these. Make the nest from a baked potato with some of the inside scooped out, break in the egg and pop back in the oven. Or choose large firm tomatoes, cut off the tops, and scoop out the insides. Into the hollows flake morsels of butter. Now pop a raw egg in each, season well, and cook on greased baking sheet for about 15 minutes at 400°F (Gas Mark 6).

EGG ROLLS

This is just right for the family. Mix 1½ lb mashed potatoes with 6 chopped hard-boiled eggs and 3 oz grated cheese. Season and add flavouring – 6–8 chopped spring onions do very nicely. Mould into 8 rolls, dip in beaten egg, coat with breadcrumbs and then fry in deep fat until golden brown.

EGG HUBBLE-BUBBLE

Fry diced cooked potatoes, and any vegetable you may have handy (mushroom, tomato or peas do very well), in butter. When cooked, pour in 3 or 4 lightly beaten seasoned eggs. Sprinkle with grated cheese. Cook very slowly, with a plate over the top, until the eggs are set.

EGG-ON-POTATO CAKES

Add an egg to about 1 lb cold mashed potatoes, season well, add (according to preference) cooked peas, cooked chopped beans or carrots, or grated cheese, mould into patties, dip in beaten egg and then breadcrumbs. Fry in shallow fat, and serve with fried, poached or scrambled egg.

ADD-AN-EGG PIE

The beauty of this dish is that it can be reheated without spoiling. If you are going out, just bake it in the morning – leave it for the family to heat up, and you will not have to feel guilty at all. Using 8 oz short-crust pastry, line the bottom of an 8 inch shallow tin, leaving some pastry for the lid. Layer with 4 sliced hard-boiled eggs, 2 peeled and sliced tomatoes, and 4 thin rashers of bacon. Season well. Cover with pastry lid and bake about 30 minutes at 425°F (Gas Mark 7). You can also use 8 oz cooked fish with this recipe, substituting for the bacon. Smoked haddock, for instance.

FLUFFY EGGS

Beat egg white stiffly and fold in some finely grated cheese. Fill individual dish, or pile up on toast. Make a hollow in the centre and drop in egg yolk. Bake at 350°F (Gas Mark 4) about 10 minutes.

SCOTCH EGGS

4 *hard-boiled eggs*   1 *beaten egg*
1 *lb sausage meat*   *Brown breadcrumbs*

Divide the sausage meat into 4 pieces. Roll out thinly, put an egg in the centre of each piece, then roll up neatly; moulding with your fingers. A little beaten egg brushed onto the join wil keep the eggs from bursting out. Dip each ball into beaten egg, roll in breadcrumbs and fry in hot fat. Allow to get quite cold, then slice and serve with salad.

FRICASSEE OF EGGS

6 *hard-boiled eggs*   1 *heaped teaspoon minced*
3 *teacups chicken or veal*   *onion*
stock   1½ *oz butter*
1 *heaped teaspoon minced*   3 *level tablespoons flour*
parsley   4 *tablespoons milk*
     Salt and pepper to taste

Shell and slice eggs. Melt butter. Stir in onion. Fry 2 minutes, then stir in flour. Gradually add stock. Stir till smooth and boiling. Season with salt and pepper to taste. Add eggs, milk, salt and pepper to taste. Mix lightly, then serve in a baked pastry case, or hollow out a mound of fluffy mashed potatoes, and pour in fricassée. Sprinkle with the parsley.

EGGS IN POTATO CASES

Take some potatoes which have been baked in their skins, cut them in halves, and scoop out all the potato pulp. Then mix it with a little butter, pepper and salt. Return the pulp to the skins, leaving a hollow in the centre. Boil some eggs soft. Shell them, and place them in the potatoes. Make a rich cheese sauce, and pour a little over each one. Place them in the oven till they are hot and a pale brown. Then sprinkle a little parsley over them, and serve them very hot.

Mrs Everard, 1911

EGG-IN-A-BED

2 *oz butter*   4 *oz Cheddar cheese, grated*
4 *oz mushrooms, sliced*   4 *eggs*
2 *tomatoes, skinned and*   4 *tablespoons single cream*
chopped   *Chopped parsley (optional)*
Salt and black pepper

Melt butter, fry mushrooms and chopped tomatoes, until tender, season to taste. Put the mixture plus half the cheese in the bottoms of 4 individual greased fireproof dishes. Break an egg into each dish. Pour 1 tablespoon cream gently over each, then top with the remaining cheese. Bake at 350°F (Gas Mark 4) for 8–10 minutes until eggs are set and cheese has melted. Serve immediately garnished with parsley.

LANCASHIRE EGGS

1 oz butter
1 teaspoon olive oil
½ lb Lancashire cheese

4 eggs
Salt and pepper

Put butter into a shallow fireproof dish with olive oil. Cover with slices of cheese, and melt over heat. Break the eggs on top and put into a moderate oven until the whites are set. Sprinkle with salt, pepper and grated cheese and brown under the grill.

EGG NESTS

1½ lb potatoes
2 tablespoons thin cream or
top milk

1 oz butter
4 eggs
1 oz grated cheese

Cook potatoes, drain well, mash with milk and butter. Divide into 4 portions and shape into round cakes. Hollow out the centre of each one, break in an egg and bake in a moderate oven for 10 minutes. Top with cheese and brown under the grill. For greater speed, poach eggs while you mash the potatoes, slip eggs into hollows, cover with cheese and brown the tops.

DEVILLED EGGS

2 tablespoons grated cheese
¼ teaspoon mustard
1 teaspoon tarragon vinegar
4 hard-boiled eggs

1 tablespoon melted butter
Salt and Cayenne pepper to
taste

Cut eggs in halves lengthwise. Remove egg yolks. Mash with cheese, mustard, vinegar, butter and enough milk to moisten. If liked, add a teaspoon grated onion or minced chives. Fill egg whites. Serve on tiny rounds of fried bread, or with sardines and potato salad as an hors-d'oeuvre course. Allow 2 halves per person.

EGGS IN PARSLEY SAUCE

6 hard-boiled eggs
2 teacups medium-thick
parsley sauce

Grated cheese to taste
Salt and black pepper to taste

Shell and slice eggs. Place in a greased pie-dish. Season with salt and black pepper to taste. Add pinch of ground mace to taste to sauce and pour over. Sprinkle thickly with grated cheese. Cover with stale breadcrumbs Dab here and there with butter. Bake in a moderate oven until brown.

CHICKEN OMELETTE

1 teacup finely chopped
chicken
1 oz butter
2 tablespoons flour

1 teacup milk
4 eggs
4 tablespoons hot water
Salt and pepper to taste

Melt butter in a small saucepan. Add flour. Stir till frothy, then add milk. Stir till smooth and boiling. Season with salt and pepper to taste. Add a rounded teaspoon of minced chives or parsley if liked, a pinch of ground mace, or grated cheese to taste. Keep hot. Beat egg whites till stiff. Beat yolks till thick and lemon-coloured. Beat in hot water and salt and pepper to taste. Fold in stiffly beaten egg whites. Melt about 1 teaspoon of butter, just enough to cover bottom of small omelette pan. When hot, add egg mixture. Cook over a slow fire till puffy and light brown below, then slip under grill or in oven till top is dry. Don't overcook or it will be tough. Loosen edges, make a dent in centre, slip on to a flat hot dish, fill with creamed chicken, and fold in 2. Serve with spinach or green peas.

MUSHROOM OMELETTE

6 eggs
Salt and pepper
4 oz mushrooms

2 oz butter
Pinch of nutmeg
3 tablespoons cream

Beat eggs lightly with a fork and season with salt and pepper. Wipe the mushrooms and chop them finely, and cook until soft in half the butter. Season with salt and pepper and a pinch of nutmeg, remove from heat and add the cream. Keep hot. Heat the remaining butter, pour in the eggs, and cook until the top is just beginning to set. Pour mushrooms on top, fold over and sprinkle with a little chopped parsley.

TOMATO OMELETTE

Peel 6 tomatoes, and cut them into small pieces. Beat up a tablespoon of flour with a little milk into a smooth paste. Add 4 well-beaten eggs, pepper, salt and the tomatoes. Put ½ oz butter into a white enamelled frying pan, pour into the pan just sufficient of the mixture to just cover the pan, let it cook quickly, fold it over, and slide it on to a hot dish, and continue cooking the rest in the same manner.

DICK'S HOLIDAY COOK-UP

When our children were small we all 11 used to cram into one moderate-sized car to go on holiday. Later when the boys grew too big to be accommodated we used to select the half-fare-sized ones to travel by British Rail while we took the dog with us. Father was always cook for this one day each year and true to fashion he cooked what his mother had done for the 8 of them (we come from long lines of big families). Her object in those hard times in the early thirties, was to make a little go a very long way, but Dick adapted it for speed before the journey. It's really quick and easy to eat.

A panful of cold potatoes squashed up and put into hot frying pan with a little, not too much hot dripping. As many eggs as can be spared. Bacon previously cooked – if there are many more mouths than slices of bacon, just snip whatever you have into small pieces and cook these first, putting the potatoes on top and mashing bacon and potato together. When potato is cooking nicely, sprinkle with salt and pepper to taste (but don't be too mean with the pepper). Now pull the potato on one side in order to fry as many eggs as you have and put them, *unbroken*, on top of the potato – you may need to use 2 pans at this stage. Place the eggs carefully on top of the nicely browned potato, and in front of the assembled company break the yolks so that they run all over the spuds. Dish up really smartly on to nice hot plates.

Babs Honey

EGG RAREBIT

6 oz *Cheddar cheese*	2 *tablespoons brown ale or*
1 *level teaspoon dry mustard*	*milk*
Pepper	4 *slices bread*
	4 *eggs*

Grate cheese; place in a medium-sized saucepan, with mustard, a shake of pepper and ale or milk. Heat gently until cheese has melted, about 10 minutes, stirring occasionally. Poach eggs and put on to buttered toast. Pour on cheese mixture and brown under grill.

1866 EGGS AND CHEESE

1 oz butter
1 teaspoon olive oil
8 oz Lancashire cheese

4 eggs
Pepper

Melt the butter and oil in a shallow dish on top of the stove. Cut the cheese into slices, reserving about 1 oz for grating. Put cheese into the dish and melt cheese gently. Break the eggs on top. Cook at 350°F (Gas Mark 4) for 8 minutes. Sprinkle with pepper and grated cheese, and brown under the grill.

BOILED CHEESE

4 oz of good mild rich English cheese cut in thin slices, a piece of butter the size of 2 walnuts, 2 tablespoons of good cream. Put all into a stewpan and keep stirring till it boils and is quite smooth. Then add the white and yolk of an egg. Stir it quickly, put it into a dish and brown it before the fire. No cheese must be used that is old or with the blue mould. Dry toast is to be sent up into it.

Mrs Garden, 1847

CHEESE AND POTATO DISH

2 lb potatoes
A little finely chopped onion
(optional)
8 oz grated Cheddar cheese
1 level teaspoon salt

½ level teaspoon pepper
½ level teaspoon nutmeg
4 tablespoons hot stock or
water

Scrub and peel the potatoes; put into cold salted water, bring to the boil and parboil for about 15 minutes. Drain and, when cool enough, cut into ½ inch dice and toss with the finely chopped onion, if used. Put alternate layers of diced potato and grated cheese into a greased fireproof dish, seasoning each layer; finish with a layer of grated Cheddar cheese. Add the stock or water, cover and place in a fairly hot oven, 400°F (Gas Mark 6). After 20 minutes uncover and brown in the oven or under the grill.

CHEESE CUSTARD PIES

If you have a little pastry left over, line as many small patty tins as your pastry will run to and fill with cheese custard. Make the cheese custard by beating together 2 eggs, a ½ pint of milk, about 2 oz grated cheese, a mustardspoon of made mustard, some pepper and salt. Bake in a moderate oven until the custard has set. Serve with a green salad.

CHEESE BALLS

Beat egg white stiff. Fold in tablespoon grated cheese. Drop spoonfuls into deep smoking fat. Drain on paper. Keep yolks for soups.

SUSSEX RAREBIT

Allow 3 oz Cheddar cheese for each person. Grate the cheese and put in a pan with some butter and a little old ale. Add some freshly ground black pepper, a teaspoon of mustard and a dessertspoon of cream for each person. Melt slowly, stirring until all the ingredients are well blended. As soon as it bubbles, serve on rounds of hot toast in deep plates into which you have poured a little spiced beer.

BOMBAY TOAST (1)

From slices of bread half an inch thick, cut out rounds small or large, as preferred, fry them a nice brown. Spread a layer of any kind of minced or potted meat on them, and place a little chutney on top of meat. Place a little grated or thinly sliced cheese on top of all and grill quickly until cheese is toasted. If liked, the cheese may be toasted separately and added last before serving.

BOMBAY TOAST (2)

2 eggs
1 oz butter
Some chopped chutney

Some rounds of buttered
toast
1 teaspoon anchovy essence
Salt and Cayenne pepper

Melt the butter in a saucepan and then add beaten eggs. Stir well and just before eggs are set add other ingredients; continue stirring until mixture thickens properly but be careful not to overcook. Spread this mixture on the rounds of buttered toast and serve very hot, immediately.

CHEESE PATTIES

Put 1 oz of butter in a saucepan over the fire with ¾ oz of flour. When mixed stir in 1½ gills of milk, let it cook well; then set aside to cool. Beat up 3 yolks and 2 whites of eggs, stir into the saucepan with salt, Cayenne, and 2 ozs of grated cheese, and mix well together. Line some patty pans with pastry, fill with the cheese mixture, and bake till the pastry is done. Serve hot.

Mrs Holt, Oldham

CHEESE FRITTERS

1¼ lb raw potatoes
2 tablespoons self-raising flour
8 oz grated Cheddar cheese

Pinch of salt
Fat for frying
1 oz castor sugar and pinch of ground mace

Peel the washed raw potatoes, mince or grate them finely. Stir in the flour and cheese. Drop tablespoons of the mixture into a pan containing ½ inch of fat at frying temperature. Fry gently, turning to brown on both sides. Lift from the fat carefully and drain. Sprinkle with sugar and ground mace, and serve hot.

CHEESE SCOTCH EGGS

6 oz grated Cheddar cheese
1½ oz flour
1 level teaspoon salt
Pinch Cayenne pepper
½ teaspoon Worcester sauce
1 egg

1-2 tablespoons milk or cream
4 hard-boiled eggs
Dried breadcrumbs
Deep fat for frying

Mix the grated cheese, flour and seasonings, add the Worcester sauce, beaten egg and milk or cream and beat well. Using wet hands coat the hard-boiled eggs completely with the cheese mixture. Roll them in dried breadcrumbs. Fry in hot deep fat to a golden brown, taking about 2 minutes to allow the cheese mixture to cook through. Drain, cool slightly and cut across in half. Garnish and serve hot with tomato sauce or cold with salad.

CHEESE ONION BAKE

4 large onions
4 slices buttered toast
4 oz grated Cheddar cheese
1 egg

¼ pint milk
1 level teaspoon salt
Pinch of paprika pepper
½ oz butter

Peel the onions and cook until almost tender in boiling salted water. Drain and cut into rings. Prepare the toast and arrange neatly in a fireproof dish. Pile on the onion rings and sprinkle liberally with the grated cheese. Beat the egg, add the milk and seasonings, and pour over the onions. Dot with butter and bake in a moderate oven at 350°F (Gas Mark 4) for approximately 30 minutes.

HOT CHEESE SAVOURY

2 eggs
¼ pint double cream
4 oz grated cheese –
Lancashire for choice

Salt and pepper
Cayenne pepper
Grated nutmeg

Beat eggs. Stir in cream and cheese. Season with salt and pepper, a little cayenne and a little nutmeg. Divide mixture between 4 individual heat-proof dishes or one small casserole. Sprinkle with remaining cheese. Bake in a hot oven at 400°F (Gas Mark 6) until just beginning to brown on top for 20–25 minutes. Serve really hot with toast.

CAULIFLOWER CHEESE

1 medium-sized cauliflower
1 oz butter
1 oz plain flour
½ pint milk or milk and
cauliflower-water
4 oz grated Cheddar cheese

½ level teaspoon salt
1 level teaspoon made
mustard
Pinch nutmeg
1 tablespoon browned crumbs

Soak the cauliflower in cold water for about 15 minutes, then break into flowerets. Cook in a little boiling salted water in a covered pan until tender and arrange neatly in a fireproof dish. Melt the butter, add the flour and cook for 1 minute. Remove from heat, add milk or milk and cauliflower water gradually. Bring to the boil, stirring well. Cook for a minute, remove from the heat, add the seasonings and 3 oz cheese, and stir until the cheese has melted. Coat the cauliflower with the cheese sauce. Mix and sprinkle over the remaining cheese and browned crumbs. Brown under a hot grill or in a fairly hot oven at 400°F (Gas Mark 6). Serve hot.

CHEESE AND ONIONS

4 medium onions
¼ pint milk

Salt and pepper
4 oz grated cheese

Peel and slice the onions. Cook until tender in very little water. Add milk and seasoning. Bring to the boil and turn into an ovenproof dish. Cover with cheese and brown under the grill. Serve with bread and butter. A nice supper dish.

EIGHTEENTH-CENTURY CHESHIRE RAMEKIN

'Take some old Cheshire Cheese, a lump of fresh butter and the Yolk of a hard boiled new-laid Egg, and beat them very well together in a Marble Mortar. Spread it on some slices of Bread toasted and buttered, hold a Salamander over them and send them up.'

CHEESE PUDDING

1 pint milk
¼ lb breadcrumbs
1 tablespoon butter
2 eggs

¼ lb grated Double
Gloucester
Pepper and salt

Pour hot milk on to breadcrumbs, adding a tablespoon of butter, leave to cool then add 2 beaten eggs, grated cheese, salt and pepper to taste. Turn into a greased pie dish and bake in a moderate oven until the mixture has set and the top is nicely browned. Time about 40 minutes.

GLOUCESTERSHIRE POTATO CAKES

½ lb cooked potatoes
2 oz flour
2 oz grated Double
Gloucester

1 egg
A little butter

Mash the potatoes thoroughly with a little butter. Work in the flour and cheese. Beat the egg and add it to the mixture. Roll out and cut into small round cakes which can either be baked in the oven, 325°F (Gas Mark 2), or cooked on a girdle or heavy frying pan.

DALE APPLE SAVOURY

Breadcrumbs
2 large apples

4 oz grated Wensleydale
cheese
¼ pint milk

Grease a baking dish and line it with breadcrumbs. Peel, core and slice the apples in rings, and layer the bottom of the dish with half the amount. Cover with half the grated Wensleydale and repeat the layers. Cover with the milk and finally sprinkle some buttered breadcrumbs on top. Bake in a moderate oven, 375°F (Gas Mark 4), for about a ½ hour until the apples are done.

WENSLEYDALE PUDDING

2 oz breadcrumbs
2 oz grated Wensleydale
cheese

1 egg
¼ pint milk
tomato

Grease pie dish. Beat egg yolk and milk. Mix breadcrumbs and cheese, and pour milk and egg yolk over this, whip egg white until stiff and fold into the mixture. Sprinkle with a little more grated cheese and a few slices of tomatoes. Bake at 400° F (Gas Mark 6) for 15–20 minutes.

CHEESE PUFFS

4 rounds of toast
2 egg whites

4 oz Wensleydale cheese
¼ teaspoon baking powder

Whip egg whites until stiff, add cheese and baking powder. Pile on to the toast and grill.

11 Vegetables and Salads

'*Tis not her coldness, father,*
That chills my labouring breast;
It's that confounded cucumber
I've ate, and can't digest.

> '*Legends of Mirth and Marvel*', Thomas Ingoldsby

First Early Vegetables

Beetroot: Try baking these for the fullest flavour. Wrap them in foil, stand on a rack, and cook in a moderate oven for about 1 hour (young roots). If the flesh yields when pressed, the beetroot is done.

Broad Beans: When young, cook in boiling salted water for 15 minutes. When old, allow 30 minutes, and slip the beans out of the skins to serve.

Carrots: Wash and scrub carrots, and cook whole in as little water as possible for 15 minutes, rubbing off the skin after cooking.

French Beans: Use very young and fresh, and if small, cook them whole or in chunks (the same applies to runner beans, as shredding dissipates flavour into the cooking water). Just cover in salted water with a lump of sugar, and cook for 15 minutes.

Globe Artichokes: Cut off stems, and invert artichokes in a deep bowl of cold water for 1 hour. Plunge into boiling salted water and cook until the leaves pull away easily. Drain very thoroughly before serving.

Peas: Cook in just enough quickly boiling, salted water to cover, with a lump of sugar and a sprig of mint, for about 15 minutes with the lid off.

Potatoes: Wash them, leaving the skins on and plunge into boiling salted water. Cook for 15–20 minutes, remove skins, and toss in melted butter.

Turnips: Peel thickly, and cook in boiling salted water for 20 minutes.

Choosing potatoes

Certain varieties of potato are more suitable for different ways of cooking than others, choose the right varieties for your dish, and see that you cook them in the best possible way.

Boiling (red or white varieties): Just cover with cold salted water, bring to the boil and when tender drain off all the water and stand the pan over a low heat allowing the steam to escape, for 2–3 minutes. If they have to be kept hot longer than this, do not put back the lid of the pan, instead cover with a crumpled tea cloth pressed well down on top of the potatoes. This will absorb any steam still left and keep in the heat.

To boil new potatoes, have ready some boiling salted water, put in the potatoes and boil till just soft.

Steaming (red or white varieties): See that the water is fully boiling before putting the potatoes in the steamer. Cook 1½–2 hours.

Mashing and Creaming (red varieties): Cook as for boiling, add hot milk and butter till you have the required consistency. Stir with a lifting movement to keep the potatoes light.

Deep Frying (white varieties for chips or crisps): Cut the potatoes into fingers or wafers, rinse well in cold water then dry in a clean cloth. Do not attempt to cook too many at one time, as the fat must be able to circulate round the potatoes.

Sauté-ing (red or white varieties): Partly boil unpeeled potatoes, peel and dice them, then fry in hot melted butter until a golden brown. Drain and serve very hot.

Roasting (red or white varieties): Put the raw peeled potatoes into really hot dripping around the joint, cook in a hot oven and baste or turn the potatoes once or twice during cooking to ensure a glistening brown crust.

Baking in skins (red or white varieties): Scrub the skins, prick with a fork or skewer and rub lightly all over with butter or cooking fat. Bake in a hot oven, 1 hour. Before serving, cut a cross in the top squeeze gently to let out the steam and press a knob of butter into the cut.

Salads (white varieties): Cook the potatoes until just done so that they do not break up. If you want the flavour of the dressing to be absorbed by the potatoes then add it while still hot. To keep the potato flavour distinct add dressing when the potatoes are cold.

1915 VICTORIA POTATOES

Peel and boil the usual amount of potatoes, but take them off the fire when they are almost, but not quite cooked. Strain them, and cut each one into thin slices. Butter a pie-dish, and put in the potato.

Make a white sauce with a $\frac{1}{2}$ oz of butter, a $\frac{1}{2}$ oz of flour, and a $\frac{1}{4}$ pint of milk, boil it up well, and pour over the potatoes. Sprinkle a $\frac{1}{2}$ oz of grated cheese over the top, and bake in a moderate oven until the top is nicely browned.

If you prefer quite plain potatoes, steam them instead of boiling. You haven't a steamer? Well, use a colander, stand it in a pan of boiling water and it will answer the same purpose.

When the potatoes are cooked, turn them into a hot dish and sprinkle them lightly with salt.

If I have any good dripping in the larder, I steam the potatoes, season and mash them up with about a $\frac{1}{2}$ oz of it.

About vegetables

If boiled potatoes have to stand awhile before being served, cover them over with a thick cloth, and stand the pan where they will keep warm, but will not scorch. The cloth absorbs the moisture, and helps to make the potatoes floury.

To remove the smell of cooked onions from a pot, fill it with boiling water and drop in a red-hot cinder.

If you wish to prevent green vegetables from boiling over, drop a piece of dripping the size of a walnut into the centre of them, just as they commence to boil.

When peeling onions, hold them under a tap of running water, or stand at an open window. No matter how weak one's eyes may be, they will not smart if onions are peeled in either of these ways.

If a cauliflower is tied up in a piece of muslin it can, when cooked, easily be lifted from the pan to the colander. There is no risk of its being broken. This will also keep it free from scum.

Miss T. Hempsall, Moorthorpe, 1913

BOILED NEW POTATOES

A root of potatoes freshly dug rarely has equal-sized potatoes on it, yet it seems wicked to cut the beautiful big young ones. So when peeled, have ready your pan of boiling salted water and put the large ones in for about 7 minutes before adding the smaller ones. About 5 minutes before they are all cooked, add 2 or 3 sprigs of freshly picked mint. Before straining off the potato water remove the mint from the pan. Dish the potatoes into a hot dish and serve with dabs of butter.

BAKED POTATOES

Potatoes for baking should have the skins brushed with melted butter or cooking fat, and pricked to allow the steam to escape. Bake 1–1¼ hours at 400°F (Gas Mark 6). To serve, mark a cross on top of the potato, squeeze gently, held in a cloth, sprinkle with salt and place a knob of butter in the cross.

The potatoes may be cut in half, the cut side wiped dry, and placed cut side down on a greased tin. This will reduce the cooking time to 30–40 minutes.

Variations for baked potato fillings

When the potato has been baked, scoop out the flesh, mash, and add any of the variations listed below:

1. Chopped cooked meat, beef, ham, bacon and garnish with parsley.
2. Flaked fish and butter.
3. Chopped grilled kidney, garnished with fried onion rings.
4. Chopped boiled egg and mayonnaise, garnished with sieved egg yolk.
5. Chopped fried mushrooms.
6. Sultanas and cubes of cheese.
7. Minced ham and savoury sauce.
8. Grated cheese and egg yolk.
9. Flaked salmon and squeeze lemon juice.
10. Chopped chives and tomato purée.
11. Flaked cooked kipper fillets and lemon juice.
12. Cottage cheese and chopped chives.
13. Scrambled egg and chopped fried bacon.
14. Minched chicken and sauté-ed chopped mushrooms.

BAKED CHEESEY POTATOES

4 *large potatoes*	1 *egg*
1 *oz butter*	*Salt and pepper*
2–3 *oz grated cheese*	

Scrub the potatoes, dry them and brush with melted fat. Bake in a hot oven for about 1 hour. Cut a slice from the top of each potato, scoop out the inside and mash well with the butter, cheese, egg yolk and seasoning. Whisk the egg white and fold into the mashed potato. Place the potatoes in the skins again, and heat in the oven for 5–10 minutes.

POTATO SAUSAGE ROLLS

Scrub average size potatoes, remove the centres from each with an apple corer. Fill cavities with sausage meat mixed with a little finely chopped onion if liked. Wrap each potato in a rasher of bacon, cover with foil, and bake at 400°F (Gas Mark 6) for 1 hour.

FOIL POTATOES

4 large potatoes   *2 medium onions*
2 oz butter   *Salt and pepper*

Peel potatoes and cut crosswise in 4 slices. Spread butter thickly between each slice and on top. Reassemble potatoes with onion slices between. Season with salt and pepper and wrap each potato tightly in double foil. Bake at 325°F (Gas Mark 3) for 1½ hours. Open foil and sprinkle with parsley, or brown in the oven. These potato parcels may be prepared in advance, then cooked at the right time.

SCOTS POTATO FRITTERS

6 large potatoes   *1 tablespoon lean ham*
2 eggs   *Dripping*
1 tablespoon breadcrumbs

Parboil the potatoes and cut them in thick slices (about ¼ inch). Beat up the eggs with the finely grated breadcrumbs and grated ham. Dip each slice of potato in this mixture and fry in plenty of good hot dripping. These are grand by themselves or for serving with any kind of fried meat.

SCALLOPED NEW POTATOES

3 oz butter   *2 oz fresh breadcrumbs*
1½ lb new potatoes (all   *Salt and pepper*
similar in size, scraped)

Melt 2 oz butter in a medium to large saucepan. Add the whole potatoes. Spread them out so they cover the base of the pan in one layer, and cover. Cook very slowly to prevent butter from burning. Turn the potatoes over, several times during cooking, so that they turn golden all over. Cook for ½–1 hour (depending on size of potatoes). When tender, add remaining 1 oz butter. Turn the heat up and add the breadcrumbs and seasoning. Cook 3–4 minutes, stirring continuously until the breadcrumbs have absorbed the butter, and have turned crisp and golden.

NORTHUMBERLAND PAN HAGGERTY

2 *lb potatoes cut in slices*   3 *oz grated cheese*
1 *lb onions sliced*   *Salt and pepper*
1 *tablespoon dripping*

Place layers of potatoes, onion and grated cheese in a heavy frying pan.
Season each layer, fry gently till brown. Keep a lid on the pan and cook
until the vegetables are brown.

DELICIOUS POTATOES

3½ *lb potatoes*   3 *oz grated cheese*
3 *oz butter*   *Salt and pepper*
1 *carton double cream (5 oz)*

Peel potatoes thinly and cut into slices ⅛ inch thick. Place on a large piece
of foil, season well, add cream, sprinkle with cheese and dot with butter.
Make a secure parcel of the foil, put into a baking tin and bake in a hot
oven for 45 minutes to 1½ hours, or until potatoes are soft. Serve as an
accompaniment to meat or savoury dishes. Oven temperature 400°F (Gas
Mark 6).

Michael Jeffs

POTATO PAN HASH

1 *lb mashed potatoes*   *Salt and pepper*
Bacon fat or butter

Heat fat or butter in a frying pan. Add potato, smooth over, and cook
gently until crisp and brown underneath. Fold over with a fish slice and
slide on to a warm plate. Serve with mushrooms, bacon, tomatoes, eggs or
a little grated cheese.

STELK

2 *lb potatoes*   *A little milk*
2 *oz butter*   *Salt and pepper*
Bunch of spring onions

Boil potatoes in salted water, drain and mash, add the butter and keep hot.
Chop onions and cook until tender in a little milk, then beat into potatoes
until light and fluffy. Pile on serving plates, and put a good lump of butter
in a 'well' in each serving. The idea is to eat from the outside, dipping each
mouthful into the pool of butter. A comforting dish for tired children.

It's also excellent with a bit of boiled bacon, or with a few crisp rashers or sausages.

WELSH POTATO CAKES

1 *lb boiled potatoes*   1 *oz butter*
4 *oz plain flour*   1 *tablespoon sugar*
1 *teaspoon baking powder*   *Pinch of salt*
1 *egg*

Mix all the ingredients except the butter. Melt the butter and mix thoroughly with the rest. Roll out 1 inch thick. Bake on a girdle, or at 425°F (Gas Mark 7) for 20 minutes. Serve hot with a lot of butter. Cold potato cakes can be fried with the breakfast bacon.

WELSH ONION CAKE

1 *lb potatoes*   4 *oz butter*
½ *lb onions*   *Salt and pepper*

Use a well-buttered cake tin. Peel the potatoes, slice them fairly thinly and arrange in a layer on the bottom of the tin. Sprinkle a layer of finely chopped onion on the potatoes, add flakes of butter, salt and pepper. Continue in layers until the tin is full, finishing with a layer of potatoes and a few flakes of butter. Cover with a lid and bake at 350°F (Gas Mark 4) for 1 hour. Eat with hot or cold meat.

POTEN BEN FEDI

2 *lb potatoes*   1 *medium onion*
½ *lb minced cooked meat*   1 *oz butter*
1 *rasher bacon*   1 *tablespoon wholemeal flour*

This is a sort of Welsh washday dish, excellent for dealing with oddments from the weekend joint. Boil the potatoes and mash them with the butter and flour, then mix in the meat. Chop bacon and onion and cook in the fat which runs from the bacon until golden. Mix well into the potatoes, season to taste, and turn into a greased pie dish. Bake at 350°F (Gas Mark 4) for 30 minutes until the top is golden.

WELSH HOT POT

1 *lb potatoes*   8 *oz bacon*
8 *oz onions*   *Salt and pepper*

This can be cheaply made with bacon pieces. Slice potatoes fairly thickly, slice onions and cut bacon in neat pieces. Arrange in alternate layers in a casserole, season with salt and pepper. Cover with a lid and cook at 325°F (Gas Mark 3) for 2 hours. Remove lid and continue cooking for 20 minutes. Another version of this made in a saucepan and with the addition of water used to be called 'The Miser's Feast', with the miser eating the mashed up potatoes one day, and saving the slices of bacon to eat a second day.

CHAMP

8 *large potatoes*	*Salt and pepper*
6 *spring onions*	*Butter*
$\frac{1}{3}$ *pint milk*	

Let the peeled potatoes stand in cold water for 1 hour. Drain and cover with cold salted water, and boil until tender. Drain well and dry off by putting a folded cloth on top and returning the pot to a gentle heat for a few minutes. Chop the spring onions very finely, using the green tops as well as the bulbs, put them into a bowl and pour on boiling water to cover them. Drain the onions and add to the milk. Bring to the boil and pour on to the mashed potatoes, with pepper and salt to taste. When very light and fluffy, pile up on individual plates, making a well in the middle, and put a piece of butter in the 'well'. The potato is scooped up into the melted butter as it is eaten. Sometimes this is known as *thump* in Ireland. Another version, called *colcannon* includes chopped boiled curly kale or cabbage. The Welsh mixture of vegetables is a *stwns*, being a mixture of potatoes and swedes; potatoes and peas; or potatoes and broad beans, sometimes with buttermilk poured over.

BOXTY

2 *large raw potatoes*	1 *teaspoon bicarbonate of*
$\frac{3}{4}$ *lb mashed potatoes*	*soda*
2 *tablespoons plain flour*	1 *teaspoon salt*

Grate the raw potatoes and squeeze out the liquid. Add to the mashed potatoes and salt. Mix the soda with the flour and add to the potatoes. Roll out $\frac{1}{2}$ inch thick in a circle. Cut in 4 quarters and put on an ungreased girdle. Cook on gentle heat for 30 to 40 minutes, turning bread once. The farls or quarters should be well browned on both sides. A teaspoon of caraway seeds can be added to the dough.

STRAW POTATOES

Cut up some potatoes about the thickness of wooden matches. Well wash and dry them on a clean cloth. Place them in a wire basket, not more than a cupful at a time, and plunge them into a bath of boiling fat. Shake the potatoes until they are quite crisp and of a golden-yellow colour. Lift them out, put them on a clean cloth to drain, sprinkle with salt, and serve on a hot dish.

PEASE PUDDING (1)

1½ *pints split peas*   2 oz *dripping*
2 *eggs*   *Salt and pepper*
½ *teaspoon bicarbonate of soda*

Soak peas overnight in hot water, to which is added the soda. Mash them and tie loosely in a muslin bag. Boil for 2 hours. Press through a sieve, re-heat and add fat, beaten eggs, pepper and salt. Tie in a floured cloth and boil for 1 hour. Serve hot.

PEASE PUDDING (2)

Put 1½ pints of split peas into a clean cloth; tie loosely in order to allow them room to swell. Place in cold water, and let them boil until tender. They should be cooked enough in 2½ hours if the peas are new. Take them from the pot, remove them from the cloth, rub them through a sieve, add pepper, salt and a knob of butter about ½ oz, beat all together thoroughly for 5 or 6 minutes, put into a floured cloth, tie it tightly, and let it boil again for ¾ hour. This dish may be served with boiled or roast pork, or boiled beef.

JEANNIE'S PEASE PUDDING

Take a small handful of peas per person and soak for a while in cold water. Bring to the boil very carefully and cook slowly until tender 2½–3 hours. Then mash well, add pepper and salt to taste, a little finely chopped onion and a good sized knob of dripping. Place in a tin and bake in good oven for 25–30 minutes until nice and brown on top. Serve with cold boiled beet-root and cold meat.

Jeannie was a Scottish orphan brought up in a home and evacuated in 1940. She said they had pease pudding served every Monday without fail with cold meat. Just the same she had quite a liking for the dish.

Jeannie's Rhyme

Pease pudding hot; pease pudding cold,
Pease pudding in the pot 3 days old (or 3 weeks old if she was remembering unhappiness).

(The traditional time was 9 days.)

GARDENER'S CASSEROLE

1 *lb lean salt pork*	2 *lb green peas (weighed*
1 *lb small carrots*	*before shelling)*
6 *small onions*	1 *lb new potatoes*
1 *dessertspoon flour*	*Parsley, thyme, bayleaf*
	Salt and pepper

Dice the salt pork and brown in a saucepan. Add the whole carrots and onions and cook together for 5 minutes. Stir in the flour, mix well, and add hot water to cover. Cover tightly and simmer for 30 minutes. Add peas and potatoes, with a good sprinkling of chopped parsley and thyme, and a bayleaf. Season to taste and simmer for 1 hour.

VEGETABLES IN THE MILKY WAY

¾ *lb young carrots (prepared*	4 *tablespoons double cream*
and sliced)	4 *tablespoons milk*
1 *medium-sized swede –*	1½ *level tablespoons*
approx. 12 *oz (prepared and*	*cornflour*
diced)	5 *tablespoons cider*
	1 *level teaspoon castor sugar*
Sauce	*Salt and pepper*
1 *oz butter*	

Cook carrots and swedes together in boiling salted water for about 15 minutes, or until cooked. To make sauce, melt butter in a saucepan, add cream and milk. Blend cornflour with 2 tablespoons of the cider, and add to the cream mixture, with the remainder of the cider. Bring to the boil, stirring continuously. Add sugar and seasonings, and simmer for 2–3 minutes. Drain vegetables and mix with sauce. Serve hot.

BUTTERED PEAS AND CARROTS

2 *lb peas (in pods)*	1 *small onion*
1 *lb new carrots*	2 *oz butter*
1 *small lettuce heart*	*Salt and sugar*

Cut the carrots in small strips and cook in boiling water for 5 minutes. Drain well. Put shelled peas, shredded lettuce, chopped onion, and a pinch each of sugar and salt in a pan with the carrots and just cover with boiling water. Cook very gently until the water is nearly absorbed, then add the butter and serve at once.

STAFFORDSHIRE SAVOURY VEGETABLE MARROW

1 *large marrow*	3 *tablespoons breadcrumbs*
1 *lb cold meat*	1 *oz dripping*
1 *oz flour*	2 *oz ham or bacon*
1 *teaspoon salt*	1 *teaspoon chopped parsley*
½ *teaspoon pepper*	1 *or 2 tomatoes*

Cut marrow through about 2 inches from the end. Remove all seed and pulp. Peel the larger part and boil for 5 minutes. Mince the meat and all the ingredients except the dripping. Moisten with stock or water, mix well. Dry marrow well on outside, stuff it with the mixture, replace the cut off end, tie on firmly, put in a baking dish, bake in a moderate oven for 1 hour basting with the dripping. Serve hot together with tomato sauce or gravy.

STUFFED CABBAGE

1 *cabbage*	*onion and parsley*
2 *tablespoons rice*	½ *lb sausage meat, seasoned to*
1 *tablespoon each chopped*	*taste*

Take a firm head of cabbage, pour boiling water over it, let stand for 15 minutes, drain cover again with boiling water, let stand for 30 minutes, drain and shake dry. Make a stuffing of the meat, onion, parsley, rice and seasoning, cut stalk out, put in some mixture, fold over 2 or 3 leaves, cover with another layer of mixture, and continue until each layer is stuffed; press all firmly together and tie in a cloth; put in a pan of salted water, and boil for 1½ hours. When cooked, remove cloth, put cabbage in a deep dish and serve with melted butter or white sauce.

CREAMED CABBAGE

Take 2 white cabbages (sometimes called cow cabbages) and shred them. Throw them into fast boiling water. Let them boil for about ½ hour until tender, drain through a colander, press them between 2 plates to drain away all moisture. Put 2 oz butter into a stewpan, pepper and salt, and work in a tablespoon of flour, adding gradually ½ pint of milk or a little cream. Stir in the cabbbage and let it cook about 10 minutes, and serve.

RED CABBAGE CASSEROLE

1 *small red cabbage*	*Salt and pepper*
1 oz *dripping*	*Flour*
1 *onion*	¾ *pint stock*
1 *apple*	*3 tablespoons vinegar*

Shred cabbage finely. Melt dripping, add chopped onion and apple, season with salt and pepper, sprinkle with flour, stir well and add cabbage. Pour in stock and vinegar. Cook with lid on for 2½ hours at 325°F (Gas Mark 3).

BRAISED CARROTS

Cut the carrots into rounds about 1 inch thick. Put them into boiling salted water and when nearly done, remove them into a stewpan with a little cayenne and 1½ oz butter. Let them simmer gently in this for about ¾ hour or less, shaking them continually to prevent their burning. Remove the carrots to a hot vegetable dish, pour the liquor over them, sprinkle with chopped parsley and serve.

MASHED CARROTS

Take 6 or more large carrots, wash and scrape them, place them in boiling water salted, and when soft remove and mash them. Replace in the saucepan with only a little of the water they were boiled in, add 1 oz butter, pepper, and a little gravy or milk. Stir them over the fire until they are nearly dry, and serve in a hot vegetable dish.

GLAZED CARROTS

Scrape and cut into even slices 6 or 7 large carrots. Throw them into boiling salted water and let them partly boil. Remove them, and place them in a saucepan with a lump of sugar, 2 oz butter, and sufficient stock to cover them. Let it boil very quickly until the stock is reduced to a glaze, shake over the fire until the carrots are covered with the gravy and serve.

MRS C's FANCY WAY WITH CARROTS

2 lb carrots   *Salt and pepper*
4 oz butter

Use a large flat saucepan. Melt the butter, add pepper to taste, and toss the prepared carrots in the melted fat. Add hot water to cover and salt to taste, and bring to boil. Simmer to taste. This is delicious. Mrs C. comes of farming stock but was left a widow with two very young children. She became a 'dinner lady' and eventually came to work for the Honey family. She was a pillar of strength, helping once or twice a week when there were 10 or more to feed every day. She managed to do a great deal of voluntary work for Boys' Clubs, Army Cadets, etc. and now runs a canteen for Old Age Pensioners in Bath.

BOILED CELERY

Cut off the outer leaves of the celery, wash it carefully, make the stalks even, put into boiling salted water, but do not cover it with the lid. Let it boil gently for ¾ hour if the celery is young or longer if older. Have ready some pieces of toast, and when the celery is cooked, dip the toast into the liquor the celery was boiled in. Place it on the toast, pour over some melted butter and serve.

BRAISED CELERY

Take the required heads of celery, cut off the roots, outer leaves, and green tops, cut into halves, and then into even lengths. Place in a saucepan 2 oz butter, and when it is melted put 2 oz each of onion, carrot and turnip in the same saucepan. Wash well and blanch the celery in boiling salted water for 15 minutes. Remove it, and place it on top of the other vege- tables. Cover with a buttered paper, put on the lid of the saucepan, and fry all together for 12 minutes. Add 1½ pints of stock, braise it gently for 2 hours, or until the celery is tender. Divide the pieces again, and place them on long snippets of bread, and serve.

TO COOK FRENCH BEANS

12 oz French beans   *Pinch of salt*
3 tablespoons butter   *Few grains of ucayenne pepper*
1 tablespoon lemon juice   *4 tablespoons water*

Cut large beans in chunks, but leave small ones whole. Cover them with cold water, and bring to the boil only. Drain the beans. Melt the butter in a heavy saucepan and add the lemon juice, salt and pepper and water. Add the beans and cook slowly for 10 minutes. This method can be used for frozen beans now, but the preliminary cooking will not then be necessary.

HARICOT BEANS

Chop 1 onion very finely, and put it into a stewpan with a little butter and flour. Let it cook until the butter is browned. Pour in a little water or stock, and stir until it thickens. Add to this the haricot beans, which have been soaking all night in water, and boil until tender. Simmer for about 25 minutes and serve hot.

HARICOT BEANS IN TOMATO SAUCE

Soak the beans overnight, put them into a saucepan and cover with cold water. Add 1 carrot, 1 onion, 1 turnip, $\frac{1}{2}$ a head of celery, pepper and salt to taste. Let them boil slowly until sufficiently cooked. Remove the vegetables, drain the beans, place them in a hot dish and cover them with tomato sauce, and serve with croûtons round the dish.

LEEKS

Leeks are delicious if fried in dripping (or butter) or roast round beef, lamb or pork (for about 25 minutes), drained and served in hot dish. The resulting fat from the draining makes a tasty foundation for the accompanying gravy, or for soup.

SAVOURY LENTILS

Wash 1 lb dried lentils overnight, and leave soaking in clean cold water. Next day drain them. Meanwhile place in a suitable saucepan the lentils, 3 or 4 rashers of streaky bacon, 1 chopped clove of garlic (if liked), 1 diced carrot, 1 chopped onion, 1 bay leaf and a sprig of thyme. Barely cover with cold water and bring slowly to the boil. When boiling, transfer the pan to the oven and allow to go on cooking gently until the lentils are quite soft. Add more liquid during this cooking if necessary. Serve the lentils with boiled ham, pork or bacon.

BOILED LENTILS

There are two kinds of lentils, the red and the green. The red are perhaps preferable. Soak the required quantity in water overnight. In the morning drain them and throw them into boiling salted water, and let them cook without breaking for about a $\frac{1}{2}$ hour, or longer if not soft enough. Drain them, return them to the saucepan, add 1 oz of butter, pepper, and a dessertspoon of vinegar, shake over the fire till hot, and serve.

LENTIL PUDDING

This is very nice with boiled pork.

Mix with a teacupful of milk 2 oz cornflour and 3 oz of lentil flour. Boil a pint of milk with pepper, salt and powdered herbs to taste. Add this to the mixed lentil flour and cornflour. When this is cool, whisk in 3 eggs, boil for 2 hours, and serve with a white sauce.

CREAMED LENTILS

Soak a pint of lentils overnight in cold water. Next day throw them into salted, boiling water, and allow them to boil for 3 hours. Strain them, and add half a teacup of thick cream, pepper, salt (if required) and simmer gently for 5 minutes. Serve very hot.

FRIED LETTUCE

Carefully wash and dry lettuce leaves. Fry them in butter until brown on both sides. Season with salt and pepper and serve as a garnish for boiled chicken or ham.

DRESSED LETTUCE

Wash and dry some crisp lettuce leaves. Shred lengthways in 1 inch wide strips. Chop a few leaves of fresh mint and sprinkle on the lettuce. Chop very finely some young onions and sprinkle on lettuce. Sprinkle with a little salt and pepper and a little sugar. Cover the whole, but do not make awash, with equal quantities of vinegar and milk to which has been added a little made mustard.

BRAISED LETTUCE

4 *small well-hearted lettuce*	1 *dessertspoon chopped*
1 *small onion*	*parsley*
1 *rasher lean bacon*	*Salt and pepper*
1 *tablespoon olive oil*	1 *lump of sugar*
1 *tablespoon butter*	*Pinch of nutmeg*
4 *tomatoes*	

Wash the lettuce but keep them whole, plunge into boiling salted water and bring water to boil again. Take out lettuce and drain them thoroughly. Heat oil and butter and add chopped bacon and onion, stir until lightly coloured, and add skinned and chopped tomatoes. Stir until the mixture begins to form a sauce, then put in lettuce, parsley and seasonings. Cover pan tightly and simmer very gently for 30 minutes. If liked add a dozen stoned olives before serving. This is very good with lamb. Most people are surprised at cooking lettuce, but it's a useful answer to the glut, and delicious.

CREAMED FIELD MUSHROOMS

Field mushrooms   *Creamy milk*
Butter   *Salt and pepper*

This simple dish is best made with field mushrooms and is very good for breakfast or supper. The mushrooms may be served with crisp bacon, or on toast. Wipe and slice the mushrooms and cook gently in a little butter until it is almost absorbed. Add a teacup of creamy milk and continue cooking for about 10 minutes. Add a little more milk and cook 2 or 3 minutes longer, so the mushrooms are in a light creamy sauce. Season to taste.

MUSHROOM SALAD

8 oz mushrooms   *1 clove garlic*
8 tablespoons olive oil   *Salt and black peppercorns*
2 tablespoons lemon juice   *Chopped parsley*

Many people have not tried raw mushrooms, but they are delicious served as a salad, in particular with shellfish.

Wipe mushrooms and slice thinly, including the stalks. Mix oil and lemon juice, crushed garlic and freshly ground black pepper. Pour over mushrooms. Leave for a couple of hours until they have absorbed most of the dressing. Just before serving, season with salt and sprinkle with chopped parsley.

MUSHRUMPS IN CREAM

1 lb mushrooms   *Salt and pepper*
3 tablespoons butter   *8 fluid oz cream*
2 tablespoons plain flour   *Parsley*
Pinch of thyme

Wipe the mushrooms and leave whole or cut in thick slices according to size. Toss in the butter until just soft. Sprinkle with flour and add thyme, salt and pepper. Add the cream and cook over very low heat for 5 minutes, stirring gently. Serve with plenty of chopped parsley. (Mushrooms were commonly referred to as mushrumps in eighteenth-century recipes.)

Eighteenth-century Recipe

BUTTERED MUSHROOMS

Take ½ lb button mushrooms; put them in a saucepan with 3 oz butter and let them get slightly browned. Sprinkle salt and pepper over them and let them cook without burning until they are quite tender. They should be served as they are, on toast, and will be found to make a nice breakfast dish.

STEWED MUSHROOMS

Trim and clean a pound of mushrooms, and put them into a saucepan with ¼ lb fresh butter, ½ pint veal stock, and salt and pepper to taste. Let this stew very gently for 1½ hours. If required, thicken with a little corn-flour. Serve in an entrée dish with snippets of dry toast around.

GRILLED MUSHROOMS

Take some large field mushrooms, peel the outside top skin, and trim the stalks. Season with pepper and salt and steep them in a marinade of oil, or fresh butter melted. Grill over a clear fire, but not too fierce, on both sides. Serve with melted butter on a hot dish, and a squeeze of lemon on each mushroom.

BAKED ONIONS

Take the required number of medium-sized Spanish onions. Remove the outer skins and boil them in salted water for 15 minutes, then throw them into cold water. Drain well, cut them in halves, and arrange on a well-buttered baking tin. Bake in a quick oven, basting them with butter until they are tender and brown, and serve.

BRAISED ONIONS

Peel 6 or more large onions, or, if preferred, choose medium ones; place them in a pan with 4 oz beef dripping, cover the pan with a closely fitting lid, and let them cook until quite soft and brown. Then take out the onions, thicken the liquor with a little cornflour, salt and pepper to taste, and the juice of ½ a lemon. Serve with steak or roast beef.

BOILED ONIONS

Peel the required number of onions and throw them into boiling salted water for 10 minutes; take them out and put them in cold water for 1 hour. Drain the onions and place them in a saucepan with sufficient water to cover them, and a little salt. Let them boil gently until quite tender, take them up, drain them and place on a hot dish with some melted butter poured over them.

ONIONS BAKED IN THEIR JACKETS

Choose decent-sized onions, 1 per person, or more for gluttons. Remove only very loose outer dried up leaves, retaining as much outer cover as possible. Place on a baking tin in the bottom of an oven and cook until tender in the middle, testing with a skewer or knitting needle. Take from the oven, cool only enough to be able to remove the onions on to a suitable dish. Eat on side plates, with a spoon, accompanied by butter, salt and pepper. Very good for children's or older people's supper dish, served with grated cheese and wholemeal bread.

IRISH BAKED ONIONS

Parboil as many onions as are needed, then drain them. Mix together some cold minced meat, chopped parsley, a little brown stock or gravy, and seasoning. Scoop out a teaspoonful from the centre of each onion, blend this with the meat mixture, and fill up the centres.

Bake the onions in a moderate oven until they are tender. Then stand each one upon a round of fried bread, and pour some thick brown, or tomato sauce round the dish, and garnish with sprigs of fried parsley.

1915

STUFFED ONIONS

4 medium-sized onions   *2 oz butter*
2 oz fresh breadcrumbs   *Salt and pepper*
6 oz grated Cheddar cheese

Peel and parboil the onions for 20 minutes. Remove from the pan and cool slightly. Take the centres out very carefully and chop them. Mix with the breadcrumbs and 4 oz cheese. Season and stuff the onion cases. Put into an ovenproof dish and dot with butter. Bake in a moderately hot oven 375°F (Gas Mark 5) for 45–55 minutes. Sprinkle the remaining cheese on top of the onions 15 minutes before end of cooking time. Serve with toast and quartered tomatoes.

ONION SAVOURY

1 *lb onions*	*2 eggs*
1 *pint milk*	*Parsley*

Cook the sliced onions in the milk, then beat in the egg yolks. Whisk the egg whites until stiff, fold them into the onion mixture, add a little chopped parsley, salt and pepper to taste. Bake in a greased dish in a moderate oven until firm.

VICTORIAN SEAKALE

An excellent vegetable and most easy of digestion. When in full season it may be bought quite cheaply. It must be well washed to free it from grit and sand, all the dark parts are to be cut away near the roots and tied into small bundles and thrown into plenty of boiling salted water; when quite soft take them up, drain thoroughly, untie the bundles and arrange on a folded napkin on a dish. Serve with melted butter.

This is a most delicious and different addition to the menu – the poor man's asparagus, in fact and as easy to grow as brussels sprouts. The leaves are a beautiful silvery blue useful in floral decorations.

VICTORIAN SALSIFY

Put into a stewpan ¼ lb beef suet, cut into small squares, add one bayleaf, 3 or 4 cloves, 1 onion, a little piece of thyme, and a teaspoon of salt. Stir it all together on the fire for about 5 minutes, then add 2 tablespoons of flour, stir well and gently add 3 pints of water. Prepare about a dozen salsify by scraping until they are white; rub them with lemon, and put them in cold water for about ½ hour before they are required. When the ingredients in the saucepan are nearly boiling put in the salsify and let them simmer till tender, which will be in about 1 hour.

SORREL PURÉE

Fry in butter 2 large onions until they are a golden yellow colour. Dredge a little flour over them, add a pinch of grated nutmeg, a small piece of sugar, salt, pepper and a ½ pint of gravy or stock. Take a peck (2 gallons) of fresh sorrel, pick away the stalks, wash it in 3 or 4 waters, and boil it for $\frac{1}{4}$ hour, or until tender in a very little water, say, $\frac{1}{2}$ pint. Drain the sorrel thoroughly, and add it to the other ingredients, stir it over a gentle fire for 15–20 minutes, rub it through a hair sieve, and place it in the centre of a hot dish, with cutlets of veal, lamb or mutton around it.

STEWED SORREL

Pick $\frac{1}{2}$ a peck (1 gallon) of sorrel leaves, wash thoroughly in several waters, drain them, and place in a fireproof dish or earthen jar, and let them stew gently in the open oven until tender. Mix 1 oz of butter with them, add pepper, salt and Cayenne to taste, beat all together until the leaves are smooth, and serve. Serve with roast meat.

BAKED TOMATOES

Well butter a flat baking-dish, and put in tomatoes cut into halves. Sprinkle over them some breadcrumbs, grated cheese, chopped onion, shallot and parsley. Place them in a hot oven, and when ready to serve, squeeze a lemon over the whole, with salt and pepper.

TURNIP TOP GREENS

When young and freshly cut they are very excellent as a vegetable. Owing to their slightly bitter taste they are considered a very healthy article of diet to eat in the spring. Cut away the stems and dead leaves, wash them in several waters, and finally let them remain in fresh water for 1 hour. After draining them, put them into a saucepan of slightly salted water, fast boiling. If young, they should be cooked and quite tender in 15 minutes or so. Strain through a colander, squeeze out as much of the water as possible, put them into a hot vegetable dish, and cut them across each way. Place a little butter, salt and pepper on top.

BOILED TURNIPS

Turnips that are to be served plainly boiled must be small and very young; the larger ones should be mashed. Put the necessary quantity of turnips into slightly salted boiling water and let them boil for 25 minutes. Drain through a colander, and serve with a white sauce poured over them.

TURNIP PURÉE

Pare and wash 6 turnips. Cut them into quarters and boil them in salted water until tender. Mash, and pass them through a hair sieve. Put them in a stewpan with 1 oz of butter and ¼ pint of cream. Dredge in a little flour, and stir it over the fire until the mass becomes stiff. Serve this purée in the centre of the dish and arrange the meat around it.

APPLE AND WALNUT SALAD

8 *fresh walnuts*
4 *crisp eating apples*

1 *gill mayonnaise, sharpened with vinegar*
A little salt

Shell and skin walnuts; peel, core and cut apples into dice. Put a thin layer of nuts into a glass dish, sprinkle very lightly with salt, and next a layer of chopped apples with a little mayonnaise over. Continue until all is used, reserving a few walnuts as garnish. Top with mayonnaise, sprinkle over remaining nuts and serve at once. This must be prepared just before serving or the apples will brown and lose their crispness. To save time, however, the apples may be peeled shortly beforehand, and if kept covered in cold water with a little salt added, they will keep white. Wash well before chopping up.

Mrs Butcher, Ely, Cambs.

APPLE AND CABBAGE SALAD

1 *small head of cabbage*
2 *small apples*
¼ *cup cream*

1 *tablespoon vinegar*
1 *tablespoon sugar*

Grate cabbage and apple. Add cream, vinegar, and sugar. Mix well.

ORANGE SALAD

2 *oranges*
2 *lettuces*

Squeeze of lemon juice
Salt and pepper
3 *tablespoons olive oil*

Peel the oranges rather extravagantly with a knife and cut out the segments of orange, leaving no pith or skin. Mix with the hearts of the lettuce. Dress with lemon juice, salt, pepper and oil. Good with cold chicken or pork.

BEETROOT AND HORSERADISH SALAD

3 or 4 beetroot, cooked and
diced
Salt and pepper
Horseradish sauce

Horseradish sauce
Juice of a lemon
1 dessertspoon vinegar
1 teaspoon mustard
Salt and pepper
Good pinch of brown sugar
2 or 3 tablespoons fresh
horseradish, grated
¼ pint double cream, whipped

To make the sauce, mix all the ingredients together and season well, cover with the whipped cream and stir thoroughly. Cover the beetroot with the horseradish sauce and stir until the sauce is consistently pink.

CELERY SALAD

1 head celery
1 large onion
A few lettuce leaves
Some chopped parsley or

chives or a little fresh
watercress
French dressing
Salt

Prepare the celery and dice it. Chop the onion very finely and mix it with the diced celery in a bowl. Put the mixture into a wooden salad bowl which has been lined with a few crisp lettuce leaves, and sprinkle with a little salt. Pour 3 or 4 dessertspoons of French dressing over the celery, onion and stir gently, taking care not to bruise the lettuce. Garnish with chopped parsley, chives or a few sprigs of fresh watercress.

12 Sauces

Ne wette hir fyngres in hir sauce depe.
Wel koude she carie a morsel, and wel kepe,
That no drope ne fille upon hire breste.

    The Prioress in 'The Canterbury Tales', Geoffrey Chaucer

Two large potatoes, passed through kitchen sieve,
Unwonted softness to the salad give.
Of mordant mustard add a single spoon
Distrust the condiment that bites so soon,
But deem it not, thou Man of Herbs, a fault
To add a double quantity of salt;
Three times the spoon with oil of Lucca crown,
And once with vinegar procured from town.
True flavour needs it, and your poet begs
The pounded yellow of two well-boiled eggs.
Let onion atoms lurk within the bowl,
And scarce suspected animate the whole:
And lastly on the flavoured compound toss
A magic teaspoon of Anchovy sauce.
Then though green turtle fail, though venison's tough,
And ham and turkey be not boiled enough,
Serenely full the epicure may say,
'Fate cannot harm me – I have dined today.'

                                 Sidney Smith

GUBBINS SAUCE

Melt ½ oz butter in a bowl over a pan of simmering water, stir in 2 teaspoons made mustard, 2 teaspoons wine vinegar, 1 teaspoon tarragon vinegar, ½ teaspoon sugar and 3 tablespoons single cream. Season to taste with salt, pepper and cayenne pepper. For chicken, turkey, pheasant and partridge.

CUMBERLAND SAUCE

Peel the zest of 1 orange and ½ lemon and shred finely, plunge in boiling water for 2 minutes and drain. Melt 4 tablespoons redcurrant jelly over a low heat and add 1 teaspoon finely chopped shallot, cook gently for a few minutes. Add ¼ pint port, lemon and orange zest. Blend together 1 teaspoon made mustard, ⅛ teaspoon cayenne pepper, ⅛ teaspoon ground ginger with the juice of the orange and lemon. Add to the port and simmer gently for 10 minutes. Adjust seasoning. For cold venison and ham.

ROBERT SAUCE

Melt 1 oz butter in a pan and gently fry a finely chopped small onion until transparent. Add ¼ pint white wine and reduce by half. Stir in ½ pint of good brown sauce, coating consistency, and bring to the boil, stir in 1 teaspoon made mustard, 1 teaspoon vinegar and ½ teaspoon sugar. For grilled meats, especially pork.

MUSTARD SAUCE

Melt 1 oz butter in a pan, add 1 oz flour and cook for a minute without browning. Draw the pan aside and gradually add ½ pint milk. Return to the heat, bring to boil, stirring, boil 2–3 minutes. Blend together 2 teaspoons dry mustard and 2 teaspoons vinegar and add to sauce. Season to taste adding a little sugar if liked. For herrings, cauliflower and boiled meats.

PIQUANT SAUCE FOR LEFTOVERS

¼ pint vinegar
2 chopped shallots
A sprig of thyme
A crushed clove of garlic

¾ pint of gravy or thickened brown stock
2 tablespoons chopped gherkins
Seasoning

Cook the vinegar and flavourings gently in an uncovered pan, remove the thyme and garlic and, when the vinegar is reduced to ⅛ pint, add the gravy and gherkins and season well. In this sauce, minced cooked meat or sliced leftover meat may be reheated. As an alternative the gherkins may be sliced and arranged as a garnish on the dish.

WILDFOWL SAUCE

2 glasses port
1 tablespoon Harvey's sauce
1 tablespoon mushroom ketchup
1 tablespoon lemon juice
1 slice lemon peel, chopped fine

1 large chopped shallot
Cayenne pepper
1 blade mace
2 cloves
1 tablespoon white roux
½ pint game stock
1 tablespoon redcurrant jelly

Simmer the chopped shallot, Cayenne, mace and cloves in the stock. Strain on to the roux in the top of a double boiler. Add the port and other ingredients. Heat and strain into a sauceboat.

BREAD SAUCE

1 medium-sized onion
1 clove
½ pint milk
2 oz fresh white breadcrumbs

Seasoning
1 tablespoon cream and ½ oz butter or 1 oz butter

Put the onion and clove in a saucepan with the milk and bring to the boil. Add the breadcrumbs and seasoning. Simmer for about 15 minutes, stirring occasionally. Remove the onion and clove and stir in the cream and butter.

1742 CUCUMBER SAUCE

2 oz butter
1 large cucumber
Salt and pepper

1 teaspoon grated onion
½ pint gravy made from pan juices
1 teaspoon lemon juice

Melt the butter. Add the cucumber which has been peeled, sliced and drained. Toss in fat until golden. Add salt and pepper, onion and gravy and simmer until the onion is cooked. Add the lemon juice and serve with mutton.

1742 HORSERADISH SAUCE

2 oz grated horseradish
1 tablespoon ground mustard
1 tablespoon sugar

4 tablespoons vinegar or oil
1 teaspoon turmeric
Salt and pepper

Mix all ingredients together and serve with beef.

1831 COMMON SAUCE

Unsalted butter
Walnut pickle or catsup

Melt the butter gently and when just soft add a spoonful of walnut pickle or catsup. Stir well and serve with fish.

1831 CELERY SAUCE

1 head celery
½ pint cream
Powdered mace

Powdered nutmeg
½ oz butter rolled in flour

Cut celery in small pieces and simmer in just enough water to cover until tender. Add cream, mace and nutmeg to taste, and the butter rolled in flour. Stir over very gentle heat until thick and well-blended, but do not boil. Serve with fowl, turkey, partridge and other game.

1831 EGG SAUCE

4 hard-boiled eggs
4 oz butter

Chop the eggs not too finely and add to just-melted butter. Very good with poached or baked cod or fresh haddock.

READING SAUCE

Take Wallnuts and beat them until thay becum a pulp. Squeeze the pulp from them and let it stand and settle the day then pour of the clear and to every pint of juice put ½ pound of anchovys 1 oz of Shallotts. Let it stand on the Fire untill the Anchovies is quite Disolved then add ¼ oz Mace ¼ oz Cloves ¼ oz Jamaica Pepper ¼ pint White Vinagar. Let all boil together Quarter of Hour. Strain it off it should Drip through the Bag jently.

Joseph Webb's Book, 1823

TARTARE SAUCE

Take yolks of 2 eggs in a basin with pepper and salt. Drop salad oil into these keeping it stirred well till quite thick and firm – then add in drops a dessertspoon of tarragon vinegar and teaspoon of chili vinegar still keeping briskly stirring. This will make it about the thickness of cream. Serve cold with salmon, soles or turbot.

Mrs Garden, 1847

HOT SAUCE

2 teaspoons French mustard
1 teaspoon common mustard
1 teaspoon anchovy sauce
1 teaspoon Harvey sauce

Half a teaspoon chili vinegar
1 teaspoon salt mixed in a
teacup full of good gravy

Boil together.

Mrs Garden, 1847

SAUCE FOR CHICKENS

Take the heads and necks of the chickens, with a small bit of scrag of veal, or any scraps of mutton you may have by you, and put them into a saucepan, with a blade or 2 of mace, and a few black pepper corns, an anchovy, a head of celery, a slice of the end of a lemon, and a bunch of sweet herbs. Put to these a quart of water, cover it close, and let it boil till it is reduced to half a pint. Then strain it, and thicken it with a ¼ lb of butter mixed with flour, and boil it 5 or 6 minutes. Then put in 2 spoonfuls of mushrooms, and mix the yolks of 2 eggs with a teacupful of cream, and a little nutmeg grated. Put in your sauce, and keep shaking it over the fire, till it is near boiling; then put it into your boats, and serve it up with your chickens.

Thomas Train, Gateshead, 1812

SAUCE FOR A BOILED DUCK

Take 1 large onion, a handful of parsley clean washed and picked, and a lettuce. Cut the onions small, chop the parsley fine, and put them into a ¼ pint of good gravy, with a spoonful of lemon juice and a little pepper and salt. When they have stewed together a ½ hour, add 2 spoonfuls of red wine. Lay the duck in your dish and pour the sauce over it.

Thomas Train, Gateshead, 1812

LEMON SAUCE FOR BOILED FOWLS

Take a lemon, and peel off the rind, then cut it into slices, take the kernels out, and cut it into small square bits. Blanch the liver of the fowl and chop it fine. Mix the lemon and liver together in a boat, pour on some hot melted butter, and stir it up.

Thomas Train, Gateshead, 1812

ORANGE SAUCE

5 tablespoons sugar
2 tablespoons water
1 tablespoon white vinegar
Juice of 2 oranges

Segments of 1 orange
Grated rind of 1 orange
1 teaspoon arrowroot

Mix arrowroot with a little orange juice. Dissolve sugar in water. Bring to boiling point until solution is golden brown. Watch carefully, remove from heat and add vinegar, remains of orange juice. Add rind and segments and blended arrowroot. Bring to boil and boil 2 minutes. Serve with roast duck.

Pat Brown, Keynsham, Somerset

VAL'S BARBECUE SAUCE

2 oz lard
1 clove garlic
3 onions
2 lemons (rind and juice)
4 oz brown sugar

¼ pint vinegar
4 tins tomato purée
4 tablespoons Worcester sauce

Cook all together to make a thick sauce. Serve with sausages or beef fondue.

Pat Brown, Keynsham, Somerset

TONATTO

A creamy sauce to serve with cold veal. This sauce is a mixture of mayonnaise made in the usual way and into which is mixed crushed tuna, anchovies, and capers to taste (but not too much), until quite smooth. It is delicious.

Signora Beglia, Italy

GREEN SAUCE DRESSING

This dressing can be served with any cold dish. Used for spaghetti only, it should be heated up quickly after it has been mixed in with the spaghetti.

You need basil, a couple of cloves of garlic, grated cheese, salt and olive oil. As it is a sauce which can be kept, the quantity may vary but the correct proportions are 1 cup of basil to 2 cloves of garlic and ½ a cup of cheese.

Mix all these ingredients together with the oil. Signora Beglia uses a mortar and works hard at it, but an electric mixer will also do the job. The sauce should be liquid with the basil and solids settled at the bottom, so when serving the spoon should dive deep in order to bring up the solid and the liquid. Well seasoned this is delicious on cold ham, cold meat or fish.

Signora Beglia, Italy

SAUCE FOR COLD CUTS FROM THE SUNDAY JOINT

Add 2 tablespoons chutney, 1 teaspoon made mustard, ¼ teaspoon curry powder and blend well.

OXFORD BRAWN SAUCE

Blend 1 teaspoon salad oil with 2 teaspoons caster sugar and 1 teaspoon dry mustard; when smooth beat in 2 tablespoons vinegar and 2 tablespoons salad oil. Season to taste. Add 1 teaspoon chopped parsley and spoon over meat slices. For cold meats and brawn.

MUSTARD CREAM SAUCE

Blend ¼ pint lightly whipped double cream with 2 tablespoons made mustard and season to taste. For herrings, mackerel and grills.

MUSTARD BUTTER

Cream 4 oz butter with 1 tablespoon made mustard. Shape into a roll, wrap in greaseproof paper, put in refrigerator, slice and use as required. For meat and fish steaks.

LEMON DRESSING

Juice of 2 lemons   *Chopped fresh herbs*
1 tablespoon clear honey

Combine all ingredients. Dress salad just before serving, or serve
separately.

SALAD CREAM

1½ pints milk   *3 heaped tablespoons sugar*
¾ pint vinegar   *1 level tablespoon mustard*
4 oz margarine   *2 eggs*
4 heaped tablespoons flour

Melt margarine in saucepan. Take from heat, add flour, sugar and mustard. Stir in milk and return to heat, stirring all the time to avoid sticking.
When mixture begins to thicken, take from heat and beat quickly to avoid
lumps. Put to cool. When cool, beat in 2 eggs and add vinegar to required
thickness. This will keep 4–6 weeks and Mrs Ball makes it before haymaking to last through the summer. She multiplied the quantity by four
to make enough for 130 people at a YFC Harvest Supper.

Mrs Ball, Compton Greenfield, Glos.

SALAD CREAM (to keep)

2 oz plain flour   *4 teaspoons salt*
4 tablespoons sugar   *1 pint cream*
6 oz butter   *½ pint vinegar*
8 egg yolks   *1 teaspoon dry mustard*

Mix dry ingredients. Add melted butter, eggs and cream. Carefully add
vinegar, stirring. Cook slowly in double saucepan, stirring frequently.

Pat Brown, Keynsham, Somerset

SALAD DRESSING

1 hard-boiled egg   *1 tablespoon oil*
1 tablespoon sugar   *Little salt*
2 tablespoons mixed mustard   *Milk and vinegar*

Mix sugar, mustard, salt, oil and egg yolk into smooth paste (mix salt,
sugar and egg first) then add by degrees alternately milk and vinegar to
taste.

Lewis' Mother's Cookbook, Mary Horrell, Exeter

SALAD DRESSING

1 egg
¼ teaspoon mixed mustard
¼ teaspoon salt
¼ teaspoon pepper

Well mix, then add 3 teaspoons Tarragon vinegar, 2 teaspoons pounded sugar. Well mixed, Add 4 teaspoons vinegar and a little Worcester sauce and ¾ teacupful cream.

Lewis' Mother's Cookbook, Mary Horrell, Exeter

MINT SAUCE TO STORE

Pick fresh young mint leaves. Warm 8 oz golden syrup and put in liquidiser. Add mint leaves and liquidise until fine. Store in jar and add vinegar as required.

Pat Brown, Keynsham, Somerset

SALAD CREAM

1 oz butter
½ oz flour
¼ pt milk
1-2 tablespoons vinegar
Salt, pepper, mustard
1 teaspoon sugar

Melt butter, add flour. Add milk slowly. Bring to the boil. Cool slightly, add remaining ingredients. This is good, but is not for keeping.

13 Packed Meals

Keen appetites and quick digestion wait
On you and yours.

Dryden

He that will have cake out of the wheat must
tarry the grinding.

Shakespeare

In the country there is always a need for packed meals. Whatever the weather, farmers may have to eat miles from home and need nourishing, compact food to last them from early breakfast to a late evening meal. In more relaxed moments, usually in the depth of winter, there is need for the handy sandwich for hunting and shooting families, and the more elaborate picnic for the numerous outdoor events in the winter calendar.

Many of the recipes throughout this book are just as good for outdoor eating, but here are some of the trusted favourites for lunch boxes of all kinds.

SAUSAGE LOAF

1 lb pork sausage meat
1 tablespoon tomato sauce
1 grated onion
Salt and pepper

Pinch of sage
2 slices bread
1 beaten egg

Mix together sausage meat, sauce, onion, seasoning, crumbled bread and egg. Press into a greased loaf tin and bake at 400°F (Gas Mark 6) for 40 minutes. Leave until cold, then wrap in foil for carrying. Eat with buttered baps.

SAUSAGE SHAPE

1 *lb beef sausage meat*
1 *lb pork sausage meat*
1 *lb cooked ham or tongue*
1 *dessertspoon chopped pickles*
1 *teaspoon mixed spice*

Pinch of freshly ground black pepper
1 *tablespoon sweet stout*
1 *tablespoon Worcester sauce*
Pinch of rosemary
Salt

Mix together the sausage meats and finely chopped ham or tongue. Add pickles, spice, pepper, stout, Worcester sauce, rosemary and salt to taste. Tie in a cloth, and cook very slowly in stock for 2 hours. Lift out and press between 2 dishes under heavy weights until cold. This may be used for sandwiches, or may be glazed when cold, to serve with salad.

PORK CHEESE

1 *lb cold roast pork*
Pinch mixed herbs
Grated lemon rind
2 *teaspoons chopped parsley*
2 *blades of mace*

4 *sage leaves*
Pinch grated nutmeg
Good stock made from meat bones and strengthened with a little gelatine.

Cut the meat into small pieces. Season well, add the herbs. Mix well and put into a greased mould, fill with the gravy, and bake in a moderate oven about an hour. Turn out when cold.

BEEF LOAF

1 *lb beef steak*
4 *oz bacon*
4 *oz white breadcrumbs*

1 *teaspoon chopped parsley*
½ *teaspoon thyme*
2 *eggs*

Mince the meat and bacon finely, and mix with the rest of the ingredients. Add the well-beaten eggs, and a little stock to moisten if necessary. Put into a greased oblong tin and steam for 3 hours. When cold, turn out and sprinkle with brown breadcrumbs. Leave to chill before cutting, as it will crumble if cut warm.

CHICKEN ROLL

Put some cold (roast) fowl through a mincer with a little ham, season with pepper, sauce, nutmeg, a little minced shallot or onion, a dessertspoon chopped parsley; moisten withh a cupful of white sauce which has been nicely flavoured and the yolk of 1 egg. Spread the mince out on a flat dish, make into rolls on a floured board, dip into a beaten egg, cover well with breadcrumbs, allowing the crumbs to harden, and fry in boiling fat. Cool and eat with crusty bread.

VEAL CAKE

Slices of cold roast veal   *Some gravy*
Slices of ham   *2 sprigs of parsley*
3 eggs   *Pepper and salt*

Cut a few slices of ham and veal *very* thin, taking off the skin from the veal, chop 2 sprigs of parsley fine, and cut the eggs hard-boiled into slices. Take any nice shaped mould, butter it, and put the veal, ham, eggs and parsley in layers until the mould is full, seasoning each layer with a little pepper and salt. Placing a few slices of egg at the bottom of the mould at equal distances, fill up with good stock and bake for 30 minutes. When cold, turn it out.

STEAMED MEAT MINCE PUDDING

½ lb minced cold meat   *1 egg*
4 oz breadcrumbs   *½ teaspoon curry powder*
2 oz suet (dripping or lard   *Stock*
would do)

Mix all together, adding a little flour if necessary; steam in greased bowl for 2 hours. Cool, and turn out.

CAMP PIE

½ lb lean ham   *¼ teaspoon Jamaica pepper*
½ lb mutton   *1 teaspoon salt*
½ lb steak   *1 egg*
½ teacup breadcrumbs   *1 teacup milk*
¼ teaspoon black pepper

Mince together the ham, steak, and mutton. Mix well all the other ingredients, put in a buttered mould, and boil for 3 hours. Serve cold.

Mrs Higgins, Falkirk, 1911

BACON AND MUSHROOM PICNIC LOAF

1 *small loaf white bread*
4 *oz butter*
4 *rashers lean bacon*
8 *oz chicken livers*

4 *oz mushrooms*
1 *onion*
Salt and pepper

Cut a 'lid' from the top of the loaf and scoop out the soft bread (this can be saved to use for breadcrumbs). Leave about 1 inch wall all round inside the bread. Melt 3 oz butter and fry the outside of the loaf and lid until golden brown and crisp and leave to cool. Chop the bacon, chicken livers, mushrooms and onion finely. In the remaining butter, cook the bacon for 1 minute, and add the onion. Cook until the onion is transparent, and add chicken livers and mushrooms. Season with salt and pepper and cook for 2 minutes. Pack the mixture into the loaf and cover with the lid. Wrap in foil and chill for 2 hours. Serve cut into slices with salad.

SHOOTER'S SANDWICH

1 *large thick rump steak*
1 *sandwich loaf*

$\frac{1}{4}$ *lb mushrooms*
Salt and pepper

Grill the steak medium rare, and fry the chopped mushrooms in butter. Cut off the end of the sandwich loaf, remove some of the crumbs, and put in the well-seasoned steak and mushrooms. Put back the crust, wrap the loaf in blotting paper, then greaseproof paper, and tie into a neat parcel with string. Put under heavy weights for 6 hours, and do not slice until needed.

SANDWICH FILLINGS

The most conventional sandwich fillings such as egg, meat, cheese and fish can be improved with imaginative additions. If you intend to freeze sandwiches, avoid hard-boiled egg, mayonnaise or salad cream, and lettuce, tomato and cucumber which do not react well to low temperatures. These can be packed into the lunch box separately. Here are the main ingredients with their flavouring combinations:

Beef: Chopped ham, lettuce, horseradish sauce. Lettuce, fried onion, cucumber. Tomato, lettuce, salad cream.

Lamb: Apple sauce, chopped mint. Mint jelly.

Pork: Apple sauce. Sliced pineapple, mustard, salad dressing. Salad dressing spiced with curry powder.

Ham: Dates and salad dressing. Hard-boiled egg, capers.

Tongue: Redcurrant jelly, lettuce. Hard-boiled egg, onion, salad cream.

Chicken or turkey: Chopped crisp bacon, lettuce, salad cream. Ham, chopped parsley, green pepper.

Crisp bacon: Chopped cooked chicken liver, tomato, mayonnaise. Mashed liver sausage, cucumber.

Egg: Sardines, lemon juice. Anchovy paste or anchovy fillets.

Cheese: Radishes, corned beef, salad dressing. Shredded raw cabbage, sliced apple, mayonnaise.

Cream cheese: Chutney, walnuts. Liver sausage, egg, chives, salad dressing.

EGG SANDWICHES

Mash hard-boiled egg with butter and curry powder, or with gherkins or anchovies. Even easier, try scrambled egg sandwiches.

BACON AND EGG SANDWICHES

Cook egg on both sides to seal yolk, and with the bacon put between bread and butter.

SAVOURY BUTTERS

These are delicious used alone for tea-party sandwiches, or as a lift to heartier sandwiches or rolls filled with salad or hard-boiled eggs.

SALMON BUTTER

Remove skin and bones from contents of 1 small tin salmon. Mash fish with a squeeze of lemon juice, plenty of pepper and salt, and work in 2 oz butter. Good with cucumber sandwiches.

SARDINE BUTTER

Mash 2 oz sardines and blend with 2 oz softened butter and a squeeze of lemon juice, pepper and salt to taste.

KIPPER BUTTER

Grill or poach 4 kipper fillets, cool and remove bones. Mash flesh with 2 oz butter, pepper and salt and a dash of Worcester sauce. Eat with plenty of crisp lettuce.

CURRY POWDER

Cream 3 oz butter and work in 1 oz chopped mango chutney, 1 teaspoon made mustard, $\frac{1}{2}$ teaspoon curry powder, a squeeze of lemon juice, pepper and salt. Useful with cold meat or poultry sandwiches.

14 Wines, Beers, Punches, Possets and Soft Drinks

From wine what sudden friendship springs!

Gay

Though gay companions o'er the bowl
Dispel awhile the sense of ill;
Though pleasure stirs the maddening soul
The heart – the heart – is lonely still.

Byron

A GALLON OF FLOWERS

Wines made from spring flowers are popular, but often a recipe calls for a 'gallon of flowers' and the weight is difficult to determine. This is best interpreted as a gallon container full of flowers under their own weight, not compressed. If a pocket spring balance is used while picking, measuring is easier. For instance, 3 lb dandelion petals only equals 1 gallon; 2 lb dandelion whole heads equals 1 gallon; 2 lb elderflower flowers stripped from bunches equals 1 gallon.

ELDERFLOWER DRINK

1 cluster of elderflowers with the pollen on it, 4 quarts cold water, 1½ lb lump sugar, 1 lemon and finely grated rind, 1 teaspoon tartaric acid. Put ingredients into a pan, stir often. After 24 hours strain and bottle. Stand bottles upright for a fortnight, then lie on side. Use screwtop bottles, or wired corks. The former are far better.

Lewis' Mother's Cookbook, Mary Horrell, Exeter

NETTLE WINE

1 gallon young nettles   *3 lemons*
3 lb white sugar   *2 oz root ginger*
1 gallon water   *½ oz yeast*

Boil the nettles, ginger, rinds and juice of the lemons together until a dark green, then strain and add the sugar. Put the yeast on toast, and put it on the wine when it is blood heat. E. Shepphard is my friend who makes it, and when she bottles it, she adds a few raisins.

Miss Mabel Nokes, Priston Mill Farm, Bath

PARKSIDE ORANGE WINE

12 large juicy oranges   *3 lb sugar*
1 gallon boiling water

Wash the oranges and slice them thinly, including the peel. Put into a china basin and pour over the water. Cover with a cloth and leave for a week, stirring 2 or 3 times a day. Strain the liquid. Heat up a pint and stir in the sugar until dissolved. Add to the remainder. Pour into bottles and cork lightly until fermentation has ceased, and then seal. Ready in 4 months.

APPLE WINE

Cut ripe apples and to each gallon of fruit allow 4 pints of water. Put on a low heat, bring to boil and simmer for 20 minutes. Cool and strain, and add 8 oz of brown sugar or honey to each quart of liquid.

Put in cask with whites of two eggs and 2 oz bruised cinnamon stick to each gallon. Let it work and bung tightly.

Ros Hill, 1864

OPPLAR COTTAGE APPLE WINE

6 *lb apples*   1 *gallon water*
2 *lb sugar*

Cut up the apples, including skins and cores. Cover with the water, and mash and stir for 2 days. Strain the liquid and heat up 1 pint. Pour this over the sugar. Stir well to dissolve, and then add the rest of the liquid. Leave to stand for 3 days. Skim, strain and bottle, corking lightly at first. Push corks in firmly later.

BRAMBLE AND ELDERBERRY WINE

Use half and half ration, i.e. 2 lb Brambles and 2 lb Elderberries – 7 pints of water – 3½ to 4 lb sugar – ½ oz yeast or all-purpose wine yeast. These proportions can be varied – 1 lb Elderberries to 3 lb Brambles – there is no hard and fast rule.

Crush the fruits, and leave to soak in warm atmosphere for 24 hours. Then strain the juice, place in pan and bring to the boil for no longer than 2 minutes. Remove the rising scum, add the sugar, and when the liquid has cooled to blood heat, add the yeast. Keep the must in a warm, even temperature closely covered until fermentation has ceased. I find that the large glass sweet jars make handy fermentation vessels and can be obtained from your local shop.

A few reminders: Never put wine into screw top bottles for fear of explosion. Incidentally, if such a disaster should occur, and I sincerely hope it never does, it is in no way an indication that the wine is extra strong and potent . . . merely that the wine has been bottled before the fermentation has ceased.

Always keep the wine closely covered – 3 thicknesses of polythene is a happy medium. Secure the neck of the jar with string.

Add one Campden tablet finely crushed to each gallon of wine; these or sulphur tablets, which kill bacteria, are obtainable from any chemist.

On one farm in Cheshire they used to bury their rhubarb wine for 40 years. Seasoned topers 'blacked out' after drinking 1 gill of its potency!

Mrs Ward, York

PARSNIP WINE

4 *lb parsnips*   3 *lb white sugar*
1 *teaspoon ground ginger*   ¾ *oz baker's yeast or* 1
Rinds and juice of 2 *lemons*   *teaspoon dried yeast*
and 1 *orange*

Scrub parsnips, but do not peel them. Cut into ¼ inch to ½ inch slices. Boil in a gallon of water with ground ginger and citrus rinds until tender. Place sugar in bucket and strain over parsnip liquid. Stir and leave to cool. When the liquid, or must, as it is called, has cooled to lukewarm, add the citrus juices and prepared yeast. Cover closely and leave for 24 hours. Pour the must into a jar. Insert an airlock and leave to ferment. When all fermentation has ceased, rack off into bottles, and store.

RICE WINE

3 lb rice
1 lb raisins
3 lb white sugar

Juice of 2 lemons and 1 orange
¾ oz baker's yeast or 1 teaspoon dried yeast

Soak rice overnight in 3 pints water. Chop or mince raisins. Mix raisins, rice, rice water and sugar in bucket; pour on 5 pints of boiling water. Stir well, cover and leave to cool. When at room temperature, add fruit juices and prepared yeast. Cover well; stand in warm place to ferment, stirring daily.

When fermentation slows, strain into fermentation bottle and fit airlock. Allow to clear, then rack off into a clean jar. Allow any further fermentation to cease before bottling.

CARROT WINE

6 lb carrots
4 lb white sugar
1 lb wheat (available from a health store)
Rind and juice of 1 lemon and 1 orange

¾ oz baker's yeast or 1 teaspoon dried yeast
4 oz raisins

Scrub and peel carrots; boil until tender in 1 gallon of water. Strain liquid into bucket over sugar, wheat and rinds; stir well. When lukewarm, add fruit juices and prepared yeast. Stir well and leave for 7 days, stirring daily.

Remove rinds, but not raisins, and pour into fermentation jar with lock. Bottle when all fermentation has ceased.

ORANGE WINE

12 medium-sized oranges
2 lemons
1 lb minced or chopped raisins

3½ lb white sugar
¾ oz baker's yeast or 1 teaspoon dried yeast or 1 champagne yeast tablet

Wash oranges and lemons. Peel half the oranges and place rinds in oven to dry crisp and brown. Squeeze all oranges and lemons and mix in bucket with raisins and sugar. Add 6 pints cold water and stir well. Cover.

Place rind from oven in a jug or bowl and pour over 2 pints of boiling water. Leave for an hour. Prepare yeast.

Strain liquid from peel into bucket and mix well. Add the yeast liquid. Cover and leave to ferment for 3 days, stirring daily. Do not strain. Pour into jar; fit airlock.

When all fermentation has ceased, rack off into a clean jar. Wait 2 weeks, to make sure all fermentation has ended, then bottle.

POTATO WINE

5 lb old potatoes
Juice and rind of 2 lemons
and 1 orange
1 teaspoon ground ginger

3½ lb demerara sugar
¾ oz baker's yeast or 1
teaspoon dried yeast
4 oz seedless raisins

Scrub potatoes and cut into large pieces. Boil in 1 gallon of water for about 15 minutes; strain off liquid while potatoes are still quite firm. Boil liquid again with rinds and ginger for 10 minutes, adding more water if level has dropped below 1 gallon mark.

Place sugar in bucket and pour over boiling liquid. Stir well, and when lukewarm, add fruit juices and yeast liquid. Cover and leave to ferment, stirring daily.

When fermentation slows, pour into fermentation jar, add raisins and insert airlock. Leave for at least 9 months, then rack off into bottles.

APPLE WINE

6 lb chopped apples
(including crab apples)
Rind and juice of 1 lemon
3 lb white sugar

¾ oz baker's yeast or 1
teaspoon dried yeast
½ lb seedless raisins, minced
or chopped

Boil apples and lemon rind in a gallon of water until soft, about 10 minutes. Strain into a bucket over the sugar. When lukewarm, add lemon juice and prepared yeast. Cover well and leave for 24 hours.

Pour into a fermenting jar; leave for 4 weeks, then rack off into a clean jar. Add raisins. Insert airlock and leave until you are sure fermentation has ceased. Cork, and leave for 6 months, then rack into bottles.

RAISIN WINE

3 *lb seedless raisins*　　　　$\frac{3}{4}$ *oz baker's yeast or* 1
3 *lb demerara sugar*　　　　*teaspoon dried yeast*
Juice and rind of 1 *lemon*

Chop or mince the raisins. Mix with half the sugar and lemon juice and
rind. Pour over 7 pints lukewarm water (half boiling, half cold will get the
right temperature). Add prepared yeast. Stir vigorously, then cover and
stand in a warm place for 10 days.

During the first 2 days, stir frequently to prevent raisins and sugar
settling. Then stir once daily.

After tenth day, boil up remaining sugar in a pint of water, allow to cool
and add to mixture when lukewarm. Stir well; do not strain. Pour into
fermenting jar and fit airlock. Keep in a warm place until fermentation
ceases, then rack off into bottles.

CIDER

This is a simple recipe. It is ready to drink just as soon as all the fermentation has ceased. Windfall and weathered apples are best, so don't be in a
hurry to bring them indoors. Try to mix varieties as much as possible.

For large quantities, cut and mash the apples so that they are thoroughly squashed; for small quantities, use a mincer. Use every part of the
fruit – skin, pips, and cores.

Put the pulp in a nylon straining bag or something similar and press out
the juice. Some people use a wooden mangle or a clothes wringer. A rolling
pin is useful, or it is possible to buy a fruit press. Keep pressing until the
pulp is 'dry', i.e. when you have extracted the maximum amount of juice
from it.

Pour juice into a fermenting jar and plug neck with cotton wool.
(Fermentation is usually fierce at first, and if you insert an airlock, the
froth may find its way up the inside.) Stand the jar on a tray in a warm
place to continue fermenting.

Renew the cotton wool if necessary. When fermentation dies down,
clean the jar and insert an airlock. Let it finish fermenting.

It is best served from the jar, otherwise use strong cider bottles.

Near almost every Somerset farm, and some other houses too, you will
notice a small orchard. There may be an eating apple or two; a cooking
apple or two; but the rest will be old, unpruned, straggling cider apple
trees. In spring they are a mass of bees and blossom, and in the autumn
they bear a crop of small bright red apples. They are not, of course, picked
in the normal way; small apples and unpruned trees would make it very

difficult. You will often see a long pole attached to a high branch and this is used to shake the apples down.

The farmer's family or workers pick up the apples into buckets and empty them into sacks. In bigger orchards this is a useful source of seasonal income for the local women. The sacks are eventually collected up and taken to the cider press in the farm buildings.

Although many of these old trees are being cut down to make way for barns and silage pits, and the farmer buys his cider, odd trees can still be seen. They are decorative in their own right; white with blossom in the spring; a welcome patch of shade in the heat of summer; red and yellow with apples and autumn leaves in the fall; and a lacy silhouette against a frosty blue sky in the winter.

They seem to be part of the old farmsteads near which they grow, and which were old when they were planted many years ago.

Mrs Berkeley, Somerset Farm Wives' Club

BEER (1)

Most beers are rather complicated to make, but this is a simple recipe for bitter beer of average strength.

To make 4 gallons of beer you will require:

¼ lb dried hops
1 dessertspoon caramel colouring
2 lb malt extract

2 lb preserving sugar
½ teaspoon citric acid
2 teaspoons dried yeast

For such a large quantity, you will need an extra-large fermenting vessel such as a small plastic dustbin.

Boil as much water as your largest pan will conveniently take. While this is heating, tie the hops in a muslin bag and add them, with the caramel colouring, when the water boils. Simmer for 45 minutes.

Warm the tin of malt extract in water to soften it a little. Remove hops.

Place extract and sugar in the dustbin and pour over the boiling liquid. Add tepid water to make up to 4 gallons, then add citric acid. Stir all the ingredients together vigorously.

Allow to cool to room temperature, then add prepared yeast. This will make a lot of froth, hence the need for a large container. Cover with dustbin lid or a sheet of polythene tightly tied, and allow to ferment for at least 3 days, but no more than 7, keeping temperature as constant as possible.

After the first day or two, remove some of the froth (this is bitter to the taste). The beer is ready for bottling when the froth has died down to a ring in the centre.

The beer will be still or only sparkling. If you want to give it more bite, add 1 level teaspoon of sugar to each quart bottle – no more or the bottles may burst.

Screw-top cider or beer bottles are best. Screw very lightly for the first day or two, then tighten up. Keep in a cool place until the beer clears. There will be a slight deposit in the bottom of the bottles, so pour the beer very carefully.

BEER (2)

2 × 1 gallon fermentation jars, 2 bored corks, 2 fermentation locks, a plastic funnel, a length of plastic tubing for syphoning. Strong bottles e.g. cider bottles (and plenty of patience).

1 oz hops	*1 lb jar plain malt extract*
½ lb demerara sugar	*½ teaspoon gravy browning*
2 oz flaked rice	*1 teaspoon granulated yeast*

All the above can be bought at Boots the Chemists.

Put the demerara sugar, malt and flaked rice into large container e.g. a 2 gallon plastic bucket, and pour on 3 pints warm water, stir till it has dissolved, meanwhile put the hops into a saucepan with 1 pint of cold water. Bring to the boil and simmer for about 10 minutes, then strain the liquid into the bucket. Put another pint of water on to the hops again bring to the boil and again strain off the liquid into the bucket. Repeat once more with another pint of water. Add the ½ teaspoon of gravy browning and stir well, put a little of the warm liquid into a cup and sprinkle on the granulated yeast. Leave for about 10 minutes until it is frothy. Make up the liquid in the bucket to 1 gallon with cold water, and when lukewarm, stir in the frothy yeast. Now pour it all into the fermentation jar and put a plug of cotton wool in the top. Stand in a deep dish in a warm place. When the first violent ferment has ceased, take out the cotton wool, wipe the neck of the jar clean, and insert a bored cork and an air lock, making sure that there is water halfway up the airlock. Leave in warm room till it has ceased working (4 to 7 days) then syphon off into a clean jar making sure you do not disturb the sediment on the bottom. Put on the airlock again and leave till liquid has cleared. Syphon off carefully into strong bottles, add 2 lumps of sugar to each bottle and screw down tight. Put in a cold place for about a week, when the beer should be ready for drinking. When syphoning the liquid from the yeasty deposits, it is better to filter it through a cloth placed in the plastic funnel. This is very, very good.

Harper Adams Agricultural College, Salop.

CORNISH MEAD

The honey used in this should be light and well ripened, and throughout the whole process the utmost cleanliness must be secured. Use 4 lb honey to each gallon of water, and allow the honey to dissolve, then put into a large boiler or copper, add 1 oz hops and $\frac{1}{2}$ oz ginger per gallon, and boil for one hour, skimming off the scum as it rises. When sufficiently boiled pour it into a wooden vessel and when its temperature is reduced to 120°F add 1 oz brewers yeast per gallon, mix well with the liquor which must then be covered and allowed to stand for about 8 hours in the same vessel. Next, pour it into a perfectly clean barrel, and as the contents ferment, the barrel must be filled with more of the liquor, an extra half-gallon having been prepared for this purpose beyond what the barrel holds. When fermentation has ceased, dissolve $\frac{1}{4}$ oz isinglass in a cupful of water, pour it into the barrel and stir well; this is to clear the liquid. After about 6 days draw off the liquor into a second perfectly clean barrel, filling the barrel completely, and drive in the bung as tightly as possible. Leave for at least 6 months, after which it may be bottled. The bottles must of course be perfectly clean, the corks new, and they should be fastened with wire and covered with tinfoil, a neat label being pasted on each bottle.

'The Practical Bee Guide', The Rev J. G. Digges, 1904

MEAD (1)

This may be made with honey straight from the bees, but can also be made with shop honey. Blend together 1 gallon of water, 1 pint of honey, and 4 oz sugar and bring to the boil. Skim and pour into an earthenware crock to cool. When lukewarm, add the peel of an orange cut in slices, the juice of an orange, and 2 oz yeast creamed with a little warm water. Put a lid on the crock, and leave to 'work' for a fortnight, stirring 3 times a day for the first 3 days. Strain, bottle and keep for 3 months before using.

MEAD (2)

1 oz dried hops	*2 gallons water*
2 lb honey	*1 oz yeast*

Put hops and honey into water and boil slowly for 1 hour. Cool and when lukewarm add the yeast spread on a piece of toast. Cover and leave for 4 days. Strain, bottle and cork loosely until fermentation has ceased, then cork tightly. Keep 1 year before using.

MR NIGHTINGALE'S WHISKEY

3 lb raisins   2 potatoes
3 lb sugar   1 gallon water
½ pint wheat   Yeast

Steep raisins, sugar, wheat and potatoes in water for one month, stirring each day. Strain, add yeast and allow to work. Restrain and bottle.

BRITISH SACK

To every quart of water put a sprig of rue; and to every gallon put a handful of fennel roots. Boil these ½ an hour, then strain it; and to every gallon of liquor put 3 lbs of honey. Boil it 2 hours, and skim it well. When it is cold, pour it off, and turn it into a cask or vessel that will just hold it.

Thomas Train, Gateshead, 1812

BRITISH CLARET

Take 8 pounds of Malaga raisins, well bruised, and put these into 6 gallons of water, and 2 gallons of cyder; place them in a warm situation, and let them stand close covered for 14 days, not forgetting to stir them well every other day. At the expiration of that time, strain off the liquor into a clean and well-seasoned cask, and add to it a pint of the juice of raspberries, a pint of the juice of black cherries, and a quart of ripe barberries. To work it up, throw in a little mustard seed, then cover it with a piece of dough, and let it stand 3 or 4 days by the side of the fire. After that, let it stand a week, and bottle it off. When it is worked fine, and is sufficiently ripe, it will have the taste and colour of common claret.

Thomas Train, Gateshead, 1812

ELDERFLOWER DRINK

Well-established idea that elderflowers are health-giving. Dry blooms and use as 'tea'.

1 *cluster of elderflowers with*   1½ *lb lump sugar*
the flower on it   1 *lemon and finely grated rind*
4 *quarts cold water*   1 *teaspoon tartaric acid*

Put ingredients into pan, stir often. After 24 hours, strain and bottle. Stand bottles upright for a fortnight, then lie on side. Use screw top bottles.

BARLEY WATER

3 oz pearl barley	2 pints boiling water
1 lemon	Sugar to taste

Wash the barley in a little boiling water. Drain off the water, and put the barley into a jug with the grated rind and juice of the lemon, and a little sugar. Pour over it the boiling water. Stir occasionally while cooling and strain before using.

LEMONADE (1)

1½ lb lump sugar	1 pint boiling water

Put ½ oz tartaric acid in a jug and pour on the hot syrup; when nearly cold add about 16 drops of essence of lemon.

LEMONADE (2)

1 orange	½ oz tartaric acid
1 lemon	3½ pints boiling water
1¾ lb sugar	

Mince orange and lemon, rind, pips and juice. Put in bowl with sugar, tartaric acid and water. Leave 24 hours. Strain through colander and sieve and bottle.

Mrs E. Jones

OLD-FASHIONED LEMONADE

3 lemons	1 quart boiling water
3 tablespoons sugar	Sprig of mint

Dice lemons and put into a jug with the sugar. Pour on boiling water, leave for 30 minutes, then strain. Put the mint into serving jug, pour on lemonade and add a few slices of fresh lemon. Serve with ice-cubes.

LEMON SYRUP

2 lemons	1 oz tartaric acid
1¾ lb lump sugar	1 pint boiling water

Peel lemons very thin. Add the peel to the lump sugar and pour on it the boiling water. Squeeze the juice of the lemons into a basin. Mix the tartaric acid with it, then stir all together. Put through a strainer and bottle off.

A drop or two of brandy or whiskey will keep it for many weeks. About 2 tablespoons to a tumbler of water.

Mrs Garden, 1847

GINGER BEER

Place 2 oz baker's yeast, or ½ oz dried yeast, in a large glass jar and add ½ pint tepid water, 2 level teaspoons each of sugar and ground ginger. When stirred it will soon begin to froth and seethe. Daily, for a week, feed the plant with 1 teaspoon each of sugar and ground ginger.

At the end of a week, strain the liquid carefully through butter muslin, retaining the residue, and add the juice of 2 lemons, 1 lb sugar and 2 pints of lukewarm water. Stir mixture well to dissolve sugar. Bottle when cool.

Carefully scrape the reserved residue into two jars, and carry out the whole process again, omitting the yeast this time. Remember, the plant won't live for more than a week or 10 days unless it is rejuvenated and started again.

The ginger beer is ready to drink in about a week. Cork lightly at first. Serve chilled.

MR JONES' PERSIAN SHERBERT

1½ *lb sugar bruised fine*	*4 oz tartarick acid*
¼ *lb carbonate soda*	¼ *oz essence lemon*

Be sure and pound it fine and sift it through fine muslin. 2 teaspoons to ½ pint Water.

Joseph Webb's Book, 1823

RHUBARB SHERBET

Cut some rhubarb into short lengths and to every pint of fruit put a quart of water and let it boil for 20 minutes; strain into a jug and sweeten with 8 lumps of sugar which have been rubbed into the rind of a lemon. When cool drink as a cooling beverage.

Lewis' Mother's Cookbook, Mary Horrell, Exeter

LAURA'S LEMONADE

4 large lemons	*1 teaspoon oil of lemon*
2 lb sugar	*1 dessertspoon tartaric acid*
2 pints water	

Squeeze the lemon juice over the sugar in a basin. Add the oil of lemon and the acid. Stir well and pour on boiling water. Stir until dissolved, and cool. Bottle when cold. Dilute to taste.

DAMSON GIN

This is a variation of the traditional sloe gin. Choose perfect fruit and wash them well, then prick them with a thick needle. Use half fruit and half gin, and to each estimated bottle add 8 oz sugar candy (or granulated sugar if the candy sugar is not available). Put fruit into a jar with the sugar and a teaspoon of almond essence and top up with gin. Stand jar in a warm place and shake or stir at least 3 times a day for a week. Store, and decant after 3 months.

CHERRY BRANDY

1 *lb Morello cherries*	½ *inch cinnamon stick*
4 *oz sugar candy*	*Brandy*
¼ *oz shredded bitter almonds*	

Remove stalks from cherries, wipe fruit and prick with a thick needle. Half-fill wide-necked jars with the fruit. Add sugar, almonds and cinnamon in the correct proportions, and fill jars to the top with brandy. Cover tightly and leave for at least 6 months. The brandy can be strained from the cherries, and the cherries are good to eat.

PUNCHES AND MULLS

Winter punches and mulls are cockle-warmers and tongue-looseners, and they can be very inexpensive, but they must be carefully prepared. Punch needs a strong spirit or wine base, and should be served very hot, preferably in handled mugs or glasses (pour it in over a metal spoon to avoid cracking). It's a good idea to heat the punch in a preserving pan which can easily be carried to a serving table and holds the heat better than a china bowl. Use inexpensive wine for punches, but use good whole spices to avoid cloudiness. As a variation on mixed drinks, try mulled wine, ale or cider, but suit the strength to the time of day.

Serve these hot drinks hot, but don't keep them on the boil, for a boiling drink soon loses its kick. Mulled wine can be poured back into the bottles after making and kept standing in hot water. For a really Olde Worlde touch, warm the mixture with a redhot poker to make the mull smoother.

MULLED WINE

Use cheap red wine for this. It's the traditional remedy for preventing or curing a cold. In Shakespeare's day, they used to add a well-beaten egg to the mull when it was taken from the fire. Heat 2 tablespoons sugar in 4 tablespoons water until the sugar has dissolved. Add 1 bottle red wine and heat to boiling point. Pour into glasses containing a slice of orange or lemon, and grate on a little fresh nutmeg.

MULLED ALE (1)

3 eggs
2 pints milk
1 pint ale

4 oz castor sugar
Little grated nutmeg

Bring the ale to the boil in a saucepan, then set aside. Beat the eggs, and stir in the milk, pour this mixture into the ale. Add the sugar and nutmeg, and heat slowly, but do not boil. Let it thicken, stirring meanwhile. Serve very hot.

MULLED ALE (2)

In a saucepan, mix together 1 quart brown ale, ¼ pint brandy, 1 tablespoon caster sugar, 4 cloves and a pinch each of nutmeg and ginger. Bring almost to the boil, add a piece of fresh butter the size of a walnut, and serve very hot.

MULLED CIDER

Boil 1 quart cider with 2 whole allspice, 2 whole cloves and 3 inch cinnamon stick for 5 minutes. Remove spices and add 3 oz brown sugar. Reheat and serve hot with a few lemon slices.

BUTTERED RUM (1)

6 lumps sugar
½ teaspoon ground allspice
½ teaspoon ground cloves

8 fluid oz rum
6 teaspoons fresh butter
6 tablespoons hot water

Dissolve the sugar in half the water. Add the other ingredients except the butter. Add remaining boiling water and pour into hot mugs. Add a knob of butter to each, and serve hot.

BUTTERED RUM (2)

For each person, warm a tumbler or mug and put 1 teaspoon caster sugar. Add ½ teacup boiling water, ½ teacup rum, and a lump of butter. Sprinkle with grated nutmeg.

RUM PUNCH

Boil 6 cloves and 1 inch cinnamon stick in 1¼ pints water for 5 minutes. Rub 12 lumps of sugar over the rind of an orange until they are yellow and full of zest. Add to the spiced water and boil for 5 minutes. Strain liquid on to 1 pint dark old rum, and serve very hot.

NEGUS

Put 1 pint of port into a jug. Rub a lemon with 12 lumps of sugar, and then squeeze the lemon juice and strain it. Mix sugar and lemon juice with the port, pour on 1 quart of boiling water. Cover the jug until the liquid has cooled slightly, then serve in glasses with grated nutmeg.

BISHOP

Stick a lemon with 12 cloves and roast it. Rub another lemon with 2 oz lump sugar and put into a bowl with juice of ½ lemon. In the bowl put the roasted lemon, 1 pint boiling water, a pinch of mixed spice and 1 quart of port which has been brought nearly to boiling point. Serve very hot.

LAMBSWOOL

Slit the skin of 4 large apples round the centre and bake them until the flesh will mash easily. Heat together 1 quart brown ale, 1 pint sweet white wine and 3 inch cinnamon stick, with ½ teaspoon each nutmeg and ginger. Mash the apples and stir them into the liquid. Take out cinnamon stick, and sieve the mixture, pressing down well. Reheat, adding sugar to taste.

WASSAIL

Slit the skin of 3 small red apples and bake them in the oven with 3 tablespoons soft brown sugar and ½ teacup brown ale, basting well until the apples are soft. Heat 1 quart brown ale with ½ pint sherry, ¼ teaspoon each of cinnamon, nutmeg and ginger, and a thin strip of lemon peel, and simmer for 5 minutes. Add the apples to the ale, with more brown sugar to taste, and serve very hot.

DR JOHNSON'S CHOICE

Heat 1 bottle red wine with 12 lumps of sugar and 6 cloves. Just before boiling point, add 1 pint boiling water, 1 wineglass orange Curaçao and 1 wineglass brandy. Serve with grated nutmeg.

CAMBRIDGE MILK PUNCH

This is a delicious, and apparently innocuous, drink, which is just the thing for maiden aunts. Put the thin rind of $\frac{1}{2}$ small lemon into 1 pint new milk with 12 lumps sugar. Simmer very slowly to extract the flavour of the lemon, take off the fire and remove the lemon rind. Stir in the yolk of an egg mixed with 1 tablespoon cold milk, 2 tablespoons brandy and 4 tablespoons rum. Whisk very thoroughly, and serve when frothy.

CARDINAL'S MULL

Make this like Bishop, but using claret or burgundy instead of port, flavouring with cinnamon and nutmeg and substituting an orange for the roasted lemon.

SIR ROGER DE COVERLEY

Heat together 1 bottle light red wine, 1 glass port and 2 tablespoons orange Curaçao, with 1 small teaspoon cinnamon, 1 small teaspoon mixed spice, a dash of nutmeg, 6 cloves and sugar to taste. Bring slowly to boiling point, simmer 2 minutes while stirring, strain and serve in warm glasses (10 glasses).

MADISON MULL

Stud an apple with cloves and bake in a moderate oven for 30 minutes. Heat to boiling point 1 pint of dry vintage cider with the apple, and 1 bottle claret. Heat without boiling, strain into a bowl and add 2 tablespoons Calvados (16 glasses).

MALMSEY MULL

Stud 1 large sweet orange with cloves and bake in a moderate oven for 1 hour. Heat 1 bottle Malmsey Madeira and 4 tablespoons apricot brandy and a pinch of ground ginger, with the orange floating on top, to boiling point. Just before serving, add $\frac{1}{2}$ pint boiling water (15 glasses).

APPLE POSSET

In each glass, put 2 tablespoons Calvados and fill up with hot apple juice, stirring with a cinnamon stick.

FLAMING PUNCH

Stick an orange with cloves and bake in a moderate oven for 1 hour. In a saucepan, combine 2 bottles claret, 1 sliced lemon, 1½ inch cinnamon stick, 2 oz blanched whole almonds, 2 oz raisins and 2 oz sugar. Add the orange and simmer uncovered for 15 minutes. Remove cinnamon stick and pour punch into serving bowl. In a saucepan, put 2 oz sugar and ¼ pint brandy. Heat very gently, ignite with a match, and while flaming pour into punch bowl (12 glasses).

OATMEAL CAUDEL

1 *pint hot water*	*Pinch of cinnamon*
2 *tablespoons oatmeal*	*Blade of mace*
Lemon rind	1 *pint ale*

Boil the oatmeal in the water with the lemon rind, and spice and enough brown sugar to taste. When thick, pour into the heated ale, stirring meanwhile.

MILK POSSET

1 *pint milk*	*Pinch of ground ginger*
A little sugar	*Pinch of nutmeg*
Squeeze of lemon	1 *glass white wine or sherry*

Heat the milk, when it froths add the wine or sherry. Strain and add lemon juice, sugar to taste, and stir in ginger and nutmeg. Serve hot.

SPICED CIDER

2 *pints cider*	1 *teaspoon ground nutmeg*
2 *tablespoons honey*	1 *teaspoon ground cinnamon*
2 *tablespoons lemon juice*	

Place all ingredients into saucepan and bring gently to the boil. Simmer 10 minutes. Strain through muslin before pouring into glasses. Garnish with apple slices and lemon slices.

SPICED RED WINE TODDY

1 *bottle good cheap red wine*
2 *oz soft brown sugar*
4 *cloves stuck into ½ large*
orange or 1 small orange
1 *teaspoon whole allspice*

Place all ingredients, except those for decoration, into saucepan and heat gently until sugar dissolves. Bring nearly to boil and simmer gently for 10 minutes. Strain before pouring into glasses. Decorate each glass with halved sliced orange and maraschino cherries.

OLD TIME MULLED CLARET

Pour into a large saucepan 3 bottles claret, ½ bottle port and ¼ bottle cognac. Add 4 spirals of lemon peel, 3 sticks of cinnamon, 1½ teaspoons of grated nutmeg, 1 dozen cloves spiked into the lemon peel. Add sugar to taste according to the dryness of the claret. Cover the saucepan with a lid and heat slowly to very hot, but not to *boil*.

MULLED BURGUNDY

2 *bottles red burgundy*
2 *limes or 1 lemon, cut into*
thin slices and seeded
½ *banana cut into slices*

Tie the fruit together with 2 sticks of cinnamon, 1 dozen whole cloves and a variety of mixed spices into a piece of cheesecloth. Put along with wine into a covered pot, simmer for not over 10 minutes. Discard cheesecloth and contents, then add 1 cup dark rum, ½ cup of brown sugar to taste and 1 cup of soda water. Stir and serve foaming, garnish with curl of lemon peel.

RED WINE CUP

3 *bottles red wine*
½ *bottle port*
¼ *bottle brandy*
Sugar, cloves and lemon rind
to taste

Heat red wine, sugar, cloves and lemon rind together. Add brandy just before serving.

HOT CHRISTMAS PUNCH

1 *bottle cider*
12 *lumps sugar*
2 *oranges*
8 *cloves*
1 *level teaspoon ground
nutmeg*

1 *stick cinnamon*
4 *tablespoons water*
2 *lemons*
1 *sherry glass rum*
1 *sherry glass brandy*

Rub the sugar over the rind of 1 of the oranges to remove the zest. Cut this orange in halves, squeeze out the juice and put into a pan with the sugar. Cut the other orange into 8 sections, stick a clove into the skin of each section and then sprinkle with the nutmeg. Add to the pan with the cinnamon, water and rind of the lemons, cut into strips. Heat gently until the sugar dissolves and then simmer for 5 minutes. Leave to cool until needed.

Remove the cinnamon, pour in the cider and heat until really hot, but not boiling. Add the rum and then the brandy and heat again for a minute. Divide the orange section and lemon rind between 8 glasses, add the hot cider and serve at once.

CIDER PUNCH

½ *gallon cider*
½ *bottle brandy*
1 *bottle red wine*
1 *lb sugar*
2 *oranges*

2 *lemons*
1 *stick of cinnamon*
Root of ginger
Cloves and nutmeg to taste

Squeeze the juice from 2 oranges and 1 lemon, put in a saucepan and add the sugar. Put remains of fruit, cinnamon, ginger, cloves and nutmeg in a cloth and boil with juice and sugar. Add cider and bring to boil. Just before serving remove cloth, add brandy and red wine and bring to boil. Serve piping hot with slices of lemon.

OXFORD PUNCH (HOT)

3 *parts rum*
2 *parts brandy*

1 *part fresh lemon juice*
6 *parts boiling water*

Add sugar to taste. Stir well.

HOT TEA PUNCH

1 *bottle rum*
1 *bottle brandy*
2 *sliced oranges*

1 *sliced lemon*
3 *pints freshly brewed tea*

Add sugar to taste. Mix well in a bowl. Mull with a red-hot poker.

WHITE WINE CUP

1 *liqueur glass orange*
Curacao
2 *liqueur glasses brandy*

1 *bottle hock*
1 *syphon soda water*

Put Curaçao and brandy in a jug with a large lump of ice. Pour on a bottle of iced hock and add soda water. Stir well and serve very cold.

SILVER WEDDING PUNCH

1 *medium tin apricots*
1 *medium tin pineapple*
6 *oranges*
1 *bottle cheap white wine*

1 *wineglass brandy*
1 *wineglass orange Curaçao*
Soda water

Mix together sliced apricots, pineapple and oranges. Add wine, brandy and Curaçao. Chill and dilute with soda water to taste.

Rene Woodhouse's recipe, as used at Oaksey Park, Cirencester

COLD PUNCH

2 *gallons best Fine Old Rum*
2 *dozen Oranges*
2 *dozen lemons*

16 *quarts spring water*
16 *lb lump sugar*
1 *pint new milk*

Pare your oranges and lemons quite thin pour the Rum on the Parings and let it stand 30 Hours then pour the boiling water on the Sugar and let that stand untill it is quite Cold. Strain the Rum from the parings to which add the Juice of the Lemons and Oranges after which add to your Ingredients the Milk put it into a cask let it stand 3 Weekes then bottle it.

NB it is proper it should be made in March then it will keep any length of time and do not foment.

Joseph Webb's Book, 1823

SNAPDRAGON

1 *lb seedless raisins*   1 *wineglass whisky or brandy*

It is an old Christmas custom to snatch hot raisins from flaming spirit. Prepare them by putting the raisins in a large shallow fireproof dish and heating them for 10 minutes in a low oven. Remove from the oven, pour over spirits, stir well and set light to the mixture. It burns steadily with a blue flame. Put the dish in the centre of the table, and let everyone snatch and eat the raisins while still flaming.

RUM AND EGG FLIP

4 *fresh eggs*   *Juice of 3 lemons*
½ *pint double cream*   ½ *lb castor sugar*
½ *pint Jamaica rum*

Place the perfectly clean whole eggs (in shells) in china bowl. Extract the juice from the lemons, and pour this over the eggs. Leave for four days, turning the eggs over daily, using wooden spoon. On fourth day, beat the eggs and juice well together, and pass through nylon, or hair sieve. Whip the cream and sugar till thick, then gradually mix in the egg and lemon juice. Beat well, and finally add rum. Stir well. Bottle and label. Store in cool place.

Miriam Ward, York

SHOOTING DRINKS

1) Strong green tea, with a little brandy in it is a capital drink for shooting.
2) Milk and whisky; quantity according to taste, the less spirit the better.
3) Melt or dissolve by a gentle heat 1 oz of black currant jelly in ½ pint of syrup (sugar and water); when cold, add the same quantity of rum (or gin if you prefer it), shake well and bottle.

The Country House Collection of Useful Information and Recipes 1867

TREACLE POSSET

½ *pint milk*   *dark treacle*
1 *tablespoon golden syrup, or*

Bring the milk to the boil and pour it over the syrup or treacle in a jug, stir well and serve very hot.

APPLE CIDER

4 lb apples (grated)   *2 gallons cold water*

4 lbs apples (grated), 2 gallons cold water. Stir every day for fortnight. Strain off. 3 lb sugar, 4 oz lump ginger (well bruised), 1 teaspoon cloves, 1 teaspoon cinnamon. Stir till sugar is dissolved. Leave a fortnight. Strain. It is then ready for use.

Mrs Kittie Lister, Chatham

DAMSON WINE

4 gallons of damsons, 4 gallons of boiling water. To every gallon of liquid allow 3½ lb lump sugar. Pour water over damsons and let stand for 4 or 5 days, stirring each day, then strain and add sugar. When this has dissolved pour into cask. It may be bottled for 12 months.

ROUGH CIDER

Leave apples to mellow and soften. Press hard between earthenware dishes, or through an old heavy mangle to extract juice. Leave tub of juice in a temperature of 60°F until frothing ceases and sediment has gone to the bottom. Remove clear liquid to a wooden cask and store in a cool place. To prevent the cider turning vinegary, put into strong clean stoppered bottles after 2 weeks and store in a cool place.

SIMPLE APPLE WINE

6 lb apples   *2 lb sugar*
1 gallon water

Cut up apples, including skins and cores. Cover with water, mash and stir every day for 2 days. Strain and heat up 1 pint of the liquid, then pour over the sugar. Stir well to dissolve sugar, and add rest of liquid. Leave to stand for 3 days, then skim, strain and bottle, corking lightly at first, then pushing corks in firmly after 3 days. This is a very light and delicious wine which stores well.

COTTAGE PERRY

10 lb windfall dessert pears   *1 lb white sugar*
1 lb raisins   *1 gallon water*
5 Campden tablets   *Yeast*

Wash fruit and slice into a china bowl with the chopped raisins and crushed Campden tablets. Dissolve the sugar in the water and pour over the fruit. Leave 3 days covered with a cloth, stirring twice daily. Cream 1 oz yeast with a little of the liquid and return to bowl, and leave in a warm room until gas bubbles no longer form. Pour off the liquid, strain the pulp through a thick cloth and add to the liquid. Put liquid into large jars, filling them and corking well. Leave in a cold room for several weeks until the perry becomes clear. Syphon off the liquid, leaving deposit behind. Dissolve ¼ lb sugar in every gallon of liquid and put into bottles (champagne bottles are best for this). Cork and tie down and store bottles on their sides in a cool place for at least 3 months.

DAMSON WINE

Bruise 8 lb damsons and pour on 1 gallon boiling water. Leave 48 hours. Strain; add 2½ lb sugar to each gallon juice.

Cover it and let it ferment. When this ceases, fill cask or bottles. Do not cork tightly till wine settles. Ready in 9 months, after straining again.

ELDERBERRY WINE (1)

Pick elderberries when quite ripe, strip from stalks, crush. Pour 1 gallon boiling water on to 8 pints berries. Stir occasionally, leave 2 weeks. Strain. To each quart of juice add ¾ lb sugar, ½ oz crushed whole ginger, 2 cloves. Boil together 25 minutes. When cool pour into tub or cask or large basin, add 1 oz yeast spread on slice of toast and allow to ferment. This takes a week or two. Strain and bottle. Do not cork too tightly. Keep 4 months before using.

ELDERBERRY WINE (2)

Put 4 lb ripe elderberries in vessel with 1 gallon cold water, let it stand until berries burst. Strain through close muslin, add 4 lb sugar to 1 gallon juice. Stir until all sugar is melted, then pour into gallon jars and let it remain until finished working. Bottle and cork tightly.

AUTUMN FRUIT WINE

Plums, damsons or blackberries make an excellent wine, particularly damsons which provide a rich, dark wine. 1 lb fruit, 1 quart boiling water. Place ripe fruit in earthenware bowl. Pour 1 quart boiling water over each pound of fruit. Let it stand for 5 days, stirring well each morning. Strain liquor, squeeze fruit well through muslin. To every quart of juice add 1 lb sugar. Put into bottles, putting over bottlenecks paper pricked with a pin. Let it stand 4 weeks. Strain again, bottle and cork well. In a week the wine is ready for use.

RHUBARB WINE

To every 5 lb rhubarb allow 1 gallon of water. Cut fruit up in small pieces. Let stand in water for 10 days, stirring every day. Strain. To each gallon of liquid allow $3\frac{1}{2}$ lb sugar, juice of 2 and rind of 1 lemon, $\frac{1}{2}$ oz isinglass dissolved in a pint of the liquor, warmed. Pour this into the wine when cool. Stir all together and let stand for 7 or 9 days. Leave to settle. Skim often during fermentation. Strain into stone jars. At end of 6 months, strain into bottles. Cork well. 2 sultanas put into each bottle will improve the wine.

BEETROOT BEER

1 *lb beetroot*   1 *breakfastcup white sugar*
1 *pint stout*

Wash beetroot and slice into bowl. Sprinkle on sugar and leave 24 hours. Strain, add stout, bottle and cork. Ready 7–14 days.

HOP BEER

1 *lb malt extract*   1 *gallon water*
1 *oz hops*   *Yeast*

Boil malt, hops and water for $1\frac{1}{2}$ hours, adding water to make up original quantity. Strain through muslin. When liquid is cool, add yeast and leave covered for 3 days. Syphon off and bottle. Put 1 lump of sugar in each, bottle and cork. Ready in 7 days.

15 Salting and Smoking

The important art of pickling or salting meat was, until refrigeration was thought up, the job which called for 'the housekeeper's best attention' to quote an early Edwardian cookery book. Nowadays, buying bacon requires very little skill, but in those days every farmer's wife was responsible for catering for enormous appetites, usually for enormous families, without the sophistication of refrigerators or deep freezers. She was compensated for this lack by having, invariably, more space, more help and in many farmhouses ample provision made for storing in cool conditions, meat and other perishable goods. This was, of course, essential since the farmer, it seemed, produced the food for his own larder before thinking of markets and other outlets for his surplus stock. Now we have, on the whole, smaller families, smaller houses and smaller profits so there are hundreds of farmers' wives who are in the (super) market for sheap food, the same as any other housewife.

GUIDE TO BACON CURING

1. If you live in Hampshire, Wiltshire or Dorset you must singe the pig – after killing it. If you live in Yorkshire, Lincolnshire or any of those northern counties you must scald the pig – this is traditional.

2. Great care must be taken in the preparation of the meat for salting. It must be carefully examined to see that it is *fresh* and *good* (i.e. sweet and wholesome smelling).

3. Having ascertained this, it must be wiped, sprinkled with salt, and afterwards left to drain a few hours before it is rubbed with the salt. *This will ensure that the meat is thoroughly cleansed from the blood.* If this is not done the meat will 'turn' and taste 'strong'.

4. It should then be placed in the pickling pan and turned every morning, it should also be rubbed with the pickle.

5. The cover of the pickling pan should fit very closely and have a weight on it to keep it down.

6. If a large quantity of salt meat is frequently required, the pickle may be boiled up, skimmed well, and when *cold* poured over any meat which has been sprinkled and well drained (as 3. above).

SWEET CURE

This is a sweet pickle for ham or bacon, using a carcass of about 8 score. Split the carcass, and from each side cut a rounded ham and a round shoulder (fore-ham). Debone the middle except for the chump end of the loin, which can be used fresh or lightly salted. To make packing easier, the middle may be subdivided into back and belly. Rub the knuckles with salt, and sprinkle salt on the joints, then pack into a crock. Pour over a pickle (for 15 lb ham or fore-ham) consisting of $\frac{1}{2}$ lb block salt, 1 lb black treacle, $\frac{1}{2}$ lb brown sugar, 1 pint malt vinegar and 2 pints old ale, with 1 tablespoon saltpetre. Turn the joints twice daily for the first week, then once daily for four weeks. Hang meat to drain for 24 hours, then encase in clean cotton bags and suspend from hooks. The hams are ready for use in 6 months and do not need soaking before cooking.

For 15 lb bacon, use a pickle of $\frac{1}{2}$ lb salt, $\frac{1}{2}$ lb brown sugar, 2 oz black treacle, $\frac{1}{4}$ pint vinegar and no saltpetre. Pack in crocks and pour over pickle, and turn joints twice daily for 3 weeks. The bacon can be used immediately after curing, or it can be soaked for 1 week with several changes of water before cooking as required.

DRY CURE

This is a dry cure method for a carcass of 16 to 20 score, using 28 lb salt and 8 oz saltpetre. Singe the flesh to remove hair and cut the carcass, removing the head, the spine with some of the back meat, and the ribs with a coating of lean meat.

Clean by sprinkling the flesh side with salt, and rubbing salt into the skin. Leave the sides, flesh side down, to drain for 24 hours, then wipe with a clean cloth. Sprinkle saltpetre on the flesh side of the shoulders and hams. Sprinkle half the salt over the sides which are placed one on top of the other. After 7 days, sprinkle half the remaining salt on, and put the top side at the bottom. After 7 more days, add remaining salt, and reverse positions of sides. The sides are in cure for about 4 weeks. Wipe off sides after curing, and hang up to dry for 7 days. Store sides whole, or for convenience cut into hams, middles and shoulders before hanging them up in clean cotton bags.

HEAVY CARCASS CURE

This is most suitable for a heavy carcass, which may be cut in three different ways. One method involves removing a chine of 6–8 inches wide and salting the 'long side'; the carcass can be simply split; or it may be cut into hams, fore-hams and middles. The ingredients for curing are 28 lb salt, $\frac{1}{2}$ lb saltpetre and 1 lb demerara sugar. Rub saltpetre in first, spreading most thickly on blood patches. Sprinkle meat with salt and pack on a layer of salt in a trough. Place hams on top and every day for a fortnight, sprinkle on salt. When meat is cured, wipe salt off and sprinkle with flour. After being dry for 3 months, pack in a bin containing slaked lime.

TO CURE BACON

Time – 3 weeks

1 *lb saltpetre*	1 *lb salprunella*
1 *lb bay salt*	1 *lb moist (brown) sugar*

Pound the salprunella and bay salt very fine, mix the coarse salt and the sugar well together, and rub it into your bacon, hams and cheeks, putting all in the same brine. Turn and rub the bacon for a week every day; afterwards every other day. Let it remain in the brine for 3 weeks, and then send it to be smoked or dried. Large sides of bacon take a month to dry, small ones 3 weeks.

TO CURE HAMS

For 2 large hams:

1 *lb common salt*	1 *lb coarse brown sugar*
3 *oz bay salt*	1 *quart stale strong beer or*
2 *oz saltpetre*	*ale*

Boil all the above ingredients in the quart of beer or ale, and when cold pour it onto the hams and turn them every day for a fortnight; then smoke them well.

MRS JEWRY'S WAY TO PICKLE PORK

One third saltpetre   *Two thirds white salt*

Mrs Jewry says some people prefer pork pickled with salt alone (the legs especially); others in the following manner: Put a layer of salt at the bottom of the tub; then mix the saltpetre and salt well. Cut the pork in pieces, rub it well with the salt and lay it close in the tub, with a layer of salt in between every layer of pork till the tub is full. Have a cover, just large enough to fit the inside of the tub, put it on, and lay a great weight at the top, then as the salt melts, it will keep it close. When you want to use it, take a piece out, cover up the tub again and it will keep for a good long time.

MRS JACKSON'S YORKSHIRE WAY
WITH HAMS, TONGUES AND BEEF

1½ *lb brown sugar*	1½ *lb common salt*
2 *oz saltpetre*	2 *oz pepper*

On the night you get the meat, rub it all over with common salt; next morning rub it well with a mixture of the above ingredients.

With hams – take them into the kitchen and rub them *before the fire* every day and turn them, every day for 10 days, then every other day for 10 days. If it is a very big thick ham, it may need a few days longer.

Mrs Jackson lives on a remote farm in the East Riding and has successfully brought up 4 sons and 2 daughters. They all had hearty appetites, so she was used to providing tables full of food. She played the village church organ for many years and filled her spare time in joining in all village activities with gusto. She is a great cook to this day and long may she continue to encourage folk to 'wrap theesen around this and ye'll not feel the wind!' as she plies one with good food.

MRS BRIDGES' GLOUCESTERSHIRE CURE

This is a very old receipt which has been handed down from generation to generation. The whole simple process is spread over 4 weeks and the result is a delicious ham of a delicate flavour.

Take one good ham. Note: the best ham is obtained from a once-farrowed 'hilt' (gilt)

First week: Put ham into trough or 'lead'. Take a bar of salt and rub salt all over ham working well into every crevice and crease. Continue the treatment every other day for 1 week.

Second week: Prepare mixture for second week's treatment. Chop 1 lb salt into a dish; add ½ lb *only* of saltpetre, 1 lb dark brown sugar and mix well together. Rub some of this mixture into the front and the back. Turn every other day for a week, gradually using more of the mixture but keeping back sufficient for the final week. When brine forms, baste this over as well.

Third week: With rind side down in brine, cover with remainder of brine mixture rubbing and pressing into the surfaces. Cover with golden syrup and leave untouched for 3 days.

Fourth week: Dust with rice flour, then hang up to dry.

Take care that no flies can get in by using plenty of butter muslin. After this, leave for 2 *years* – if you can.

Jim Woodhouse, Oaksey Park, Glos.

W. ARNOLD'S PICKLING RECIPE

For Beef and Pork

1 *gallon water*	½ *oz saltpetre*
6 *oz coarsest raw sugar*	¾ *lb bay salt*

Hams and Tongues

2 *quarts water*	1 *oz saltpetre*
3 *oz coarsest sugar*	14 *oz bay salt*

Boil till no more scum rises, then set by till quite cold. Let the meat be entirely covered and if you have reason to keep it long it will be necessary to boil the pickle every 6 weeks and to move the scumming as before and adding to the above quantities ½ oz coarset moist sugar and 2 oz of common salt. If these instructions are carefully attended to the Pickle will keep for 12 months. In extreme hot weather it is necessary to rub the meat with a little salt and let it remain a few hours that all the blood may be drawn from it before it is put into the pickle. Meat thus cured never becomes hard and dry as when salted in the usual way.

Mrs Garden, Slough, 25 September, 1861

FOR PICKLING A HAM WITH BOILING PICKLE

For a ham 26 lb.

5 quarts water
3 lb common salt
1 oz saltpetre

1 oz salt prunella
1 lb moist sugar

Put all in the water to boil, and throw it while boiling on the ham. Keep a month in pickle and smoke – if preferred.

Lewis' Mother's Cookbook, Mary Horrell, Exeter

EVERYTHING BUT THE SQUEAK

How to deal with the rest of the pig

Liver: The liver of the pig is particularly good for highly seasoned patés. If cooked as a main meal, it is excellent seasoned with sage, onion and apple.

Pork Fillet: This is the lean strip of meat lying beneath the loin, weighing 8–12 oz. It is a delicious piece of meat. The fillet may be slit, stuffed and roasted in a hot oven for 45 minutes, before serving with a good gravy. The meat is best wrapped in bacon, and well basted with a little dripping, and should be cut diagonally to serve. It is also delicious if cut in small pieces and tossed in oil or butter with chopped mushrooms, onions and green peppers until golden and cooked through, then served in its own juices with rice or mashed potatoes.

Ears: Leave them for 24 hours in coarse salt, then wash well and scald. Make a stuffing with 4 oz sausage meat, 4 oz bread soaked in stock, 4 oz chopped mushrooms, 1 small onion, 1 egg. Fill the ears with this stuffing putting one ear on top of the other to contain the stuffing, and tie up. Brown in a little fat, then simmer in good stock for two hours. Serve in the reduced liquor with pease pudding, lentils or butter beans.

Trotters: Wash, scrape and singe the trotters thoroughly. Cut them in half, and leave covered in salt for 24 hours. Wash very thoroughly, match up the halves again, and tie each tightly in a clean cloth. Put in a pan of cold water with a good bunch of mixed herbs, a carrot, an onion stuck with cloves, salt and pepper, bring to the boil, then simmer for five hours. Leave to cool in the stock remove when just tepid, and leave until completely cold before taking out of cloth. Roll each trotter in melted butter or in oil, and then in breadcrumbs. Grill slowly for 20 minutes.

Head: The head makes superb stock, and if this is left to chill, lard may be removed from the top of the stock. The meat from the head can be eaten in many ways, but its best known use is in brawn.

Chitterlings: Cut 'tubes' in lengths of about 4 inches and clean thoroughly under running water. Scald in boiling water for 30 minutes. Thoroughly rinse again by running cold water through. Soak in salt and water for 5 days, then rinse thoroughly again. Some people like to eat these cold with salt, pepper and vinegar; others fry them and season with salt and pepper.

Brains: Leave brains in cold running water for an hour. Put in a pan of cold salted water and bring to the boil. Boil for 5 minutes, remove from heat, and leave to cool in the liquid. A good way of serving these is to dip walnut-size pieces in batter and deep-fry them, serving with a sharp sauce.

Heart: Thoroughly wash the heart, removing core and piece at top. Make 4 deep cuts into the flesh, wash again in cold water and stuff the cuts with sage and onion stuffing. Skewer together, sprinkle with salt and pepper, and wrap in foil. Put in a dish and bake at 350°F (Gas Mark 4) for 2 hours. Serve with rich gravy.

HOME SMOKING

Smoked food has been a tradition in Britain for centuries. From the humble haddock, bloater and kipper to the grand salmon and trout, and from the everyday rasher to the succulent ham, there is a delicious smoked food for any meal of the day.

Those with good supplies of fresh meat and fish, wonder whether they might not try their hand at home-smoking. It is possible to tackle the job on a do-it-yourself basis, but good results are only obtained by careful attention to detail.

The point of smoking is to remove moisture from the food very slowly, like drying, and to give additional flavour and to preserve. Smoking which is meant to preserve food for a length of time needs space, skill and scrupulous hygiene.

It is necessary to build a smoke-house, though this can be of a simple type, or to adapt a farmhouse chimney with a smoke box. Foods which can be smoked include eel, herring, salmon, trout, sprats, cod's roe, ham and bacon, tongue, turkey, goose, duck and chicken, and a variety of home-made sausages. Some of these items need brining before smoking; ham, bacon and salmon need elaborate preparation and are not really practical to smoke on a small scale.

If an individual flavour is required for home-produced or home-caught products, it may be preferable to prepare the meat or fish with an individual cure but get it smoked by a local bacon factory.

In addition to the basic smoke-house, there must be a good supply of wood. The best smoke is produced by slow combustion hardwood shavings; oak, beech, birch and hornbeam are excellent, with additional flavour provided by juniper and bay. The addition of thyme, sage or heather makes a good variation.

Resinous woods should be avoided because they can give an unpleasant flavour. The object of creating the smoke is to make fumes which solidify the albumen in the meat. This halts decomposition; the flavour is a bonus.

The simplest form of smoke-house can be constructed in a 10-gallon drum with the bottom cut out and a replaceable top which has a few holes punched in. This is particularly good for smoking trout or haddock, suspended over a concentrated source of heat and smoke. Haddock should be split, cleaned and beheaded, rubbed inside and out with salt, and left overnight, then dried in the open air for 3 days. Trout need not be split or beheaded, but the gut should be removed.

The fish should be suspended by the tail on a rod across the top of the drum, and tied with a piece of wire at least 1 foot from the fire. The drum should then be upended over the fire – best made between bricks on which the drum stands. The heat must be evenly maintained during smoking – which will take from 9 to 12 hours.

A slightly more elaborate smoke-house can be constructed for permanent use. This can be a drum or a packing case which has been made smoke-proof at the joints, standing across a trench. The trench should be about 10 ft long, 1 ft deep and 1 ft wide, dug in the direction of the prevailing wind, with old paving stones or sheet iron to roof it over. If the lid of the house is hinged, it will be esaier to use, and it should have small holes or a tube inserted as a vent.

To use this type of smoke-house, light a fire at the end furthest from the box, cover with stones or iron sheets, and open the lid of the box. When the fire is red-hot, draw it to the end of the trench and put a load of hardwood sawdust between the fire and the box. Leave a little flue space, cover the trench and seal all spaces with earth. The food can be hung across the box and the lid closed and not opened for 48 hours.

The idea is to build up a progressively dense smoke which dries and flavours the fish gradually; if the first smoke is too dense it will form a dry coating on the food which will not be penetrated by the later smoking.

For this type of smoking, the food should be brined first in a strong brine (with enough salt to float a potato). A small fish need only be brined for 20 minutes, but a salmon needs several days, and elaborate preparation.

The smoking method which is most likely to appeal is the one using the old-fashioned farmhouse chimney, which can be used for hams and sausages. These must be prepared first, and are then best left to hang and dry for two or three days before smoking.

The food to be smoked can be hung above the opening of a bread oven so that the smoke gently enfolds them; the temperature should never rise above 90°F at which point the fat melts and meat is spoiled. The fire should be smouldering, not flaming. On the first day, the meat should be smoked for 30 minutes, then rubbed down with pepper, thyme and chopped bay leaves, which will cling to the fat.

After cooling and drying for 48 hours, the meat should be smoked again for 1 hour. After further drying for 48 hours and 1 hour's smoking, a light flavour will be obtained.

The meat should be hung in the chimney for 2 or 3 weeks before being stored in a cool dry place. The meat will lose about $\frac{1}{4}$ of its weight in smoking.

The wide chimney can be used for complete smoking, with the meat suspended high up on a bar, or on hooks on wire, but the fire will need careful attention.

Smoke the meat for about an hour a day, allowing a total of at least 3 weeks for complete smoking.

The best method of regulating the smoke-flow is to construct a smoking box for the fireplace, to fit on a wall above the fire. A sheet of metal has to be fitted across the whole chimney with a piece of piping going through it and the wall into the smoking-box. A second piece of piping should then go out of the top of the box and back into the chimney. Meat in the box needs about 2 hours a day for 8 consecutive days.

16 Freezing

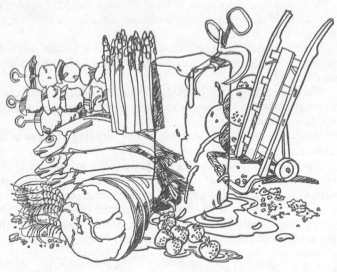

St James's Park

'As Lately Improved by His Majesty'

(on the royal ice well)

Yonder, the harvest of the months laid up
Gives a fresh coolness to the Royal Cup;
There ice, like crystal firm, and never lost,
Tempers hot July with December's frost;
Winter's dark prison, whence he cannot fly,
Though the warm spring, his enemy, draws nigh.
Strange! that extremes should thus preserve the snow.
High on the Alps, or in deep caves below.

Edmund Waller, 1606–87

GARDEN PRODUCE

APPLES

Firm apples for freezing in slices; fluffy apples for purée or sauce. For slices, peel and core fruit and put into basin of cold water, then slice medium apples into twelfths, large ones into sixteenths. Use dry sugar pack for preference (8 oz sugar to 2 lb fruit). Freeze baked apples in individual waxed tubs or foil dishes. Make apple sauce in the oven with a minimum of water, adding a squeeze of lemon juice. Storage time for baked apples: 1 month. Storage time for slices, pulp or sauce: 1 year.

ARTICHOKES (GLOBE)

Remove outer leaves, trim stalks, remove 'chokes' and wash artichokes very thoroughly. Blanch in sizes in 4 quarts boiling water with 1 tablespoon lemon juice for 7 minutes. Cool in ice water, and drain upside down. Pack in boxes (polythene will tear). If preferred, blanch only bottoms for 5 minutes. To cook whole artichokes, plunge into boiling water and boil 5 minutes. Storage time: 1 year.

ASPARAGUS

Remove woody portions and small scales and wash well. Sort into sizes, and blanch each size separately (small spears: 2 minutes; medium: 3 minutes; large: 4 minutes). Cool and drain and pack in boxes lined with moisture-vapour-proof paper, or wrap in freezer paper. To cook: allow 5 minutes in boiling water. Storage time: 9 months.

BLACKBERRIES

Fully ripe, dark glossy berries. Wash in chilled water and drain on absorbent paper. Pack dry and unsweetened, or in dry sugar pack (8 oz sugar to 2 lb fruit) or in 50 per cent syrup. Storage time: 1 year.

BEANS (BROAD)

Small young beans with tender outer skins. Blanch $1\frac{1}{2}$ minutes, cool and pack in cartons or polythene. To cook, allow 8 minutes in boiling salted water. Storage time: 1 year.

BEANS (FRENCH)

Tender young beans left whole or cut in 1 inch pieces. Blanch whole beans 3 minutes, cut beans 2 minutes, and pack in polythene. Cook whole beans for 7 minutes in boiling salted water, cut beans for 5 minutes. Storage time: 1 year.

BEANS (RUNNER)

Tender young beans cut in pieces (not shredded, as they become pulpy and tasteless). Blanch 2 minutes and pack in polythene. Cook 7 minutes in boiling salted water. Storage time: 1 year.

BROCCOLI

Compact heads with tender stalks not more than 1 inch thick, of uniform green colour. Discard woody stems and trim outer leaves. Wash very well and soak in salt solution (2 teaspoons salt to 8 pints water) for 30 minutes, then wash in clean water. Cut in sprigs and blanch 3 minutes for thin stems, 4 minutes for medium and 5 minutes for thick stems. Pack into bags or boxes (alternate heads in boxes). Cook 8 minutes in boiling water. Storage time: 1 year.

BRUSSELS SPROUTS

Small, compact heads, graded for size before blanching. Blanch 3 minutes for small sprouts, 4 minutes for medium ones, and pack in cartons or bags. Cook for 8 minutes in boiling water. Storage time: 1 year.

CHERRIES

Red varieties freeze better than black. Firm cherries in chilled water for 1 hour, then dry, and remove stones which may flavour fruit. Pack in glass or plastic containers, as the acid in cherry juice tends to remain liquid in freezing and may leak through cardboard. For pies, pack cherries in dry sugar (8 oz sugar to 2 lb pitted cherries or in syrup depending on tartness). Storage time: 1 year.

CAULIFLOWER

Firm compact heads with close white flowers, broken into sprigs not more than 1 inch across. Add juice of 1 lemon to blanching water and blanch for 3 minutes. Pack in lined boxes. Cook for 10 minutes in boiling water. Storage time: 6 months.

CORN ON THE COB

Fresh tender corn, frozen as cobs or kernels. Remove leaves and 'silk' and grade cobs for size, cutting stems short. Blanch small cobs for 4 minutes, medium 6 minutes and large 8 minutes. Cool and dry in paper. Pack individual ears in freezer paper and freeze immediately in coldest part of freezer. Store quantities in bags for easy handling. Kernels can be scraped from cobs and packed in containers. Storage time: 1 year.

Correct cooking after freezing is very important for corn. Either put frozen cobs in cold water to cover, bring to fast boil, and simmer for 15 minutes, or thaw in packaging in refrigerator, plunge in boiling water and cook for 10 minutes.

CURRANTS

Black, red and white currants should be stripped from stems, washed in chilled water, and dried. For jam making, pack dry in bags. For later cooking, use dry sugar pack (8 oz sugar to 1 lb berries, mixing sugar until dissolved). *Boskoop Giant* and *Wellington* are good for freezing. Storage time: 1 year.

GOOSEBERRIES

Wash in chilled water, dry, and freeze without sweetening. For future jam-making, freeze fruit slightly under-ripe. Purée can be made with little water, sieved and sweetened. *Careless* is a good variety for freezing. Storage time: 1 year.

HERBS

Wash parsley, mint or chives, chop finely, pack into ice-cube trays and fill with water. Freeze, wrap cubes in foil, and package in bags. Flavour is not strong, though colour is good. Do not freeze herbs in sprigs for garnishing, as they go limp on thawing.

PLUMS

Plums, greengages and damsons can be treated in similar ways. Chill fruit in chilled water, dry well, cut in halves, removing stones, and pack in 40 per cent syrup. Damson skins can be very tough, and they are best frozen in pulp form. Very good plums can also be frozen in a dry sugar pack. Storage time: 1 year.

PEAS

Young sweet peas, not old starchy ones. Shell and blanch for 1 minute, lifting basket in and out of water to distribute heat evenly between layers of peas. Chill and pack in polythene bags or cartons. Cook in boiling water for 7 minutes. Storage time: 1 year.

POTATOES

Young new potatoes can be scraped and washed, blanched for 4 minutes, cooled and packed in polythene bags. Cook in boiling water for 15 minutes. Storage time 1 year. Or slightly undercook, drain, toss in butter, cool, pack and freeze. Cook by plunging frozen bag in boiling water, removing pan from heat and leaving 10 minutes. Older potatoes can be frozen as mashed potatoes, chips, or baked potatoes, for no longer than 3 months.

RASPBERRIES

Discard hard, seedy fruit, and wash in chilled water. Freeze in dry pack, or in sugar, allowing 4 oz to each lb raspberries. *Norfolk Giant* and *Lloyd George* are best for freezing. Storage time: 1 year.

RHUBARB

Young pink sticks can be frozen unsweetened for pies. Pack in cartons or polythene or foil. If lightly blanched for 1 minute, stems will pack more easily. Also can be packed in 40 per cent syrup, or in purée form. Storage time: 1 year.

STRAWBERRIES

Strawberries are best frozen dry, when they will be less pulpy when thawed. If packed in dry sugar or syrup, slice or lightly crush fruit (dry sugar pack: 4 oz sugar to 1 lb fruit or 40 per cent syrup). *Cambridge Vigour*, *Cambridge Favourite* and *Royal Sovereign* are best for freezing. Storage time: 1 year.

Apricots, blueberries, cranberries, fresh figs, grapes, melons, peaches and quinces may also be frozen.

SPINACH

Young tender spinach without heavy leaf ribs. Remove stems and wash very well. Blanch for 2 minutes, moving container to separate leaves. Cool, press out excess moisture, and pack in rigid containers or polythene bags. To serve, cook 7 minutes in a little melted butter. Storage time: 1 year.

TOMATOES

Tomatoes cannot be frozen for salad use. For cooking, they can be frozen whole, after wiping clean, in polythene bags. Thaw for 2 hours at room temperature before using. Storage time: 10 months. Tomatoes can be frozen as pulp, by removing skins, pips and cores, then simmering tomatoes in their own juice for 5 minutes before sieving and packing in cartons. Storage time: 1 year. Tomato juice is made by simmering ripe tomatoes in a covered container for 15 minutes, then putting juice through muslin and packing in containers. Juice should be thawed in containers in refrigerator. Storage time: 1 year.

FARMYARD AND FIELD

POULTRY

Birds to be frozen should be in perfect condition, and should be starved for 24 hours before killing, then hung and bled well. When the bird is plucked, it is important to avoid skin damage; if scalding, beware of over-scalding which may increase the chance of freezer-burn (grey spots occurring during storage). The bird should be cooled in a refrigerator or cold larder for 12 hours, drawn and completely cleaned. With geese and ducks, it is particularly important to see the oil glands are removed, as these will cause tainting.

A whole bird should be carefully trussed to make a neat shape for packing. Birds may be frozen in halves or joints. When packing pieces, it is not always ideal to pack a complete drum in each package; it may be more useful ultimately if all drumsticks are packaged together, all breasts or all wings according to the way in which the flesh will be cooked. *Giblets* have a storage life of 2 months, so unless a whole bird is to be used within that time, it is not advisable to pack them inside the bird. Giblets should be cleaned, washed, dried and chilled, then wrapped in moisture-vapour proof paper or bag, excluding air; frozen in batches, they may be used for soup, stews or pies. *Livers* should be treated in the same way and packaged in batches for use in omelettes, risotto or pâté.

Bones of poultry joints should be padded with a small piece of paper or foil to avoid tearing freezer wrappings. Joints should be divided by two layers of Cellophane. Bones of young birds may turn brown in storage, but this does not affect flavour or quality.

Geese and ducks have a storage life of 6–7 months; turkey and chicken frozen whole 8–12 months, and in pieces 6–10 months. Giblets and livers should not be kept longer than 2 months.

Stuffing can be put into a bird before freezing, but it is not advisable as the storage life of stuffing is only about 1 month. Pork sausage stuffing should not be used, and if a bird must be stuffed, a breadcrumb stuffing is best. It is better to package stuffing separately, but this is unnecessary as a stuffing may be prepared during the thawing time of the bird.

GAME BIRDS

All game birds should be kept cool between shooting and freezing; care should be taken to remove as much shot as possible, and to make sure shot wounds are thoroughly clean. Birds should be bled as soon as shot, kept cool and hung to individual taste. After plucking and drawing, the cavity should be thoroughly washed and drained and the body wiped with a damp cloth. The birds should then be packed, cooled and frozen, as for poultry. Game will keep in the freezer 6–8 months.

HARES AND RABBITS

Hares and rabbits should be beheaded and bled as soon as possible and hung for 24 hours in a cool place. Skin and clean, washing cavity well, and wipe with a damp cloth. Cut into joints and wrap each piece in Cellophane, excluding air, then pack joints together in moisture-vapour-proof bag or paper, seal, label and freeze. Hares and rabbits will keep in the freezer 6–8 months.

VENISON

Venison needs careful butchering, but if help is not immediately available, the carcass should be kept in good condition, the shot wounds carefully cleaned, and the animal kept as cold as possible. The venison should be beheaded and bled, skinned and cleaned, and the interior washed and wiped. Hanging should take place in a very cool place (preferably just above freezing point) with the belly propped open so air can circulate. 5 to 6 days' hanging will make the meat tender. The meat should be cut in joints, packed like meat, sealed, labelled and frozen. Since this is a large animal, it is best to keep only the good joints whole. The rest of the meat can be minced to freeze raw for later use as hamburgers and mince, or can be casseroled or made into pies and frozen in this form. Since the meat is inclined to dryness, it is often marinaded before cooking. The marinade should be poured over the meat while it is thawing. Venison will keep in the freezer 8–10 months.

HAM AND BACON

Cured and smoked meats are best stored in a cool atmosphere, protected from flies and dust, and there is no advantage in freezing them. They may, of course, be frozen, and are then better in the piece rather than slices, but storage time is limited to 3–4 months. Meat stored in this way should be overwrapped. Sliced bacon may for convenience be stored in the freezer, wrapped in moisture-vapour-proof wrapping, but storage time is limited to 3 weeks.

MEAT

Good quality meat should be chosen, and hung for the required time. Meat should be packed in quantities suitable for use on one occasion. If possible, meat should be boned and surplus fat removed so as not to take up unnecessary freezer space; if bones are not removed, ends should be wrapped in several layers of greaseproof paper to avoid piercing freezer wrappings. Meat should be packed in polythene for easy identification, and labelling is very important as with all freezer items. It is most important to exclude air from packages so that the freezer wrap stays close to surface of meat. If a whole animal or a variety of different meats are being prepared for freezing at one time, begin with the offal, then pork, then veal and lamb, and finally beef as this will keep best under refrigeration if delays occur. Normally, no more than 4 pounds of meat per cubic foot of freezer space should be frozen at one time for best results.

It is important that wrapping for meat should be strong, since oxygen from the air which may penetrate wrappings affects fat and causes rancidity (pork is, of course, most subject to this problem). In addition to moisture-vapour-proof wrapping, an overwrap of brown paper, grease-proof paper or stockinette will protect packages and will guard against punctures from projecting bones or other packets. It is worth taking this precaution, since meat is likely to be the most costly item stored in the freezer.

BAKING DAY

COOKED YEAST MIXTURES

Bread, buns and rolls freeze particularly well when 1 day old. Freeze in polythene bags. Thaw in wrapping at room temperature; $1\frac{1}{2}$ lb loaf takes about 3 hours. In emergency, bread can be thawed very quickly in a moderate oven, but will become stale very quickly.

SCONES

These may be frozen cooked or uncooked; unbaked ones will only store for 2 weeks, otherwise 2 months. If scones are unbaked, they can be baked in a hot oven without thawing, or partly thawed and then cooked.

CRUMPETS AND MUFFINS

These bought seasonal delicacies can be frozen in polythene bags for future use. Thaw at room temperature and toast.

PANCAKES AND GRIDDLE CAKES

Thin pancakes, griddle cakes and drop scones should be cooled before packing. Stack large pancakes with layers of Cellophane or greaseproof paper between, then wrap in freezer paper or polythene. Separate while frozen, or thaw in one piece at room temperature. Wrap around filling and heat in a low oven, or on a plate over steam covered with a cloth. Thaw griddle cakes or drop scones before buttering.

SPONGE CAKES

Fatless sponges can be stored for 10 months; those made with fat can be stored for four months. Delicate sponges can be frozen in freezer paper or polythene, then packed in boxes to avoid crushing. Thaw baked cakes in wrappings at room temperature unless they are iced (see Icings and Fillings).

FRUIT CAKES

Rich fruit cakes store well in tins, so there is little point in taking up freezer room. Dundee cakes, sultana cakes and other light fruit mixtures freeze very well. Thaw in wrappings at room temperature.

SMALL CAKES

Small fruit cakes and sponge drops may be frozen in polythene bags. Small butter-iced cakes are best made in paper or foil cases, iced and frozen in single layers, then packed in boxes with greaseproof paper between layers. Choux pastry and meringues can be frozen well, if unfilled, and should be frozen in single layers, then packed in boxes.

BISCUITS

Baked biscuits store well in tins. Unbaked biscuits freeze very well. Make up batches of biscuit mixture, form into cylinder shapes and freeze in freezer paper, polythene or foil. To use, thaw in wrapping in refrigerator for 45 minutes, cut in slices and bake. These unbaked biscuits will store for 2 months.

ICINGS AND FILLINGS

Do not fill cakes with cream, jam or fruit. Be sure a butter-iced cake is absolutely firm before wrapping and freezing. The easiest packing method is to put the cake on a board or cardboard plate, and slip it into a polythene bag. Foil wrappings can also be used. Remove wrappings before thawing to avoid smudging icing. If sponge or flavoured cakes are to be packed ready for future icing, put layers together with Cellophane, foil or grease-proof paper between.

FLAVOURINGS AND DECORATIONS

Use only pure flavourings, vanilla in particular. Highly spiced foods develop off-flavours, so avoid spice cakes, though gingerbread will be satisfactory if stored for no longer than a month. Chocolate, coffee and fruit-flavoured cakes freeze very well. Do not decorate with nuts, coloured balls, sweets or grated chocolate before freezing, or moisture may be absorbed and the cake icing show colour changes.

SLICED CAKES

It is usually most convenient to pack cakes whole. It can happen that a cake may be started, but the remainder might be left for some time, when it can then be frozen in slices for future use. It is also useful to have meal-size wedges or individual pieces for lunch boxes. Pieces can be wrapped and frozen individually. It is easier to slice the whole cake in wedges before freezing, and withdraw slices as they are needed without thawing the whole cake.

PIES AND FLANS

Pies and flans can be stored baked and unbaked. Do not use custard fillings which separate, or meringue toppings which toughen and dry during storage. Baked flan cases, patty cases and vol-au-vent cases are usefully frozen, and can be thawed at room temperature before filling.

UNBAKED PIES

Pies may be prepared with or without a bottom crust. For fruit fillings, brush surface of bottom crust with egg white to prevent sogginess, for meat pies, brush crust with melted lard. Do not cut air vents in pastry before freezing. To prevent sogginess, freeze unbaked pies *before* wrapping them. Make fruit pies with cooked or uncooked fillings; apples tend to brown after 4 weeks, even if treated with lemon juice. Meat pies are best made with cooked filling and uncooked pastry; to bake, cut slits in top crust and bake unthawed as for fresh pies, allowing 10 minutes longer than normal cooking time.

BAKED PIES

Cook pies in normal way, cool quickly and freeze. These are best prepared and frozen in foil containers, packed in freezer paper or polythene. Pies may be eaten thawed but not reheated. A cooked pie should be heated in a moderate oven for 45 minutes (double crust) or 30 minutes (single crust).

FRESH FRUIT PIE FILLINGS

Surplus fruit may be frozen in the form of pie fillings which can be used with fresh pastry when needed. Simply combine fruit with sugar to sweeten, and add 1 tablespoon lemon juice and 2 tablespoons tapioca flakes to each lb of fruit, leave to stand for 15 minutes, then put into a pie plate with foil lining, leaving a rim of foil to fold over. Fold over foil and freeze, then remove filling from pie plate and store in freezer. To use, line pie plate with pastry, put in fruit filling, dot with butter, cover with pastry lid, make slits in top crust, and bake at 425°F (Gas Mark 7) for 45 minutes.

COMPLETE MEALS

FIRST COURSES

Keep a small selection of prepared starters. Vegetable soup, kidney soup and tomato soup are worth keeping in the freezer. Chicken stock or meat stock can be quickly turned into clear soup with a few fresh vegetables. Pâté is another good first course. Keep a roughcut one which will make a complete meal, and a smooth chicken liver or fish pâté for grander occasions.

MAIN COURSES

Main courses can be prepared in batches for freezing, though most people prefer to cook a double quantity, serving half fresh and freezing the rest for future use. Steak and kidney pies and chicken pies are excellent frozen. If they are completely cooked before freezing, they can also be taken out to eat cold for a packed meal. Steak and kidney pudding or game pudding can be either large or individual sizes. Shepherd's pie is most easily prepared with a cooked meat base and cooked mashed potato, frozen before the final browning process. All casseroles are successful, but thicken with cornflour if necessary. Meat balls and meat loaves can be made in large batches to use in a number of ways. Left over meat and poultry are best sliced and covered in sauce or gravy before freezing.

ACCOMPANIMENTS

Even the quickest freezer meal loses its point if potatoes have to be peeled or sauces prepared. Freeze rice, spaghetti and macaroni when slightly undercooked and well-drained, packed in bags. They may be reheated in the oven or in boiling water. Potatoes are good if mashed and formed into croquettes, or piped into pyramids which can be quickly browned in the oven or deep-fried; plain mashed potatoes should be reheated in a double saucepan with a little hot milk.

Later in the year, freeze large baked jacket potatoes wrapped individually in foil. Bread from the freezer is always useful, after heating in the oven, to go with soups or salads. Sauces can be prepared well in advance when there is more time for simmering and stirring.

PUDDINGS

Pastry flan cases and sponge flan cases can be made ready for filling with fruit or ice cream. Ready-cooked fruit pies and mincemeat can be used for packed meals. Fruit with sponge toppings and fruit crumbles freeze well. These are best with the fruit partly cooked and the topping raw to cook during the reheating.

All kinds of steamed puddings, sponge and suet varieties can be frozen with jam or syrup toppings, dried fruit, or chocolate flavouring. I like to cook these for slightly less than the full time before freezing, then complete cooking during the reheating. Light mousses and fruit whips are excellent for hot evenings. Milk puddings and custards do not freeze well.

17 Buttermaking and Cheesemaking

But huswives, that learne not to make their owne cheese;
with trusting of others, have this for their feese.
Their milke slapt in corners their creame al to soat;
their milk pannes so slotte that their cheeses be lost.

Thomas Tusser

Butter and hard cheeses are not easy to make at home these days, for large quantities of fresh untreated milk are needed, and the sort of equipment not often found in today's kitchens. Small quantities of butter, yoghurt, clotted cream, and soft cheeses, can, however be made with little equipment. Some of the very old traditional recipes for these foods can still be easily used.

DIRECTIONS TO THE DAIRY-MAID

The business of the dairy-maid is of the most beneficial nature, as by her knowledge and industry we are furnished with several of the most essential articles necessary for the preservation of our existence. We shall therefore give such directions as may enable the inexperienced to become proper proficients in so valuable an employment.

Directions for making butter

When you have got a sufficient quantity of cream, strain it through a clean linen cloth into the churn, which must be put to stand in the coolest place of the dairy, in summer; but in winter it must stand in the warmest. When you churn, let it be with solid heavy strokes, for they will make the butter much better than slight quick ones. When you find the butter begins to break, cleanse the inside of the lid, and then strike the church-staff more softly, to prevent the butter from heating. If the summer is hot, it would be proper to set the churn in a leaden cistern filled with cold water, and in winter before a slow fire. When the butter-milk is drained off, let the butter be taken out and washed in clean cold water, and it will be ready to be made up in rolls for present use.

To make Common Cheese

Take as much milk as you have ready, and when it has been made milk-warm, take a calf's bag that has been washed clean, and put in it some salt with curd. Keep it fastened with a skewer, and when you use it, put it in a pan of water mixed with salt, then boil it, and make small holes in it to let out the liquor, which must be poured into the milk. Take great care the milk be not too warm, otherwise you will spoil your cheese; for it should not be warmer than when it comes from the cows. When it has curdled, pour the whey from it, and let the rest be pressed out; then let it stand a day to dry, when it must be carefully crumbled as small as possible; then put to it a little salt properly mixed, and then put into the mould. If the cheese is pressed hard it will keep much longer than what is pressed soft; but the latter, when new, will have a better taste.

To make Cream Cheese

Put 2 spoonfuls of rennet into 12 gallons of milk, just as hot as when it comes from the cow, and in a ½ hour it will be curdled. Break the curd with a delf plate, and take care to keep it from getting to the bottom; then let it stand a ½ hour, when you must draw a plug fixed to the middle of the vessel to let the whey run out. When it is properly drained, put the curd into a clean canvas bag, and roll it up and down till the rest of the whey is drained off, then hang it up till it be dry, when it must be put in a thick mould, and a flat stone laid over it. When you take it out of the mould, cut it in slices of an inch thick, by drawing a silken thread gently and regularly through it. Put the slices thus cut up on a clean board, and sprinkle a little salt over them, taking care to turn them twice each of the first 4 days. Then lay them on strewed nettles 8 days more, when they must be set up to dry. They will be ready to eat in a few days.

To make Sage Cheese

Prepare the curd in the same manner as before, and squeeze as much of the juice out of sage and spinnage as will give it a fine greenish colour; put it to the curd, with which it must be properly mixed, then put it into the mould, and press it in a moderate manner; then put it by about 6 months, and it will eat fine.

To make Cheese as in Cheshire

Instead of breaking the curd, you must draw it gently to one side with your hands, and press it as softly as possible, that the whey may run out without hurting the milk. When you have got out the curd, put it in a vat, and keep turning it, and mixing with it a great deal of salt; then mix the curd as small as possible, and put it in a mould 8 inches deep. It must be pressed very hard, and when taken out, let it be put upon a shelf and turned once every day for a month; then cut a hole in the middle and pour in a $\frac{1}{2}$ pint of sack, which will immediately dissolve through the cheese, when you must put in the piece that was taken out, so close that it may not be damaged; then set it in the cellar, and in a year it will be ready for use.

To make Cheese as in Gloucestershire

When you have prepared the curd, let it be taken off gently, and put it into a vat covered with a clean linen cloth till it is dry. Then cut it into small pieces, and put it into boiling water mixed with salt; then take it out, and, having wrung it from the water, let it stand a day longer in another vat, only that you must turn it several times. Put it into the press, and when it has laid 24 hours, take it out and set it up. Turn it several times for a month and in 8 months it will be ready for use.

1812

INSTRUCTIONS TO A DAIRY-MAID

To Make Cheese

Put the milk into a large tub, warming a part till it is of a degree of heat quite equal to new; if too hot, the cheese will be tough. Put in as much rennet as will turn it, and cover it over. Let it stand still completely turned; then strike the curd down several times with the skimming-dish, and let it separate, still covering it. There are 2 modes of breaking the curd; and there will be a difference in the taste of the cheese, according as either is observed; one is, to gather it with the hands through the fingers till it is cleared, and lading it off as it collects. The other is, to get the whey from it by early breaking the curd; the last method deprives it of many of its oily particles, and is therefore not advised.

Put the vat on a ladder over the tub, and fill it with curd by the skimmer; press the curd close with your hand, and add more as it sinks; press the curd close with your hand, and add more as it sinks; and it must be finally left 2 inches above the edge. Before the vat is filled, the cheese-cloth must be laid at the bottom: and when full, drawn smooth over on all sides.

There are 2 modes of salting cheese; one by mixing it in the curd while in the tub after the whey is out; and the other by putting it into the vat and crumbling the curd all to pieces with it, after the first squeezing has dried it. The first method appears best on some accounts, but not on all; and therefore the custom of the county must direct. Put a board under and over the vat, and place it in the press; in 2 hours turn it out and put a fresh cheese-cloth; press it again for 8 or 9 hours; then salt it all over, and turn it again in the vat, and let it stand in the press 14 or 16 hours, observing to put the cheeses last made undermost. Before putting them the last time into the vat, pare the edges if they do not look smooth. The vat should have holes at the sides and bottom, to let all the whey pass through. Put on clean boards, and change and scald them.

To preserve Cheese sound

Wash in warm whey, when you have any, and wipe it once a month, and keep it on a rack. If you want to ripen it, a damp cellar will bring it forward. When a whole cheese is cut, the larger quantity should be spread with butter inside, and outside wiped to preserve it. To keep those in daily use moist, let a clean cloth be wrung out from cold water, and wrapt round them when carried from table. Dry cheese may be used to advantage to grate for serving with macaroni, or eating without. These observations are made with a view to make the above articles less expensive, as in most families where much is used there is waste.

To make Sage Cheese

Bruise the tops of young red sage in a mortar, with some leaves of spinach, and squeeze the juice; mix it with the rennet in the milk, more or less according as you like for colour and taste. When the curd is come, break it gently, and put it in with the skimmer, till it is pressed 2 inches over 1 vat. Press it 8 or 10 hours. Salt it, and turn every day.

Cream Cheese

Put 5 quarts of strippings, that is, the last of the milk, into a pan, with 2 spoonfuls of rennet. When the curd is come, strike it down 2 or 3 times with the skimming-dish, just to break it. Let it stand 2 hours, then spread a cheese-cloth on a sieve, put the curd on it, and let the whey drain; break the curd a little with your hand, and put it into a vat with a 2 lb weight upon it. Let it stand 12 hours, take it out, and bind a fillet round. Turn every day till dry, from 1 board to another; cover them with nettles, or clean dock-leaves and put between 2 pewter-plates to ripen. If the weather be warm, it will be ready in 3 weeks.

Another – Have ready a kettle of boiling water, put 5 quarts of new milk into a pan, and 5 pints of cold water, and 5 of hot; when of a proper heat, put in as much rennet as will bring it in 20 minutes, likewise a bit of sugar. When come, strike the skimmer 3 or 4 times down, and leave it on the curd. In an hour or 2 lade it into the vat without touching it; put a 1 lb weight on it when the whey has run from it, and the vat is full.

Another sort – Put as much salt to 3 pints of raw cream as will season it; stir well and pur it into a sieve in which you have folded a cheese-cloth 3 or 4 times, and laid at the bottom. When it hardens, cover it with nettles on a pewter-plate.

To a quart of fresh cream put a pint of new milk warm enough to make the cream a proper warmth, a piece of sugar, and a little rennet.

Set near the fire till the curd comes; fill a vat made in the form of a brick, of wheat-straw or rushes sewed together. Have ready a square of straw, or rushes sewed flat, to rest the vat on, and another to cover it; the vat being open at top and bottom. Next day take it out, and change it as above to ripen. A ½ lb weight will be sufficient to put on it.

To Make Butter

During summer, skim the milk when the sun has not heated the dairy; at that season it should stand for butter 24 hours without skimming, and 48 in winter. Deposit the cream-pot in a very cold cellar, if your dairy is not cool. If you cannot churn daily, change it into scalded fresh pots; but never omit churning twice a week. If possible, put the churn in a through air; and if not a barrel one, set it in a tub of water 2 feet deep, which will give firmness to the butter. When the butter is come, pour off the butter-milk and put the butter into a fresh-scalded pan, or tubs which have afterwards been in cold water. Pour water on it, and let it lie to acquire some hardness before you work it; then change the water, and beat it with flat boards so perfectly that not the least taste of the butter-milk remain, and that the water, which must be often changed, shall be quite clear in colour. Then work some salt into it, weigh, and make it into forms; throw them into cold water, in an earthen pan and cover. You will then have very nice and cool butter in the hottest weather. It requires more working in hot than in cold weather; but in neither should be left with a particle of buttermilk, or a sour taste, as is sometimes done.

To Preserve Butter

Take 2 parts of the best common salt, 1 part of good loaf sugar, and 1 part of saltpetre; beat them well together. To 16 ozs of butter thoroughly cleansed from the milk, put 1 oz of this composition; work it well, and pot down, when it will become firm and cold.

The butter thus preserved is the better for keeping, and should not be used under a month. This should be kept from the air, and is best in pots of the best glazed earthenware, that will hold from 10 to 14 lbs each.

To Preserve Butter for Winter, the best way

When the butter has been prepared, as above directed, take 2 parts of the best common salt, 1 part of good loaf-sugar, and 1 part of saltpetre, beaten and blended well together. Of this composition put 1 oz to 16 ozs of butter, and work it well together in a mass. Press it into the pans after the butter is become cool; for friction, though it be not touched by the hands, will soften it. The pans should hold 10 or 12 lbs each. On the top put some salt; and when that is turned into brine, if not enough to cover the butter entirely, add some strong salt and water. It requires only then to be covered from the dust.

To manage Cream for Whey Butter

Set the whey 1 day and night, skim it, and so till you have enough; then boil it and pour it into a pan or 2 of cold water. As the cream rises, skim it till no more comes; then churn it. Where new-milk cheese is made daily, whey-butter for common and present use may be made to advantage.

To scald Cream, as in the West of England

In winter let the milk stand 24 hours, in the summer 12 at least; then put the milk-pan on a hot hearth, if you have one; if not, set it in a wide brass kettle of water, large enough to receive the pan. It must remain on the fire till quite hot, but on no account boil, or there will be a skin instead of a cream upon the milk. You will know when done enough, by the undulations on the surface looking thick, and having a ring round the pan the size of the bottom. The time required to scald cream depends on the size of the pan, and the heat of the fire; the slower the better. Remove the pan into the dairy when done, and skim it next day. In cold weather it may stand 36 hours, and never less than 2 meals. The butter is usually made in Devonshire of cream thus prepared, and if properly, it is very firm.

Butter-milk

If made of sweet cream, is a delicious and most wholesome food. Those who can relish sour butter-milk, find it still more light, and it is reckoned more beneficial in consumptive cases. Butter-milk, if not very sour, is also as good as cream to eat with fruit, if sweetened with white sugar, and mixed with a very little milk. It likewise does equally for cakes and rice-puddings, and of course it is economical to churn before the cream is too stale for anything but to feed pigs.

To keep Milk and Cream

In hot weather, when it is difficult to preserve milk from becoming sour and spoiling the cream, it may be kept perfectly sweet by scalding the new milk very gently, without boiling, and setting it by in the earthen dish, or pan, that it is done in. This method is pursued in Devonshire, and for butter, and eating, would equally answer in small quantities for coffee, tea, etc. Cream already skimmed may be kept 24 hours if scalded without sugar; and, by adding to it as much powdered lump-sugar, as will make it sweet, will be good for 2 days, keeping it in a cool place.

To choose Butter at Market

Put a knife into the butter if salt, and smell it when drawn out; if there is any thing rancid or unpleasant, it is bad. Being made at different times, the layers in casks will vary greatly, and you will not easily come at the goodness but by unhooping the cask, and trying it between the staves. Fresh butter ought to smell like a nosegay, and be of an equal colour all through; if sour in smell, it has not been sufficiently washed; if veiny and open, it is probably mixed with staler or an inferior sort.

To prepare Rennet, to turn the Milk

Take out the stomach of a calf as soon as killed, and scour it inside and out with salt, after it is cleared of the curd always found in it. Let it drain a few hours; then sew it up with two good handfuls of salt in it, or stretch it on a stick, well salted; or keep it in the salt wet, and soak a bit, which will do over and over by fresh water.

From Mrs Bing Smith, Lancaster, 1900

CORNISH CREAM

Put new milk into rather deep straight-sided pans, enamel if possible. Leave it to stand for 24 hours, and set over a slow fire. Heat very slowly to a temperature of 150°F. Remove from heat without shaking the cream, and leave to stand in a cold place for 24 hours. Skim off the cream.

DEVONSHIRE CREAM

Leave the milk to stand for 12 hours after milking, or 24 hours in the winter, for the cream to rise. Put the pan in a second pan of boiling water and let the water simmer gently, until the cream on the surface of the milk is thick and yellow, and small air bubbles come to the surface. When a ring appears on the cream inside the rim of the pan, remove it from the heat. Leave to stand for 12 hours, and skim off the cream. A note on this old recipe says that a pinch of saltpetre, put into each basin with the milk strained over it, will take away the taste of turnips.

BUTTER WITH AN ELECTRIC MIXER

Use 4-day-old double cream. Put into mixing bowl and mix with a heavy beater at low speed. As soon as the butter begins to form, reduce speed and continue until the butter comes into one lump. Drain off buttermilk. Wash the butter in cold water until the water remains clear. Squeeze to extract water. Salt to taste and pat butter into shape. 1 pint cream is the most practical quantity to use.

BUTTER WITH AN ELECTRIC BLENDER

Blend top milk or fresh cream at high speed for 1 minute. Drain off buttermilk. Put clean, cold water into the blender goblet, and blend for a few seconds. Drain off water, and squeeze butter to exclude moisture.

To remove the taste of turnips from butter

Dissolve 1 tablespoon saltpetre in 1 breakfastcup boiling water. Put a tablespoon of this liquid into a 10-pint pail and milk the cow into the pail. At once put the pail into a copper of boiling water and leave for about 3 minutes until the milk reaches 104°F. All taste of turnip will disappear. (This recipe dates from 1909.)

CONSTANT YOGHURT

Bring a pint of milk to the boil, bubble gently 1 minute and allow to stand 15 minutes in a warm kitchen. Meanwhile take 4 empty cartons or small jars, and an ovenproof dish or cake tin to stand them in. Fold a clean tea-towel in 2, lay it in the dish and place a cork mat on top.

Take 1 spoonful of commercial yoghurt and blend with 3 of hot milk. Divide the rest of the milk among the jars and stir in a spoonful of yoghurt and milk mixture. Place the jars on the cork mat, cover with another mat and wrap the ends of the towel over the top. Cover all with a lid or a plate and leave in a warm part of the kitchen 6 to 8 hours, disturbing as little as possible.

YOGHURT

Boil 1 pint milk then cool to blood heat. Add carton of plain yoghurt. Tip into coffee jar and wrap. Leave for 24 hours. Next day take ½ a carton of this mixture and add to 1 pint boiled milk. Continue indefinitely to make supplies.

COTTAGE CHEESE

Put sour milk in a warm place until thick. Add ½ teaspoon salt to each pint of milk. Put into a muslin bag and leave to drain overnight. Press between 2 plates for an hour, and then mix with a little fresh cream to serve.

SOUR MILK CHEESE WITH HERBS

2 pints thick sour milk   *1 fluid oz cream*
1 oz butter   *Salt and pepper*
1 tablespoon salt   *Chopped fresh herbs*

Scale the sour milk until the curd separates from the whey, but do not boil. Add all the other ingredients except the herbs and beat well. Add herbs to taste.

EIGHTEENTH-CENTURY CREAM CHEESE

Put a wet double napkin into a pewter soup plate. Put in a pint of cream, cover it and let it stand for 24 hours, unless the weather is very hot. Turn the cheese, add a little salt and leave 12 hours. Put into a dry napkin, salt the other side and leave another day. Some keep it in nut leaves to ripen.

FRESH CHEESE

Use 2 pints of warm new milk with a pint of sweet cream and 2 spoons of good rennet. Cover and leave to stand until it is a hard jelly. Break this up and put into a hair sieve. Let the whey drain off. Put the cheese in a dish with a beaten egg yolk and sugar to taste. Serve with sweet thick fresh cream and more sugar.

TWENTY-FOUR HOURS CREAM CHEESE

Leave 3 pints of cream to stand for 24 hours until thick. Put into a thick cloth and press with 4 oz weight, turning every hour until it is thick, and putting in a clean cloth each time. Chill in dairy or on ice.

HERB CHEESE

Heat some creamy milk to blood heat. Add just enough rennet to curdle, and let it coagulate. Hang in a muslin bag to drip. When the curd is firm, add plenty of chopped chives or parsley to make a green cheese.

DRY CREAM CHEESE

Take 1½ pints of very thick fresh cream, and put it into a cloth. Put this on a board and put another board on top, weighted with 4 lb. Leave for an hour and remove the cream to a bowl. Add a little salt and put into a clean cloth. Repeat pressing, and changing the cloth 3 times more until the cheese is firm.

FRESH CREAM CHEESE

Put 2 pints very thick sweet cream into a muslin cloth and hang it up all night. Next mornng, line a small hair sieve with fresh nettles and put a square of fine-mesh netting on the nettles. Pour in the cream, fold a cloth on top, and cover with nettles. Put in cold dairy, or on ice. When well chilled, put a piece of fresh wet muslin into the sieve, cover with nettles and put cream upside down on them. Cover with more nettles and 8 oz weight. Put back in dairy or on ice until the evening.

TO MAKE STILTON CHEESE

Take 60 quarts of new milk, and 6 quarts of cream. When lukewarm, put rennet, as for other cheeses. Press the curd in the usual manner, and when put into the cheese-vat, turn it over 4 or 5 times a-day into clean cloths. The cheese-vat should be 10¼ inches deep, and 8¼ inches over. Stilton cheeses are seldom used till 2 years old. See that the rennet is perfectly sweet, for on that the flavour of the cheese greatly depends.

1872

18 Potted Meat and Fish and Pâtés

What a breakfast ! Pot of hare; ditto of trout;
pot of prepared shrimps; dish of plain shrimps;
tin of sardines; beautiful beef-steak; eggs, muffins,
large loaf, and butter, not forgetting capital tea.

'Wild Wales', George Borrow

Potted meat and fish have been popular in Britain for many hundreds of years. They were traditionally eaten for breakfast, but are now more acceptable as a first course for luncheon or dinner, or for high tea or supper. Many delightful litttle china pots were produced to hold these delicacies, but today the same mixtures can be pressed into small soufflé dishes or ramekins. Originally 'potting' was a useful method of preserving meat, game and fish, and the dishes were covered with clarified melted butter to keep out air. This same method can be employed today, but once a 'pot' has been started, it should be eaten quickly.

More hearty pâtés are also included in this chapter, since they contain so many similar ingredients. They can be covered with butter also, or with aspic. Pâtés and 'pots' freeze well, but the butter or aspic coating should not then be used. These finishes may be added after thawing for serving. Both types of recipe are useful for using up meat, game and fish from other dishes, or for preserving a surplus quantity. They are nicest eaten with thin bread and butter, or with fresh toast, while some of the firmer mixtures may be sliced and eaten with salad.

POTTED BEEF

1 *lb shoulder steak (beef)*	$\frac{1}{8}$ *teaspoon pepper*
1 *teaspoon salt*	4 *oz butter or margarine*

Wash and dry the meat and cut into very small pieces. Season and place in a stone jam jar or in a basin; cover with aluminium foil or greased grease-proof paper and stand in a pan of water. Cover the pan and simmer for $2\frac{1}{2}$ hours. Strain the liquid into a bowl and add 3 oz of the margarine. Mince the meat several times till very fine. Mix with the liquid. Put into a clean jar or bowl and pour on the remaining melted margarine. Keep in a cool place and use within 2 days.

MRS JEWRY'S POTTED BEEF

Allow yourself about $3\frac{1}{2}$–4 hours to complete this task, she says, but 'be assured it is well worth the time spent'. (Actually, most of this time involves the meat being cooked.)

$2\frac{1}{2}$ *lb lean beef*	*Pepper, salt and mace*
5 *oz butter*	

Take a piece of lean beef and remove carefully the skin and gristle; put it into a covered stone jar with 3 dessertspoons of hot water, and stand it in a deep stewpan of boiling water to boil slowly for *nearly 4 hours*, taking care that the water does not reach the top of the jar. When done, take it out and mince it fine, then pound it in a mortar with a seasoning of pepper, salt and mace (also pounded). When smooth like a thick paste, mix in some clarified butter and a very little of the gravy from the jar. Press it into pots, pour over butter on to the tops and tie down for use.

POTTED LIVER

8 *oz calves' liver*	1 *hard-boiled egg*
1 *medium onion*	1 *tablespoon double cream*
2 *oz butter*	*Salt and pepper*

Cut the liver in small pieces and chop the onion. Cook them slowly in the butter until the onion is soft but not brown. Mince liver, onion and egg, with the pan juices. Add the cream and season to taste and put into small pots. Serve on toast or in sandwiches.

POTTED PORK

1 lb hand, shoulder or blade
of pork
1 lb pork sausage meat
¼ teaspoon garlic salt
¼ teaspoon basil
¼ teaspoon black pepper

¼ teaspoon salt
¼ teaspoon marjoram
Pinch of nutmeg
1 pint water
1 oz gelatine

Cut the pork into very small pieces and put into pan with the sausage meat, seasonings and water. Bring to boil. Put lid on, reduce heat and simmer for about 1 hour. Strain off the liquid. Dissolve gelatine in a little cold water and stand over hot water until gelatine is syrupy. Add gelatine to liquid and leave until cold. Skim off fat and add meat mixture to liquid. Put into 2 lb loaf tin or dish and leave until set. Cut in slices to serve with salad or in sandwiches.

TO POT OX CHEEK

When you stew an ox cheek, take some of the fleshy part, and season it well with salt and pepper, and beat it very fine in a mortar, with a little clear fat skimmed off the gravy; then put it close into your potting-pots, and pour over it clarified butter, and keep it for use.

Thomas Train, Gateshead, 1812

MRS HILLIER'S POTTED OX-TONGUE

1½ lb cooked tongue
6 oz butter
Nutmeg and cloves

1 small spoon mace
A little Cayenne pepper

Take about 1½ lb from a boiled tongue and remove the rind. Pound it as fine as you can with the butter and the spices. When the meat is nice and smooth and free from bits and the spices are properly worked into the meat, press the mixture into little suitable pots and pour melted butter over them. You can add a little cold roast meat with the tongue such as lamb or veal. It all helps the flavour.

Mrs Hillier is now very old indeed, over 90, but she still works hard and it is always a pleasure to hear her talking of the good old days when her husband was a vet. in some pretty hard hunting country. She had long, lonely days when her husband was out hunting, but she found plenty to occupy her time; there were many parties around the various farmhouses where the large kitchens would be cleared and dancing would begin after supper and carry on to the early hours, when the horses would take them safely home.

POTTED MEAT (1)

Procure 1 lb of lean hock and a nap or kneebone. The hock costs little and the knee even less. Wash the hock and nap carefully, and place in a large pot, covering the whole with cold water. Bring to the boil, and skim well; then boil slowly for 4 hours. Take out the meat and bone. Mince the meat very finely, also any small pieces of soft gristle adhering to the bone, but these can be left out if liked. Put back the minced meat into the liquid again, and boil for another ½ hour, adding salt to taste and also 2 teaspoons Jamaican pepper (red pepper). Dish into bowls of fancy shapes, and leave until cold.

POTTED MEAT (2)

1 pig's cheek   *1½ lb shin of beef*
1 cow heel   *Seasoning*

If the pig's cheek is too salt, boil it by itself; when cooked cut into small pieces and add it to the cow heel and beef, which should be boiled until the meat comes freely from the bones. Cover the cow heel and shin with water, boil a bag of pickling spices with these for about an hour of the cooking time – cook the meats until very tender. The bag of spice consists of 1 tablespoon peppercorns, 12 cloves, 3 blades of mace, or a little nutmeg, ½ teaspoon Cayenne pepper, and 3 bayleaves; tie in a muslin bag and suspend from saucepan handle with string into the liquid.

Remove all meat from bones and chop or mince very finely. Place in basins or moulds and cover with the liquid, which you have previously reduced, by boiling, until only a little remains. Stir these juices into the minced meat and leave to set. It is advisable to rinse moulds or basins with cold water.

POTTED MEAT (3)

1½ lb beef   *Pepper and salt to taste*
2 tablespoons anchovy sauce   *4 oz salt butter*
½ gill water

Cut the meat up into cubes and put in an earthenware pot with the water. Let it simmer for 5 hours. Put through a mincer twice and mix well with the sauce, seasoning, and 2 oz butter. Fill small jars with the mixture. Melt remainder of the butter and pour over the top.

WILTSHIRE MEAT PASTE

1 *lb lean beef, the better the*
cut, the better the paste
1 *tablespoon anchovy paste*
or sauce

¼ *teaspoon pepper*
Salt to taste
¼ *grated nutmeg*

Put all in a basin when thoroughly minced and steam for at least 2 hours, or according to the cut of the beef. Suitable for spreading on home-made scones or bridge rolls, or on snippets of dry toast.

LIVER PÂTÉ

Get very fresh calves' liver, parboil it, pass it through a mincing machine, mix the same weight of cold tongue, which must be cut into dice, 2 dozen button mushrooms cut into small pieces, 2 onions minced and fried in butter; salt, pepper and parsley to taste.

Line a dish with well made puff pastry, fill with the mixture and cover with a thin layer of pastry. Bake from ¾ to 1 hour.

SIMPLE PÂTÉ

¾ *lb pig's liver*
2 *lb belly pork*
3 *heaped tablespoons onion*
softened in butter
1 *large egg beaten with*

1 *heaped tablespoon flour*
Salt and pepper
Nutmeg
Bay leaf

Mince or chop liver and pork and mix all ingredients together, seasoning to taste. Put into terrine (or loaf tin). Cover with lid or foil and bake at 350°F (Gas Mark 4) for 1½ hours (the terrine should stand in a baking tin of water). The pâté will be cooked when a metal needle or skewer comes out clean. Cool for an hour, then weight gently until next day. The pâté may be finished with meat jelly; or with a layer of lard for storage in a cool dry place. Before the pâté is cooked, the terrine may be lined with pieces of pork fat, or with thin strips of streaky bacon.

CHICKEN LIVER PÂTÉ

Equal quantities by bulk of cooked livers (I do them inside the birds when roasting or simmer with the stock), butter and stock from chicken carcasses. Press livers through a sieve. Mix thoroughly with melted butter and as much of the stock as you like. The full quantity may make it too wet for some tastes, but I find that an hour in the fridge makes it pretty solid. Season to taste with salt and fresh ground pepper and ring the changes with thyme/parsley/chives.

Useful for supper for 2 when the family have had roast chicken for lunch.

Mrs Chaplin, Finsthwaite, Lancs

PORK AND SAUSAGE PÂTÉ

½ pig's liver
½ lb pork sausage meat
1 oz white breadcrumbs
Salt and black pepper
4 oz lean bacon

4 oz mushrooms, finely
chopped
¼ teaspoon sage
1 dessertspoon tomato
chutney

Remove the gristle from liver and rinds from the bacon. Mince liver and bacon and then mix them together, stirring in all the other ingredients. Mix thoroughly. Press into a 1½-pint sized basin, cover loosely with foil and bake at 325°F (Gas Mark 3) for 1½ hours. Leave loaf in basin until cold.

PRESSED FOWL

Old boiling hens are often obtainable at small country markets and are more tasty, as well as being a better buy, than frozen chicken. Place a dressed fowl (i.e. ready-for-cooking) in a saucepan with cold water, to cover and let it simmer gently over a moderate fire until the meat falls off the bone, about 2–3 hours. When done pick to pieces – this is best done with only the fingers, when the bird is cool enough to handle. Put the bones back in the liquor in saucepan and boil until the content is halved; then strain. Season with salt and pepper, and pour the strained liquor over the "picked" meat and mix well again. Pour the whole into a mould. When quite firm turn out and slice thinly.

BUTTERED GROUSE

The birds (young ones are essential) are rubbed with butter, a lump of butter is put inside them, and they are wrapped in a piece of fat bacon. Roast them in a preheated oven at 425–450°F (Gas Mark 7 or 8). Baste frequently. They will take 30–35 minutes. Remove from the oven, cut each bird in half, and arrange neatly in a pie dish. Pour the hot juices from the roasting pan into a saucepan, add, for 2 birds, ½ lb of butter. Let it melt, season with a very little mace, cayenne pepper and salt. Pour over the birds, and eat cold next day.

POTTED GROUSE

2 *old grouse*
1 *carrot*
1 *onion*
2 oz *streaky bacon*

Butter
Bunch of mixed herbs
Salt and pepper

Slice the carrots and onions, and cut the bacon in neat pieces and fry in butter until golden. Put into a casserole with the herbs and plenty of salt and pepper, and put the grouse on top. Cover with stock and cook at 300°F (Gas Mark 2) for 2½ hours. Remove the carrot. Take meat from the bones of the grouse, and put the mixture through a mincer, then pound, sieve or put in a liquidiser. Press into a shallow dish and cover with melted butter. A small glass of port improves this dish. Serve with hot fresh toast.

POTTED GROUSE

2 *grouse*
Salt and pepper
6 oz *butter*

¾ *pint jellied consommé*
1 *wineglass red wine or sherry*

Salt and pepper the birds and put a knob of butter into each. Pack into an earthenware casserole and pour over the consommé (this may be home-made or canned). Add the wine or sherry and remaining butter. Cover tightly and bake at 325°F (Gas Mark 3) for 2 hours. Leave until cold and set when the birds will be in wine-flavoured jelly with a firm butter top. Serve half a bird to each person with toast, and small pickled gherkins or reducrrant jelly.

DEVON TERRINE OF HARE

Line an earthenware terrine with slices of bacon. Remove all bones from the hare and cut up into small pieces. Place it in the terrine with ½ lb pickled pork, cut into small pieces, and flavourings of thyme, marjoram, parsley, one shallot, 1 clove of garlic, salt and pepper to taste, and then pour over the whole a glass of Madeira or sherry. Close the lid tightly with an edging of paste, and put it in the oven – a slow one – to bake gently for 4 hours.

HARE PÂTÉ (1)

1 *lb cooked hare, removed*
from bones
2 oz *mushrooms*
1 *thick slice bread soaked in*
milk
Rich gravy

2 oz *butter*
2 *egg yolks*
6 *tablespoons brandy or*
Madeira
Pepper and salt
1 *bayleaf*

Strip the hare from the bones and cut up meat in small pieces. Mix with sliced mushrooms cooked in butter and the soaked bread. Mince and pound until smooth. Moisten with a little gravy and mix with butter, egg yolks, brandy or Madeira and seasoning. Put the bayleaf in the bottom of a dish, put in the meat mixture, cover and steam for 2 hours (the dish may be placed in a tin of water and cooked at 325°F, Gas Mark 3, for 2 hours). Leave until very cold under a weight. This pâté will keep for several weeks in a refrigerator.

HARE PÂTÉ (2)

Joints of hare
2 *onions*
Bayleaf
Mixed herbs

1 *lb fat bacon, cut in cubes*
3-4 *rashers bacon*
$\frac{1}{2}$ *pint red wine*
Lemon juice

Put the hare, fat bacon, onions, bayleaf and herbs into a pan and cook very slowly until the meat will just leave the bones. Take out and remove meat from bones, put hare and bacon through the mincer, add more seasoning and lemon juice. Lay some rashers of bacon on the bottom of a fireproof dish, press the minced meat into the dish, add the red wine and some more rashers of bacon on top. Put the dish, standing in a baking tin containing water, into a moderate oven 300°F (Gas Mark 3) for 2–3 hours. Take out and apply light pressure until the pâté is cold.

HARE PÂTÉ (3)

Crisp 1 lb fat diced bacon in a large pan before adding and browning the jointed hindquarters of a hare. Then pour in $\frac{1}{4}$ pint dry red wine and $\frac{1}{2}$ pint of chicken stock. Add a dozen peppercorns, bayleaf and thyme, simmer, covered for 1 hour adding 6 oz thickly sliced calf's liver to cook for the last 5 minutes. Let cool, strip the hare flesh from the bones and double mince together with the liver, bacon, 1 medium onion and 2 garlic cloves. Thereafter cream the mixture with the fat from the cooking liquor together with some of the liquor itself, 2 tablespoons brandy and seasonings to make a medium-stiff purée. Turn this into a greased casserole, cover with foil and bake for an hour in a moderate oven, first seating the casserole in a shallow pan of water.

HARE PÂTÉ (4)

Joint the hare, and stew until tender with an assortment of herbs and vegetables until the meat is ready to fall off the bone. Then take the meat and mince finely, or put it through a sieve. Add a glass of port or brandy, and 2 tablespoons of redcurrant jelly. Mix well, put into jars, pour melted butter on the top.

POTTED HARE

Remains of jugged hare   *Butter or aspic*

Put the remains of a jugged hare through a sieve or mill with just enough of its sauce to moisten it but not so much as to make it runny. Press down in a dish. Cover with melted butter or liquid aspic. Put in the refrigerator.

HARE TERRINE

Put all the joints but the saddle into a casserole with 2 or 3 sliced onions, a bayleaf, a teaspoon of marjoram and 2 lb of fat bacon, cut into cubes. Add enough stock to cover all ingredients, or, if you have it, use stock and half a bottle of cheap red wine. Cover closely and cook in a slow oven, 45 minutes. Let it cool, then put all the meat, including the bacon, through the fine plate of the mincer.

Season well with ground black pepper, salt if needed, more herbs and a little grated lemon peel.

Grease a mould. This should be a 2-pint terrine, that is a straight-sided china mould, but if you have not got such a thing use a basin or a straight-sided fireproof dish, do not use a metal mould.

Put the meat into the mould, do not press it down. Put a few rashers of bacon on the top and moisten with some of the stock in which you have cooked the joints. Put greaseproof paper on the top and stand the mould in a pan of hot water. Put this pan into a low oven and cook for $1\frac{1}{2}$–2 hours. When you take the pan out of the oven press evenly down on the greaseproof paper so that all the meat is consolidated, leave the paper on top while the terrine cools, it can then be stored in a cold larder until required.

If wanted to be kept for 2–3 weeks, run melted butter over the top of the meat; when cold cover with tinfoil. It can then be safely kept for 2–3 weeks.

POTTED PARTRIDGE

2 partridges   ½ pint stock
8 oz butter

Season the birds inside and out and put a lump of butter in each. Put into a casserole with some good stock and the rest of the butter, cover with double cooking foil and a lid and cook at 350°F (Gas Mark 3) for 1½ hours. Leave until cold, when the butter will form a seal on top. Do not uncover until they are to be eaten; they will keep several days. Serve garnished with parsley, and with redcurrant jelly.

PHEASANT TERRINE

1 pheasant   ½ wineglass Madeira
1 lb fat pork   ½ wineglass brandy
½ lb thin-cut streaky bacon   Salt and pepper
rashers   Mixed herbs (parsley, chives,
1 wineglass white wine   basil, tarragon, garlic)

This is a rather expensive recipe but makes a large quantity of a very superior pâté and is well worth while for a special occasion. The recipe may be used for other game birds, hare, duck or chicken, and the mincemeat layers can consist of chopped-up poultry or game, pork, liver or tinned liver pâté.

Take the breast and thighs from a plump pheasant, cut the meat in slices and leave for 24 hours in the wine, Madeira, brandy and herbs. Mince the pheasant trimmings and liver with pork and season well with salt and pepper. Line a terrine (if you haven't the correct dish, use a deep pie dish or an earthenware casserole) with rashers of bacon. Put in a layer of the mincemeat, then the pheasant slices, and continue in layers, finishing with a layer of mincemeat. Cover with bacon rashers and put on a lid. Stand the dish in a tin of water and cook at 325°F (Gas Mark 3) for 1½ hours. Leave until cold with a weight on top. This makes an excellent beginning for a shooting picnic.

POTTED PIGEONS

2 pigeons   8 small onions
1 oz butter   ½ pint stock
2 rashers streaky bacon   Salt and pepper

Brown the birds all over in the butter, then take out the pigeons, and cook the onions and the bacon cut in strips in the fat. Put onions and bacon in a casserole and add pigeons split in half. Season well with salt and pepper and add stock. Cook at 350°F (Gas Mark 4) for 1½ hours.

PIGEON PÂTÉ (can be made from either young or old birds)

3 pigeons	**Small teaspoon grated thyme**
1 cup red wine	**Grating of nutmeg**
½ cup vinegar	**Salt and pepper**
Bayleaf	**4 finely chopped onions**

Make a marinade of the seasonings, the herbs, the wine and the vinegar, add the chopped onion, and pour all this over the jointed birds. Leave to soak, 3–4 days. Take the meat from the birds, 8 oz sausage meat, 8 oz bacon rashers, seasoning, little milk and 1 slice of bread (crusts removed). Mince the meat twice, mix with the sausage meat, add seasoning. Soak the crumbled bread in enough milk to moisten it, then beat this in to the meat mixture. Have ready an ovenware dish with a close fitting lid. Lay some rashers of bacon at the bottom, press in the meat mixture, put more rashers on top, put on the lid and bake in a moderate oven 2–2½ hours.

RICH PIGEON PÂTÉ

10 pigeon breasts	**½ glass wine, sherry, brandy**
½ small onion	**or whisky**
1 teaspoon mixed herbs	**Salt**
(including basil and	**Ground black pepper**
rosemary if possible)	**Garlic (optional)**
½ oz streaky bacon	**6 crushed juniper berries**
4 oz lard	**(optional)**
4 oz butter	

Cut the pigeon breasts into cubes about 1 inch square. 'Melt' bacon and onion in butter and lard in a thick frying pan so that they are cooked but not browned. Turn up heat and sauté the pigeon breasts. This should take only a few minutes, and they should be faintly pink inside. Remove from the pan and put aside. Add the herbs, seasoning (plenty of black pepper) and wine to the butter and let it bubble for a few seconds. Add to the pigeon and place in a liquidiser until well pounded. (If you do not possess one, simply pass the meat through a fine mincer and then beat in the butter and wine with a fork.) Put into an earthenware dish or terrine and cover with melted butter. Place in a refrigerator. Serve well chilled with piping hot toast.

Mrs. Archie Coat

312

PIGEON WALNUT PÂTÉ

Separate the flesh from the bones of 2 pigeons that have simmered till quite tender in a little stock and then mince it up. Mix it together with ½ lb double minced dry walnuts, garlic and onion, creaming in at the same time a little of the greatly reduced stock in which the pigeons cooked, together with seasonings and a good dash of Cayenne.

POTTED RABBIT

Joint a rabbit and put into a casserole with tightly-fitting lid. Add 2 oz butter, 1 lump sugar, 1 onion stuck thickly with cloves, 12 allspice, 6 peppercorns, and a good sprinkling of nutmeg. Put on lid and cook in a slow oven till the meat leaves the bones easily. Cool the meat, remove the bones and put through a mincer twice. Beat in ½ lb butter, 1 dessertspoon Worcester sauce and a pinch of sugar. Put into small pots, covering the tops with melted butter. This is delicious on toast, and will keep in the refrigerator for a few days.

POTTED ROOKS

4 rooks *Gelatine*
Salt and pepper *1 oz butter*

Skin and clean the rooks and cut away the backs and ribs, leaving the breasts with the 2 upper wing bones attached, also the 2 legs without the feet. Put into a double saucepan with salt and pepper to taste and butter. Cook slowly until the meat comes away from the bones, which may take 8 or 10 hours. Take the meat off the bones and put into a jar. Put the bones back in the liquid and continue simmering for 2 hours. Strain liquid and add very little gelatine. Pour over the meat and leave until cold. Cover with a layer of melted butter.

TO POT WOODCOCKS

Pluck 6 woodcocks, draw out the train, skewer their bills through their thighs, and put the legs through each other, and their feet upon their breasts. Season them with 3 or 4 blades of mace, and a little pepper and salt: then put them into a deep pot with 1 lb of butter over them; tie a strong paper over them, and bake them in a moderate oven; when they are tender enough, lay them on a dish to drain the gravy from them;

then put them into potting-pots, and take all the clear butter from your gravy, and put it upon them. Fill up your pots with clarified butter, and keep them in a dry place.

Thomas Train, Gateshead, 1812

POTTED KIPPERS

Remove all skins and bones from some cooked kippers, mash the flesh until nice and smooth, then add sufficient melted butter to work into a soft paste. Add pepper, and salt if required, and a pinch of nutmeg. Fill some empty paste pots with the mixture and seal with a thin layer of melted butter. This is very acceptable to someone who has been ill and needs a change of diet.

POTTED PERCH

Take the heads off your perch and the tails, and take out the insides unless the fish are less than 2 inch long. Butter a baking dish and lay them in – packing them as tight as possible. Dot with butter, sprinkle with a pinch of salt, black pepper and mace and cook very slowly with the lid on over a piece of foil for 4 hours. All the bones will have melted by this time. You can serve them in the dish in which they were cooked or pound them up and put them into individual ramekins and run clarified butter over them. For tea serve from the dish with large hunks of new bread and butter – for dinner for a first course in ramekins with thin brown bread and butter or with toast.

Mrs Chaplin, Finsthwaite, Lancs

SALMON PÂTÉ

Mince and pound cooked salmon till it will go through a sieve, then put into a dish leaving $\frac{1}{2}$ inch headroom. Pour over half the weight of the fish in butter, melted, with pinch of mace, black pepper and salt to taste, while the fish is still warm. Serve as for Potted Perch.

Mrs Chaplin, Finsthwaite, Lancs

POTTED HERRINGS

6 herrings slit down back. Do not remove tails. Remove bones; wash; dry and season; pepper and salt. Roll up; skin outside and tails uppermost. Place in pie-dish, add 2 tablespoons vinegar and 2 of water. Cover dish. Bake very slowly for 1 hour or more. Serve cold; garnish parsley.

TO POT SALMON

Let your salmon be quite fresh, scale and wash it well; dry it well with a cloth, split it up the back, and take out the bone. Season it well with white pepper and salt, a little nutmeg and mace; let it be 2 or 3 hours, then put it in your pot, with ½ lb of butter; tie it down, put it in the oven, and bake it an hour. When it comes out, lay it on a flat dish, that the oil may run from it; cut it to the size of your pots, lay it in layers till you fill the pots, with the skin upwards; put a board over it, lay on a weight to press it till cold, then pour over it clarified butter; when you cut it, the skin makes it look ribbed. You may send it to the table either cut in slices, or in the pot.

Thomas Train, Gateshead, 1812

Index

325